PANCHO VILLA AND
BLACK JACK PERSHING

Pershing and Villa in happier days. John J. Pershing, Francisco Villa, and Alvaro
Obregon—August 27, 1914 [National Archives].

PANCHO VILLA AND
BLACK JACK PERSHING

The Punitive Expedition in Mexico

JAMES W. HURST

PRAEGER

Westport, Connecticut
London

Library of Congress Cataloging-in-Publication Data

Hurst, James W.
Pancho Villa and Black Jack Pershing : the Punitive Expedition in Mexico / James W. Hurst.
    p.   cm.
    Includes bibliographical references and index.
    ISBN–13: 978–0–313–35004–7 (alk. paper)
    1. United States. Army—History—Punitive Expedition into Mexico, 1916.
2. Mexican–American Border Region—History—20th century.   3. Pershing, John J. (John
Joseph), 1860–1948.   4. Villa, Pancho, 1878–1923.   I. Title.
    F1234.H95   2008
    972.08'16—dc22   2007036163

British Library Cataloguing in Publication Data is available.

Library of Congress Catalog Card Number: 2007036163
ISBN–13: 978–0–313–35004–7

First published in 2008

Praeger Publishers, 88 Post Road West, Westport, CT 06881
An imprint of Greenwood Publishing Group, Inc.
www.praeger.com

Printed in the United States of America

The paper used in this book complies with the
Permanent Paper Standard issued by the National
Information Standards Organization (Z39.48–1984).

10 9 8 7 6 5 4 3 2 1

For my parents,
George William and Isabelle Gordon Hurst, where it all began,
and for
Charles A. Bill, "Mr. Bill," an extraordinary teacher who touched a young
man's life and shaped his future.

CONTENTS

PREFACE

My introduction to Francisco Villa and the Punitive Expedition came as a result of a visit to Pancho Villa State Park in Columbus, New Mexico. I had then (what seems to me in retrospect) the same vague notions about what had transpired in Columbus in March 1916 as most of the people with whom I have since spoken: A Mexican bandit raided, burned, and looted this small border town for reasons not clearly understood, and in retaliation the United States Army was sent into Mexico to apprehend him and bring him to the bar of justice. Furthermore, the expedition was a failure. The bandits made fools of the Army, the entire episode was one giant fiasco, and since it was such an embarrassment we would all be better off if we forgot about it. This was, after all, what I had gleaned from the little reading I had done in magazines and books, and I had no reason to question these tidbits of conventional wisdom.

My curiosity about this incident in American history, little noted outside of the American southwest and virtually unknown east of the Mississippi River, was aroused not by Villa, Pershing, or the Expedition, but by the fate of the Villista raiders who were taken prisoner during and immediately after the raid and of those who were brought back from Mexico by the Army upon its return. I began the research that led to my book, *The Villista Prisoners of 1916–17*, and as so often happens, investigation in one subject leads to discoveries not directly related to the point of inquiry. While at the National Archives in Washington, DC, I ran across documents dealing with the Expedition that offered what to me was a new perspective. I decided that when time permitted

I would follow the primary sources to see what light they shed on the already established narratives in the surprisingly plentiful secondary sources. First, however, I had to climb the mountain of books, essays, and pamphlets, which dealt with the Punitive Expedition.

The genesis of this book was a paper I read to the 2000 Annual Meeting of the Historical Society of New Mexico at the Valencia Campus of the University of New Mexico. The paper was titled, "The Pershing Punitive Expedition of 1916–17: Mission Misunderstood," in which I argued what is the basic thesis of this book: that *judged by the criteria of its orders* to proceed promptly across the border in pursuit of the Mexican band, which attacked the town of Columbus, and that the work of these troops would be regarded as finished as soon as Villa's band (or bands) are known to be broken up, the Expedition was a success. This argument, which runs counter to most accounts in the vast body of literature dealing with the subject, will be developed in greater detail in the course of the following narrative.

The United States Army of the Punitive Expedition, contrary to the assertions of some contemporary writers, was not a bunch of bungling amateurs thrashing about in confusion and frustration. Nearly two-thirds of Pershing's officers were veterans of the Philippine War, and a number were also veterans of the Indian Wars. Many of these men had key positions in the Expedition[1] and were familiar with what has been called the "guerilla technique" of warfare: when confronted by regular forces, irregular bands react in similar ways. They flee from strength, attack weakness, prey upon small isolated garrisons and poorly defended supply trains, kill the lone sentry or unwary patrol, live off the land with the aid of their people, and terrorize those among their own who refuse to cooperate or join with the enemy. One of a number of techniques successfully employed by the Army against irregulars dated from the days of General Crook and the Apache Wars: it was the use of highly mobile, self-contained units to pursue the enemy relentlessly and to force him to disband or be destroyed. This would prove to be a key strategy in the Expedition's campaign against the Villistas.

Armies in the field have always relied heavily on gathering information about their opposition, and the Pershing Punitive Expedition was no exception. In addition to local informants and the Army's traditional reconnaissance resources, the Expedition's intelligence officer, Major James A Ryan, had at his disposal aircraft, motor vehicles, and "radio tractors." The underpowered aircraft, with a new aerial camera at their disposal, proved ineffective in the altitudes of Mexico's Sierra Madres and were rendered useless within the first two months of the Expedition's presence in Mexico. The motor vehicles were used mostly for logistical links to the supply base in the United States, but several were used for the first time in limited capacities for gathering intelligence. The "radio tractors" made it possible for the Army to monitor Mexican radio transmissions, a source of valuable information not only about the de facto government's deployment of troops but also about the diplomatic climate between the de facto Carrancista government and the Wilson administration.

Pershing referred to his intelligence gathering organization as the Intelligence Section, and in addition to Major Ryan the department included Assistant Chief of Staff Captain W. O. Reed, 6th Cavalry and Captain Nicholas W. Campanole, 6th Infantry. The Punitive Expedition's intelligence officer interrogated prisoners, recruited guides, interpreters, and informers, and organized a secret service of Mexican expatriates who were more than willing to provide their services against Villa. There were a number of Japanese who were employed with mixed results, and a few reliable local Mexicans were employed in the Secret Service with fairly good results. Pershing learned early on that the Carranza regime had no communication code in universal use and local commanders used their own. In a short time the local codes were deciphered and through tapping telegraph and telephone lines the Information Department was able to monitor key government communications. Wireless transmissions were also monitored with satisfactory results. Few reliable maps of Chihuahua, Mexico, were available at the beginning of Pershing's march south, but cavalry officers and engineers made sketches and maps at every opportunity and the Expedition left a cartographic legacy that is little short of amazing.

The focus of this book is the Expedition, the Villistas, and their leader Francisco "Pancho" Villa. During the active phase of the Expedition, March through June, 1916, Villa was in flight and in hiding, but his presence was felt even as his influence began to decline. The book's narrative is itself a reflection of the success of the Intelligence Section in gathering information in the field and preserving what was gathered in detailed, written reports. The reports would not have been possible without the cooperation of the local population, particularly in the Guerrero district and specifically in the pueblo of Namiquipa. Both were hotbeds of Villista sentiment, and early Expedition reports stressed the hostility of the locals. Within a matter of weeks of its arrival, however, the local situation had changed radically. Local farmers were collaborating with the Americans, selling their labor and supplies to the troops and, more importantly, furnishing the invaders with military intelligence. I have made substantial use of these reports in the hope of drawing the reader closer to the essence of the subject, the human dimension, while at the same time dissipating some of the myths and, in some cases, absolute silliness regarding the Expedition.

The archival sources used in the narrative are from American repositories, and they are listed for the reader at the end of the narrative. The perspective is, therefore, an American one: the newspapers, the press, the papers of the major figures involved in the episode, books, and articles both by and about the participants, and the documents generated by the United States Army. The narrative is aimed at the general reading public and not at the specialist; therefore the paraphernalia of academic citations are kept to a minimum.

NOTE

1. Gen. Pershing, Expedition Commander (Indian, Philippine, and Moro Wars); Lt. Col. De Rosey Cabell, Chief of Staff (Geronimo campaign); Col. George Dodd, Cavalry Brigade Commander (Indian and Philippine Wars, former commander of Indian Scouts); Col. James B. Irwin, Cavalry Column Commander (Philippine Wars); Lt. Col. Henry T. Allen, Cavalry Column Commander (Philippine War, former Chief, Philippine Constabulary); Col. William C. Brown, Cavalry Column Commander (Indian and Philippine Wars and former commander of Indian Scouts); Col. Herbert J. Slocum, (Indian, Philippine, and Moro Wars and former advisor to the Cuban Rural Guard); Maj. Frank Tompkins, Cavalry Column Commander (Philippines and Texas border patrol); and Col. Robert Howze, Cavalry Column Commander (former commander of Indian Scouts and the Puerto Rico Regiment).

Villa   Pershing

Carranza

The Protagonists [National Archives].

ACKNOWLEDGMENTS

When writers think about the individuals and institutions that assisted them in their work, they pay homage, whether they realize it or not, to an old aphorism: "We have all drawn water from wells we did not dig." I hope that in the following paragraphs I have managed to thank all the well-diggers whose work has made this book possible.

Brian P. Graney, Senior Archivist, and Sibel Melik, Archivist, at the State Records Center and Archives, Santa Fe, New Mexico, for their assistance in securing the prison photographs of the Villistas sentenced to the State Penitentiary for their participation in the raid on Columbus, New Mexico. Terri M. Grant, Library Information Specialist II, and Imira Ramirez of the Border Heritage Center, El Paso Public Library, El Paso, Texas, for their assistance in using the library's photographic holdings. The Staff of the Libraries of New Mexico State University, Las Cruces, New Mexico for their patience in answering my many questions and for their assistance in finding microfilm and microfiche relating to my research.

A large portion of gratitude goes to Professors Charles H. Harris III and Louis R. Sadler, History Department, New Mexico State University, Las Cruces, NM, not only for their pathfinding research and publications that got me started in all of this in the first place, but for their subsequent willingness to offer help whenever requested. They are, it may be said without exaggeration, a historian's historians.

For Mitchell Yockelson, Archivist, Modern Military Records Branch, National Archives and Records Administration at College Park, MD, a special thanks for the time and effort in answering my e-mail inquiries, telephone calls, and most of all for digging out the boxes and boxes of documents and having them ready for me when I got to the archives. His vast knowledge of the archival holdings in regard to the Punitive Expedition is a gold mine for the researcher, and he is a reminder that behind any researcher's success is a good archivist. Many thanks also to the staff of the photographic services for their help in locating so many of the photographs that appear in the text.

I owe a tremendous debt to Robert H. Bouilly, PhD, Historian, Sergeants Major Academy, Fort Bliss, Texas. Bob has been more than generous with his time and resources. His staff rides to Columbus, New Mexico, continue to infuse life into an event now over eighty years past, his collection and reconstruction of maps of Villa's raid are themselves a valuable resource, and one would be hard-pressed to find a more knowledgeable guide to just what really happened on that early morning of March 9, 1916. Through his willingness to share his collection of documents, books, photographs, and maps, Bob in a very real sense made this book a reality.

Much is owed to Robert Ferrell who generously spent time with the manuscript, and whose suggestions in matters of style and narrative presentation were invaluable. His carefully typed four-by-six index card annotations to the text were a mine of valuable nuggets from which I profited immensely.

Many thanks are due my wife, Annabelle, for her understanding of and patience with a husband who, infected by Clio's charm, spent many hours in libraries, archives, and museums sifting and sorting through old documents and photographs. Her understanding extended to my need to spend many more hours secluded in writing and rewriting the manuscript, and in selecting and editing old photographs. My son Jonathan accompanied me to Columbus, New Mexico, to participate in one of the Sergeants Major Academy's staff rides, and his photographic skills proved to be a valuable resource.

Many thanks are due to Elizabeth A. S. Demers, Senior Editor, and to Bridget Austiguy-Preschel, Senior Project Manager, both of Greenwood Publishing Group, for their assistance in the editorial process. Thanks are also due to Saloni Jain, Project Manager, Aptara, New Delhi, India, for assistance as project coordinator.

While it is obvious that many individuals contributed to this book, I hope it is just as obvious that any errors are mine and mine alone.

INTRODUCTION:
THE REVOLUTIONARY BACKGROUND TO THE
PERSHING EXPEDITION

We are sleeping under the cool but harmful shade of a poisonous tree . . . we should not deceive ourselves, we are heading for a precipice.

—Francisco I. Madero

The words of the young Francisco I. Madero, a wealthy landowner in the frontier state of Chihuahua, would prove to possess oracular accuracy. The poisonous tree of Madero's metaphor was the long reign of Porfirio Díaz who, defeated in the presidential election of 1875, had seized power and ruled as president for thirty years. The long reign of "Don Porfirio," as most Mexicans respectfully entitled him, was named the Porfiriate and was distinguished by his program of "Peace, Order, and Progress," which had by the turn of the century created numerous *revoltosos* (émigrés or exiles in revolt) groups in the United States and Canada. The ideological range of the exiles spread from the radical Left amalgamation of anarchists and socialists to the reactionary Right's conglomeration of counterrevolutionaries and pro-Church conservatives. They were perhaps the first indication that Madero's "harmful shade" of the Díaz regime was spreading to the United States, and few if any Americans could foresee just how deeply they were to be affected by the precipice that was beginning to open south of the Rio Grande River.

The administration of Porfirio Díaz was characterized by the facade of democracy, an admiration for the type of modernization he thought the United States embodied, and a view of government in which all authority was in the hands of those who governed. In short, he embraced a policy of *pan o palo* ("bread or the club"). Díaz justified his long autocratic reign with the argument that he brought political and social stability and pointed with pride to Mexico's economic growth. His support of the *científicos* (educated and technological elites) had, he argued, brought the blessings of industrial progress to a poor and backward country. He came to believe that only through the application of capital and technology to Mexico's vast resources could she be brought into the quickly approaching twentieth century. At the turn of the century foreign capital was pouring into Mexico, particularly into petroleum, mining, and transportation. Had Díaz been a student of nineteenth-century Europe, he might have foreseen some of the problems that modernization and industrialization bring in their wake.

As in Europe's Industrial Revolution, those first hit by the effects of modernization were the rural poor and the urban laborers. Under Diaz's policies more and more land, particularly communal lands of Indians, came under the control of foreigners. In agriculture this resulted in more profitable export crops such as sugar and coffee, but lowered the production of the basics necessary to feed the Mexican people. The rural population saw its standard of living drop, and in the urban areas industrial and craft workers found that even the prevailing seventy-two hour week was not enough to maintain their already meager standard of living. Díaz resisted any thought of land reform for Mexico's long-suffering rural poor, and any movement toward collective action by urban workers was fiercely resisted. Mexico was a country seething with discontent, and from exile the *revoltosos* were waiting for a moment when the possibility of revolt would present itself. In one of history's paradoxes, the possibility presented itself with the presidential election in 1910.

Diaz was so convinced that his program of foreign investment, domestic order, and economic progress were so firmly established in Mexico that he welcomed Francisco Madero's challenge for the presidency. The government's budget was showing a surplus, the silver peso was a stable currency, and Mexico's credit ranked alongside the world's major industrial powers. With good reason, Diaz could look back at unprecedented growth and stability and look forward to more of the same. He did not, however, realize the extent of nationalist disaffection among Mexico's literate middle classes, nor did he sense the growing anger among his nation's working classes. And both groups had a common focus for their dissatisfactions: the growing presence and influence of foreigners in Mexico's national life.

When he realized that Madero's candidacy was not an idle threat but a rallying point for his opponents, Díaz had Madero arrested. Following the summer election, the official results of which were certified in early October and in which the unopposed incumbent won a crushing victory, Madero was released from jail and departed for San Antonio, Texas. From exile among *revoltosos* he would later come to oppose, he issued his "Plan of San Luis Potosí" (named after the city in which he had been jailed): the summer elections were voided, Madero was declared provisional president until new elections were arranged, and all citizens were to be prepared to take up arms against the Porfiriate. The Plan even had a specific time for the revolt to begin: 6:00 PM on Sunday, November 20, 1910. San Antonio was a cauldron of émigré activity with political clubs, American adventurers, and arms and ammunition smugglers who worked on both sides of the border. Against this background of revolutionary fervor, Madero departed for Mexico on the evening of November 19.

The November reception in Mexico was so disheartening that Madero returned to San Antonio. When several rebellions against the Porfiriate broke out in Mexico under the banner of Madero's slogan of "Valid Voting, No Reelection," Madero returned to assume ostensible control of the rebel movements. In spite of the growth of rebellion against the Porfiriate, it never spread to include all of Mexico. The northern area (Chihuahua for the most part) allied itself with Francisco Villa and Pascual Orozco; the southern area (Morelos for the most part) was most closely connected to Emiliano Zapata. Both regions were virtually continuous war zones. In the south, Zapata was calling for land reform ("Land and Liberty" was the essence of *Zapatismo*): land for the Indians and the virtually landless peasants. His fighters were drawn for the most part from Indians and the peasantry. In the north, Villa's growing forces came from the ranks of ranch workers, under-and unemployed artisans, and cowboys.

The capture of Ciudad Juárez in early May (May 10) by Villa and Orozco was the end of the Porfiriate. Juárez was the entrance to El Paso, Texas, and its possession by the rebels guaranteed access to the supplies needed to equip their forces. Díaz agreed to resign at the end of the month, and Madero agreed to allow the Porfiriate bureaucracy to retain its integral place in the new government to be formed. An interim president, Francisco de la Barra, was selected to preside until elections could be held in the fall. The October elections found Madero the easy victor in a field with no strong challenger. On November 6, 1911, Mexico had a new president, one whose ideals were widely accepted but whose moderation would prove to be unacceptable to both the radicals and the conservatives. The revolutionary tiger so feared by Porfirio Díaz was about to be unleashed.

In an attempt to defuse the potentially explosive situation he found himself in, Madero sought to disband the rebel forces. He believed that order could best be maintained through keeping the federal army intact and moving cautiously in matters of social reform. His caution triggered a *Zapatista* revolt during which Zapata issued his *Plan de Ayala*, calling for the transfer of land to peasant proprietors in order to free them from control by the haciendas. Further revolts followed: Pascual Orosco, disappointed that Madero had ignored him; Feliz Díaz, the old dictator's nephew, and an ambitious member of Mexico's old Porfiriate power structure hoped for a restoration of his family's lost supremacy. The revolts were put down successfully, but at the cost of Madero's presidency and ultimately of his life.

A military coup d'état led by General Victoriano Huerta and his close allies overthrew Madero's government, and on February 22, 1913, Madero and his vice president, José Suárez, were arrested and murdered. It appeared that the forces of reaction had triumphed, but in reality the tiger had slipped its leash and began to vent its fury on the enemies of reform. In the south, Zapata, who had never really trusted Huerta's commitment to land reform, rallied his *campesinos* to the banner of "Land and Liberty." In the north a triumvirate developed that was to prove not only Huerta's undoing but was also to plunge Mexico into the worst days of her long and bloody revolution: Álvaro Obregón of Sonora, Venustiano Carranza of Coahuila, and Francisco Villa of Chihuahua.

They were the "Men of the North," the men of Mexico's "Wild West." Born and bred in the desert and mountains they were every bit as tough as the land that spawned them. They have been colorfully described as superstitious, ignorant, stubborn, part pagan and part Christian, suspicious of change and any way of life other than their own, strangers to formal education, but endowed with an exceptional natural intelligence of their own world. These three men, as uncomfortable with each other as any ancient Roman Triumvirate had ever been, were held together only by their desire to destroy Huerta. They proclaimed themselves "Constitutionalists" because they sought a constitutional solution to Mexico's problems, and they accepted Carranza's leadership, albeit with reservations.

In addition to his domestic enemies, Huerta had alienated President Woodrow Wilson. Huerta's coup was unacceptable to Wilson who, while championing a nation's right to self-determination, was appalled by the murders of Madero and Suárez. Wilson not only refused to recognize Huerta's legitimacy, but he also began actively to undermine Huerta's regime. Wilson's offer of financial assistance in return for elections in which Huerta could not be a candidate was refused, and Wilson ordered an arms embargo followed by the occupation of the port of Vera Cruz by American troops (April 1914). The arms embargo did not apply to Constitutionalist forces that could import arms and munitions from the United States. Huerta's situation was indefensible, and on July 14, 1914, he resigned and went into exile.

Victory for the Constitutionalists brought neither peace nor an end to the revolution. After months of arguing, the victors met in the Convention of Aguascalientes on October 5, 1914. They hoped to be able to unite behind a president, but irreconcilable differences destroyed that hope. Neither Venustiano Carranza (First Chief) nor Alvaro Obregón was interested in land reform. For Emiliano Zapata the land question *was* the Revolution; for Villa the *political* future of Mexico was of primary importance. Obregón referred to the differences as a lover's quarrel, but it was more a difference of passions and personalities than of belief or ideology. The passions and personalities of the "lover's quarrel" destroyed the Convention and plunged Mexico into a violent and bloody civil war.

As First Chief of the Constitutionalist Army, Carranza announced he would accept retirement only under conditions that called for the resignation and exile of both Zapata and Villa. Zapata marched toward Mexico City and his forces occupied it in November 1914. In December Villa and his followers were welcomed into the city. Forever the land reformer, however, Zapata returned to Morelos that month to continue and expand upon land redistribution. Villa lingered for a time in the city, and in the early months of 1915 he began his journey down the path to defeat at the hands of Obregón and Benjamín Hill. Following a series of seven consecutive defeats in the Bajío, Villa was forced to retreat into Chihuahua. In late summer the Constitutionalists forced Zapata's army from Mexico City, and the United States government recognized Carranza as the de facto First Chief of the Republic of Mexico on October 19, 1915.

The recognition of Carranza by the Wilson Administration had been planned by Secretary of State Lansing for several months, and by October concerns over southwest border disturbances prompted him to solidify his plan to recognize Carranza as the first step in establishing relations between national governments. Only a legitimate government, Lansing and President Wilson believed, could be held accountable for border disturbances; revolutionary factions could not be depended upon. Recognition, however, ended any hope for rapprochement with Villa. When he first received the news he could not believe it. He declared that he was through with the United States, through with protecting American citizens, and through with protecting their property. He said that he would take no responsibility for future events, an ominous remark coming from a man like Villa.

One

DÉNOUEMENT, DEFEAT, AND THE MARCH TO COLUMBUS

The recognition of Venustiano Carranza as "First Chief" of the provisional government of the Mexican Republic by the Wilson Administration was the primary reason for the development of Villa's antagonism toward the United States. American residents in Mexico had earlier emphasized the friendliness Villa had shown them, and Villa realized that his successes had been largely due to the support he had received from Americans both in Mexico and in the Unites States. As many as fifty Americans had fought with Villa on numerous occasions, and he believed that both the American people and the government of Woodrow Wilson looked to him as Mexico's salvation from chaos. His belief that the ruler of Chihuahua was the rightful ruler of Mexico, plus his belief in the invincibility of the vaqueros of the north, led him to see himself as the natural choice to lead Mexico through her revolutionary difficulties. His disappointment and anger over the recognition of Carranza gave way, however, to a deadly hatred as the result of his campaign in Sonora.

The American embargo had made it increasingly difficult for Villa to supply his men with guns, ammunition, and provisions. He believed that a successful campaign in Sonora offered a number of advantages:

(1) it increased the possibility of securing arms and ammunition because with control of additional border territory the chances for successful smuggling increased;

(2) the acquisition of territory on the west coast of Mexico made possible shipments of war materiel from Japan through arrangements already made with Japanese shippers;

(3) the cooperation of the Sonora Yaqui Indians, who it was believed had already declared for Villa; and

(4) the cooperation of Emiliano Zapata who had control of the states extending west to the Pacific coast and Colima.

Within two weeks of Carranza's recognition, Villa began his movement toward Sonora from Torreon, and by early October 1915, he had concentrated about 13,000 men and 42 field pieces at Casas Grandes on the Mexican Northwestern Railroad. Most of the men, some 9,000, had been transported by train from Juarez and the remaining 4,000 had crossed the Sierra Madre under General Rodolfo Fierro.

This concentrated force of 13,000 left Casas Grandes October 15, 1915, and its advance guard reached Agua Prieta in late October. Villa camped east of Agua Prieta on the ranch of John Slaughter, a retired lawman, and a Villa sympathizer. In the days following its arrival, the army grew to perhaps 15,000 strong and included women, children, Indians, peasants, and *Dorados*. The women nursed their infants, cared for the children, and cooked for the multitude. The Yaqui Indians smoked marijuana and danced away the nighttime hours in wild abandon. The peasants drank *sotol*, and whiled away the hours in song and conversation; the *Dorados* patrolled the area and attempted to maintain a semblance of order.

Unaware that the United States had assisted Carranza by allowing 6,000 troops and their supplies to pass through Eagle Pass to Sonora on the railroad in New Mexico and Arizona, on November 1 the attack was launched with disastrous results. Colonel Plutarco Elías Calles had his troops behind walls, and the open areas were covered with barbed wire and strewn with mines. Three frontal assaults were broken by Carrancista artillery and machine gun fire. An assault that evening under cover of night was decimated when searchlights from Nogales, Arizona, bounced their beams off clouds and illuminated the battlefield. The Yaqui Indians who led the attack were stoned on marijuana, and they made no attempt at subterfuge; as they charged into the illuminated barbed wire they were simply slaughtered. Villa retreated to the west, to Naco and Cananea, then south past Magdelena and Santa Ana toward Hermosillo, the capital of Sonora. The final days of the once invincible Division of the North were at hand.

On November 22, 1915, Villa, having learned nothing from his defeats at Celaya, León, and Agua Prieta, attacked Hermosillo in a direct frontal assault. There was no cover of darkness this time. His men, exposed to fire from concealed machine guns and a deadly rifle fire from the city's rooftops, attacked with a desperate, suicidal bravery. The punishment produced by the Carrancistas' firepower was, however, more than they could bear. The assault slowed, and then stopped. Seized by panic, the engaged Villistas fled, leaving a field strewn with their dead and wounded comrades. They became a vicious irrational horde, and as they made their flight toward Nogales their hallmark became arson, rape, pillage, and anarchy. Villa realized the futility of continuing his fight in Sonora and toward the end of November ordered a guarded retreat into Chihuahua.

In his retreat from Sonora, Villa utilized all the practicable passes in the Sierra Madre, which connected Sonora and Chihuahua but covered only the Delores and Pulpit Passes with rear guards. Villa had preceded his retreating forces and arrived in Madera, Chihuahua, on December 10, 1915, and brought with him about thirty *Dorados*. Stragglers continued to come in until December 25. A large part of his army had retreated to Casas Grandes, and most went from there to Juarez to accept Carranza's offer of amnesty. Only six of his forty-two artillery pieces returned from Sonora. Of the 13,000 men he had mustered for his conquest of Sonora in October, approximately 8,000 came back to Chihuahua (and that included the men who amnestied themselves from Casas Grandes). The remainder deserted, joined the victorious Carrancistas at Hermosillo, or simply elected to remain in Sonora. His battle casualties were a greater psychological defeat than they were a numerical defeat: the manner in which they were inflicted was devastating to his followers' morale.

The defeats and desertions suffered by Villa in Sonora only further embittered him toward Americans. On December 13 he left Madera for Chihuahua City, passed through Guerrero, and arrived at his new headquarters on December 15. He remained in Chihuahua for seven days and during those days lost no opportunity to denounce both the gringos and their government. In a public address given on December 21, he stated in essence the following: the United States had been unfair to him in recognizing Carranza; that Carranza had sold the Mexican people into bondage to the United States; that the United States would intervene and invade Mexico and Carranza would be too weak to resist; that he would always love the Mexican people and protect them; and that from this date on his ammunition would only be used against the Americans and not one round would be fired against his fellow Mexicans. He left the following day by train for Hacienda de Bustillos for a conference with his generals.

The Bustillos Conference, also known as the Conference of the Twenty-Seven Generals (See Appendices), was a gathering of his most trusted advisors.

The object of the conference was to evaluate whether or not to continue to support Villa's cause, and it had been called as a result of a petition sent to Villa by his leading generals. Villa was present and listened to the debate only a short time because it was apparent from the beginning what the outcome would be. He informed those present that they were free to do as they wished, but that he would never seek amnesty from his hated rival, Carranza. With that said he left the meeting and departed by carriage that evening for Rubio. Accompanied by a mistress and the wife of Colonel Nicholas Fernandez, he arrived at Rubio in the early evening of Christmas Eve. Among the generals who attended the meeting and proclaimed their continued allegiance to Villa were Francisco Beltran, Gregorio Beltran, Cruz Dominguez, and Juan Pedrosa.

At Rubio, Villa's army consisted of 100 men and 200 horses. Perhaps reflecting the spirit of Christmas, he did not at this time oppose individual soldiers who wished to secure Carranza's amnesty. He required, however, that those who decided to leave must surrender their arms to General Julio Acosta who was in charge of supplies for the Guerrero district. This order was generally disregarded because part of the amnesty plan was a bounty on each firearm surrendered. On the morning of December 26, Villa left Rubio accompanied by Colonel Nicholas Fernandez and about eighty men. At El Valle on the afternoon of December 28, Villa found Generals Rodriguez, Hernandez, Cenisero, and Lopez with 300 men. The following day the combined force left El Valle southbound with San Geronimo as its objective. While enroute, Villa visited General Pedrosa at Cruces and Colonel Candelario Cervantes at Namiquipa and left both men in command of their respective posts. Villa continued on his way to San Geronimo and arrived there January 2, 1916.

During the first week of January, Villa was quite generous in permitting his men to visit their homes. They were simply required to leave their arms in camp when they departed. There was a great deal of movement to and from the camp at this time, detachments were sent out either on reconnaissance or to enlist recruits. Perhaps the most important incident at this time was the loss of General Rodriguez. He had been dispatched with thirty men to Madera and was trapped and captured on January 8 by Carrancista General, Maximiano Marquez. On orders from Marquez's superiors, Rodriguez was shot. To add to Villa's woes, General Manuel Hernandez left with eighty men for Durango and General Cenicero left with his men and neither remained in communication with Villa. The reconnaissance patrols, the recruiting expeditions, and the permits granted to men to visit home exacted a heavy toll on available forces.

When he ordered a move from San Geronimo to Los Tankes on January 7, 1916, he had 130 men. During the night march about thirty of those men deserted, and when he arrived he found he had seventy *Dorados* under Colonel Ramon Tarango and about thirty followers of Colonel Nicolas Fernandez. The detachments of General Juan Pedrosa at Cruces (forty men) and Colonel Candelario Cervantes at Santa Clara (twenty men) constituted Villa's total reserve force. On January 9 General Jesus M. Rios entered camp with his detachment of ten men. The next fortnight saw Villa in camp and the men working on the slaughter of cattle and the preparation of jerky in expectation of a move in the immediate future. The men who had been permitted to make home visits failed to return, and this created a great deal of unrest and discontent among the rank and file.

On January 15 Pedrosa and Cervantes were ordered to recruit all able-bodied men in the vicinities of Cruces and Namiquipa and to then concentrate their forces at Santa Clara. Villa made his intentions clear to his own force on January 18 when he assembled the entire command and told them that in the morning they would leave to attack the American border town of Presidio, Texas, in the vicinity of Ojinaga. He assured them that they would be reinforced prior to the attacks by large detachments of troops, and promised them that they would be free to return to their homes and would not regret their participation in what he called the last expedition to attack the Americans. What he had in mind here (large numbers of reinforcements) perhaps came from a letter he had written to Emiliano Zapata on January 9 in which he blamed his defeat at Agua Prieta on a corrupt bargain between Carranza and President Wilson and asked Zapata to come north with all his troops. Together, the letter continued, they would undertake the reconstruction and improvement of Mexico as well as punish their "eternal enemy," the United States of America. Apparently, Villa neither took into consideration the difficulties Zapata would face in marching an army hundreds of miles through hostile territory, nor did he consider Zapata's reluctance to send his men out of their native state of Morelos. In either case, the "large number of reinforcements" did not appear, and Zapata remained in Morelos.

Villa left the following morning with approximately one hundred men to the previously designated concentration point at Santa Clara. At San Geronimo, Villa was joined by Colonel Martin Lopez and seventy-five men, and the combined detachments proceeded to Santa Clara to rendezvous with Pedrosa and Cervantes. January 22 and 23 were spent in making preparations for the march to Ojinaga. The force numbered a total of 240 men, divided as follows: Villa, his headquarters staff and escort, 50 men; General Pedrosa, 40 men; Colonels Fernandez, Lopez, Cervantes, Perez, and Cardenas, 150 men.

Aware that a Carrancista force in the rear would constitute a grave threat, Villa ordered Pedrosa and his detachment to establish themselves as a garrison force at Cruces. The force that departed Santa Clara on January 24 consisted of approximately 200 men, many of whom were openly skeptical about the wisdom of attacking the United States. The first night's march saw considerable desertion, when Colonel Perez and a portion of his detachment of twenty men deserted. The march was temporarily halted from January 26 to 28, and Colonel Cardenas was dispatched to recover the deserters. During the second night of the halt several more deserted, and desertions continued throughout the day. By the third day Colonel Cardenas had not returned, and the number of desertions had reached thirty. The march was resumed January 29 and reached Las Varas, near San Lorenzo, where camp was made for the night. Villa was aware of the discontent, and changed his plans to meet the new situation. He ordered an early morning march to La Laguna, a town with a railroad station.

The remnant arrived at La Laguna at daylight, and the Carrancista telegraph operator at the railroad station was replaced with a loyal Villista. The past several weeks had taught Villa that his desertion-wracked contingent was not strong enough to attack the United States, and that he needed to return to San Geronimo and recruit a larger, more dependable force. Before returning, however, he thought it necessary to somehow reward the men who had followed him this far. He decided the best way to reward them was to provide them with enough loot to take their minds off the frustrations of the past several months. His telegraphic operator at the train station informed him that a train would leave Juarez the following morning, January 31. Villa's opportunity to provide his men with loot was on its way.

The Juarez train on the Mexico Central railroad pulled into La Laguna at 11:00 AM The station was covered by Villistas. It was allowed to stop as usual, and then the passengers were required to leave the train while it was looted. Among the passengers was General Porfirio Ornelas who had taken part in the Bustillos Conference the past December. He had since accepted amnesty under Carranza's proclamation and when Villa saw him he immediately shot him, killing him instantly. The loot was divided among the Villistas, and that which could not be carried on their mounts was abandoned. Dissatisfaction was widespread, however, as most of the loot could not be taken due to lack of wheeled transportation. Villa was later heard expressing regret at having killed Ornelas, telling an aide that ingratitude was one fault he could not abide. By February 2, after a long and arduous march, the detachment made its way to Santa Clara.

For the next several days the horses were rested, while General Pedrosa was dispatched with part of Villa's force to scout Carranza forces reported to be near Cruces. Pedrosa learned that the Carrancistas were at the Babicora Ranch where they had occupied the main houses. This ranch, which traced it origins to a Jesuit settlement, was purchased by United States Senator George Hearst in the late nineteenth century. The original purchase was 500,000 acres, which was the area of the principal plain of San José de Babicora. When the Senator died in 1891 his widow Phoebe Apperson Hearst purchased an additional 500,000 acres, about half of which adjoined the principal plain on the east on the headwaters of the Santa María River. The other half, to the west of the main property and on high drainages to the Yaqui River, contained the areas then known as Naguerachic, Tascates, and San Pedro. On the eve of the Mexican Revolution, the ranch held 75,000 head of cattle, 2,000 horses, and 6,000 sheep. It was, after years of revolutionary upheaval, a shell of its former self.

An argument broke out among the Villistas over who was in charge of the detachment and finally Pedrosa, because of his age and rank, was chosen. Those who opposed Pedrosa threatened to desert, and only the thought of Villa's revenge prevented them from doing so. After resting their horses on February 5 and 6, preparations were made for a forced march to attack the Carranza troops. On the morning of February 8, Pedrosa sent three columns under Cervantes, Fernandez, and Martin Lopez to attack the Carrancistas, who had taken shelter in the ranch buildings. The fight lasted for an hour and a half and broke off when the attacking Villistas gave way and retreated in disorder in the direction of San Geronimo. The attackers lost three (who were killed), and several were wounded. The next day the stragglers reached Namiquipa and awaited the gathering of the remainder of Villa's scattered forces.

On February 7, the small army departed Santa Clara and marched to San Geronimo, where General Beltran with about eighty men and General Pablo Lopez with close to a hundred men were camped. The force was now an estimated 400 men, the largest of which were Pablo Lopez's command (100) and Beltran's detachment (80). There were, however, serious uncertainties. The mission that they had spoken of at Los Tanques in January, an attack upon the United States in order to provoke American intervention in Mexico, had proven unpopular with not only some of his officers but also among the rank and file. The desertions and the loss of fighting élan demonstrated at the Babicora Ranch just days earlier caused a reexamination of assumptions that had been made earlier. It was apparent that the men were willing to fight against Carranza on Mexican territory, and that they were willing to fight in Mexico against Mexicans. They were, however, apprehensive about the prospect of fighting Americans *in* the United States. Villa needed a plan of action that would ingratiate him with his officers and men as well as the general population upon whom he would be calling for volunteers.

On the afternoon of February 10 the Lopez brothers, whose combined commands totaled 150 men, were dispatched to the Santa Ana Ranch. The ranch, owned by William Randolph Hearst and abandoned for several months, was to provide the cattle and sheep that would be the foundation of Villa's future largesse. Some livestock were slaughtered and the rest were driven down the Santa Clara Valley as far as Casas Grandes where they were given to the populace. The livestock on the Bustillos Ranch, also American-owned, were disposed of in a similar manner. During the two weeks that Villa had his headquarters at San Geronimo, approximately 5,500 cattle and 1,000 head of sheep were taken and disposed of among the general population. Confiscation and distribution met the twofold purpose of revenge upon Americans and of winning over the farm workers as a base for future "volunteers" in case they were needed.

Plans for an attack upon the United States had not been abandoned by Villa, and he now took steps to rebuild his command. He dispatched Colonel Tarango and an escort with personal letters to both Colonel Julian Perez and Colonel Julian Cardenas asking them to rejoin him at San Geronimo. Villa's forces, it should be noted, consisted of dozens of generals, hundreds of officers, and few enlisted men. He did not tell them of his plans to attack the United States, but told them he had 500 men (in reality he had less than 400) and soon would have thousands. His motives here probably had less to do with the presence of Perez and Cardenas than it did with his belief that their presence would help put an end to the continuing problem of desertion. Perez could not be reached as he had already gone to Chihuahua to seek amnesty; Cardenas replied that he would rejoin Villa as soon as he finished recruiting as many men as he could (Cardenas did not rejoin Villa until March 24 at Rubio, after the attack on Columbus).

On the evening of February 12, probably in collusion with Villa, the Lopez brothers went to San Geronimo and kidnapped the three daughters of Señor Camaduran, an American sympathizer and resident of the United States. The oldest girl, age eighteen, was taken to Villa at Los Tankes where he was waiting for her, and the other two were taken and raped by Pablo and Martin Lopez. Relatives of the Camaduran family provided General Cavazos, the Carrancista commander at Guerrero, with detailed information about the locations of the Villistas along with a report on the conduct of the officers. Villa ordered the Lopez brothers to return the two girls to their mother. Sources indicate that the mother appeared appeased and was satisfied that the other girl was living with Villa. The Camaduran family was one of influence in the area, however, and the circumstances surrounding the incident were wired to Chihuahua where plans were made to attack the Villistas at Santa Ana.

Several days later Colonel Lopez's contingent at Santa Ana was attacked by Carrancistas under General Cavazos, commanding officer of a force of 450. The Villistas, approximately 140 men, retreated to the old barracks and prepared for Cavazos' attack. The attackers were deployed to encircle the barracks and to form a perimeter facing southeast and east. Villa's main force arrived about 6:00 AM and were deployed with a view to flank Cavazos' right, while at the same time cutting off his retreat. Cervantes arrived from Namiquipa with about forty men and engaged Cavazos on his left. After about an hour of fighting, the demoralized Carrancistas fled in a panic. General Cavazos escaped to San Juanito with a few of the Babicora Ranch force, and at Santa Ana the Villistas killed all Carrancista prisoners along with the wounded. It was estimated that 250 of General Cavazos' men were killed in what is called the Battle of Santa Ana. Villa's force returned to San Geronimo the same day to continue his plans for a strike on the United States.

The success of his forces at Santa Ana suggested to Villa an auspicious moment. On February 20 Villa handed Colonel Candelario Cervantes a letter in which he ordered the immediate mobilization of all men in the districts of Namiquipa and Cruces who had earlier been in his service. The men would be assigned to the command of Cervantes, and those who refused to report for duty would be shot. In addition, the families of any men who concealed themselves and were not found would pay a penalty (presumably death). Cervantes left San Geronimo for Namiquipa and on the following day detailed Lt. Colonel José Boncamo for Cruces and Lt. Colonel Cruz Chavez for Santa Ana to carry out Villa's proclamation. These orders were accompanied by further orders to prepare large quantities of jerked beef for the journey northward to the United States border.

The Lopez brothers, who were at Santa Ana, were ordered to report to San Geronimo; they were further ordered to burn the ranch houses before departing. They joined Villa at San Geronimo, as did about fifteen men recruited by Cervantes at Namiquipa. The next day a complete reorganization of the forces present at San Geronimo took place. Villa knew from experience that the best results were obtained by grouping men from each locality under officers known to them, and in keeping with this principle the assignments on February 21 were made as follows: the headquarters unit and escort, 80 men, under Colonel Ramon Tarango; General Pablo Lopez 100 men; General Francisco Beltran, 125 men; and Colonel Nicholas Fernandez, 60 men. About 20 men, sick and wounded, were left behind. This reorganized force of 365 men left San Geronimo on February 23.

General Pershing's intelligence officers later took statements from participants in the march, and these statements varied in regard to the destination the marchers were given. Some mentioned El Valle, others said Palomas, but border towns in the United States did not appear to have been mentioned as objectives. The reason for this is rather simple: based on experience, Villa was reluctant to suggest to his rank and file that his plans included crossing the border into the United States. In an effort to maintain high morale, Villa was heard to say to members of his escort that they would be more than pleased upon their return from this expedition. He promised good horses and loot, rewards worthy of an army under the command of Pancho Villa.

Upon arrival at Namiquipa, Villa established himself in the City Hall and was pleased to learn that Cervantes was able to recruit about sixty men including those he had sent to San Geronimo a few days earlier. All detachments and leaders were billeted in town. The following day equipment was secured for the new men, fresh mounts were collected, and provisions were packed. A comprehensive organization could not be concluded until Cruces was reached, because General Pedrosa and his detachment were waiting there to be included into the expedition. The detachments left Namiquipa for Cruces via the Santa Maria River route in columns of two, each detachment separated from the others by about one-half mile and in the following order of march: (1) Fernandez (2), Cervantes (3), Pablo and Martin Lopez (4), Villa with his headquarters unit and body guard, and (5) Beltran. Ten pack mules laden with jerky brought up the rear.

When the lead detachment entered Cruces, Villa and his *Dorados* occupied the schoolhouse, and the other detachments were billeted in various parts of the town as they arrived. Billets had been arranged by Colonel Pedrosa in advance and the occupation went smoothly. The final arrangements for the march were made there; a day and a half was spent in arming and equipping the new men. All available mounts, pack mules, and saddles in Cruces were confiscated, and corn was collected to be transported as emergency rations. In the final organization of Villa's force at Cruces, a number of observations may be made, particularly in regard to Cervantes' detachment.

About eighty in number, the Cervantes detachment consisted of men from Namiquipa, Cruces, and vicinity. These men had had previous service in the Villista armies and were, to a large extent, seasoned campaigners. They stood in fear of Cervantes and in all matters his word was law; he brooked no opposition, and his men knew better than to offer any. His control was total, and many men were indebted to him for past kindnesses. Many of these men were familiar with the roads leading north from Cruces to the American border. Colonel Cruz Chavez and Major Carmen Ortiz were knowledgeable about the roads and conditions along the border, and particularly well informed about Columbus. For these reasons Cervantes' detachment was the perfect choice for advance guard for the march, and with the exception of one day at Colonia Pacheco, it led until the actual attack on Columbus. Villa had greater confidence in Cervantes than in any other of his other leaders.

Fernandez's detachment was composed of men whose original leaders had abandoned Villa. Unlike their former leaders, these men were completely dependable, as they chose to follow Villa because of their intense loyalty to him. They came from all areas of Mexico and included the men left by Cardenas and Perez when they departed just prior to the Laguna raid. Fernandez was among the first to proclaim his loyalty to Villa after the Bustillos Conference, and he was Villa's close friend. He was in command of sixty men in the attack on Columbus.

In Villa's staff and in the *Dorados* were men who would choose death rather than to desert their leader. Among them were members of Villa's family as well as his closest political advisor, Colonel Manuel Baca. *Dorados* was a term coined by Villa to designate his bodyguard. The only distinguishing part of their uniform was a bronze insignia about the size of a half-dollar upon the upper edge of which was inscribed "Constitutionalist Army," in the center was the word *Dorado*, and along the lower edge were the words "Command Officer." Officers in addition wore their insignia of rank on their hat. *Dorado* signified "Golden One," "Browned" (i.e., accustomed to hard service and indifferent to discomfort). Colonel Tarango, commander of the *Dorados*, was one of Villa's most devoted followers and like Fernandez preferred death to separation from Villa. He died March 27, 1916, at Guerrero in an encounter with Carrancista forces (a skirmish in which Villa was wounded). With few exceptions the *Dorados* were from the state of Durango and more than half of them were officers.

General Pablo Lopez with about 150 men joined Villa at San Geronimo after the Santa Ysabel massacre. In the reorganization and allocation of assignments at San Geronimo prior to the march to Columbus, his brother Martin and he were given command of the hundred-man contingent from San Andres. There was no question about the loyalty of the Lopez brothers; they were totally committed to Villa and his cause.

General Juan Pedrosa's forty men were from the state of Durango. His detachment had remained virtually unchanged since the earlier days prior to Villa's last campaign in Sonora. General Francisco Beltran's was composed of men from the Yaqui section of Sonora and he was widely known as *El General de los Yaquis*. Statements taken from Villista prisoners following the Columbus attack indicate that only six Yaqui Indians participated in the raid. At the time Beltran acquired the name, however, he commanded 3,000 Yaquis.

The preparations for the march to Columbus were completed by the evening of February 26, and the movement began before daybreak the next day. The formation that was adopted for the march and that would remain with few exceptions until the attack on March 9 consisted of an advance guard of 80 men under Colonel Candelario Cervantes, the main body of 405 men, which included Villa's headquarters staff and escort, and a small rear guard of 10 men in Francisco Beltran's detachment from the main body. In the advance guard were the scouts and guides under the command of Lt. Colonel Sisto Valenzuela, a resident of Palomas, the small town just south of the border and several miles from Columbus, New Mexico.

As it marched out of Cruces, the column counted 200 officers and 285 enlisted men. They were armed with 7 mm Mauser rifles, a large number of 30–40 caliber rifles, and a few 30–30 Winchesters. The rifles were not only in an assortment of calibers, but they were also in an assortment of physical condition, which ranged from dilapidated to reasonably well cared for. Each man carried between thirty and one hundred rounds of ammunition for his rifle, and no extra ammunition was issued. Because of the variety of calibers in the weapons carried by the Villistas, ammunition was always in short supply. There was, therefore, no possibility for systematic practice with their rifles. This probably accounted for their reputation as poor marksmen. The first night's camp was made at La Hacienda del Arco, about thirty miles west of El Valle and east of the continental divide. The campsite was reached in mid-afternoon, and all the serviceable mounts in the area were confiscated. Five beef cattle were killed to be distributed among the camps. Later in the evening orders were given that desertion would be punishable by death. The march to Columbus had begun, and there would be no turning back.

THE MARCH TO COLUMBUS

The narrative of Villa's march northward to Columbus was recorded in General Pershing's "Report of Operations." The report was compiled from statements taken by intelligence officers from Villista officers who had participated in the raid on Columbus and who were later captured by soldiers of the Punitive Expedition in Mexico. According to Pershing's intelligence officers, the statements taken were all verified by cross-reference to other statements and it was believed that the facts were essentially correct.

On February 28, the Villistas left El Arce camp shortly after sunrise and marched over a very rough, narrow, mountain trail all day to a place called Rancheria de San José de Armitas, a distance of about thirty-five miles. They arrived there in the early evening and proceeded to requisition horses and cattle. The subsequent march proved to be something of a plague to the local populations, as Villa and his men simply requisitioned what they wanted. Depending on the attitude of the locals whose property was taken, receipts and primitive IOUs were issued. More often than not, Villa's actions amounted to simple theft.

The next day, the Villistas broke camp early and traveled on a trail leading northwest, crossed the Mexican Northwestern Railroad track at Palanganas, about twenty miles south of Pearson and arrived at their camp at La Maga at about mid-evening without incident. The trail was so rough on this day that the major portion of the distance was traveled on foot, and thereby the horses were spared the punishment. The distance from the camp on the previous night was estimated at thirty-five miles. The camp was on the ranch owned by the Hearst Estate and Cervantes was anxious to press into service the cowboys employed there. When the Villistas arrived, however, the place was deserted and everything of value had been removed. Two cattle found in the mountains were brought in and killed.

Since the camp that night was not more than two miles from the railroad track, Villa and his officers were wary of discovery by the Carranza force they believed to be in the vicinity. So cautious was Villa that when a southbound passenger train was observed he called a conference of his officers to discuss their options. Villa and Cervantes favored an attack on the train, but the majority was opposed. While they debated the issue, the train passed on without incident. In earlier times there would not have been a debate, Villa would simply have ordered the attack. His caution was an indication of his realization that desertion among the rank and file was a constant possibility, and he increasingly called upon his officers for advice.

On March 1 Villa ordered the march to begin at 5:00 AM, before daylight brought the possibility of discovery by Carrancista forces. In the darkness the Villistas marched to "La Laguna," a lake at a very high altitude in the Sierra Madre, about fifteen miles west of Palanganas. The march was a very difficult one and half of the time was taken up in a brutal ascent of a high peak on which they situated their camp for the night. The campsite provided an unobstructed view of the surrounding countryside. Despite the hardship of the march nothing of importance occurred, and the men felt relaxed and secure. For the first time, however, they were compelled to rely upon their own beef for food, and Villa realized that he had a balance of security to observe: camp in remote areas and be relatively free from Carrancista interference, but be forced to rely on what food and water could be transported; or camp near settlements that could easily be plundered and thereby run the risk of an unwanted confrontation with government forces.

The next day the Villa broke camp well before dawn and marched across country, due north, to Ceinega Bonita. Lieutenant Colonel Cruz Chavez and Lieutenant Colonel Don Sisto Valenzuela were so familiar with the country being traversed that Villa could undertake night marches without the least anxiety of getting lost. He reached his next campsite at about four o'clock in the afternoon, having covered only fifteen miles. The main reason for the short march was that some of the horses were beginning to show signs of fatigue. Villa dispatched riders to search for fresh mounts, and ten horses were confiscated to replace those mounts that were too exhausted to be ridden. Villa decided against an early start the next day, and he remained in camp until early afternoon in order to give the horses time to graze and rest.

An afternoon and evening trek on Friday, March 3, took the Villistas to Colonia Garcia, an American Mormon colony. They arrived there roughly before midnight and found the colony deserted. Villa had always treated the Mormons with respect, but word of his new anti-Americanism had spread and the Mormons were not taking chances with a man notorious for his mercurial nature. The hungry Villistas found nothing to eat and were forced to fall back upon the supplies carried by the pack train. The supplies had rapidly diminished, and of the pack train's load assembled in Namiquipa only a small amount of corn remained. To make matters worse, the intermittent rain that had followed the column to Colonia Garcia became a full-scale rainstorm that settled in and drenched everything and everyone in the camp. Soon the campsite was flooded, and the Villistas made use of the deserted houses for the night's shelter. The next morning the rain was gone, and the sunshine was used to dry clothes and equipment.

Villa ordered the march to resume in mid-morning, and the column marched to Colonia Pacheco, a distance of about ten miles, where it halted for an hour's rest. During the halt a detachment from Cervantes' column brought in three Mexicans who were captured a short distance from the line of march. It developed later that these men were hunters from Pearson, a small American ranch near Colonia Hernández, about 120 miles south of the border. Presently one other member of the same party appeared, an American woman, Maude Hawkes Wright. She and her husband, Edward J. Wright, had worked the small ranch since shortly before the outbreak of the Revolution. She was soon joined by her husband and another American, Frank Hayden. Maude, Edward, Hayden, and the Mexicans were informed that they were prisoners of the Army of the North. The following morning Edward and Frank were taken before Villa, but were given neither a reason for their captivity nor an indication of what their fate would be. Shortly thereafter, the men were led away, and Maude never saw either of them again. She later learned that they had been murdered.

Only two horses and one mule were seized at the colony, but no food. The march resumed and camp was not made until a place called Chimeneya was reached in the early evening. At this camp Cervantes' detachment was well provided with meat, as he had killed a deer and divided it among members of his command. Food, generally speaking, was now quite scarce, and Villa became more and more concerned with possible desertions. The next morning, March 5, the Villista column departed Chimeneya and marched in a northerly direction to a place some five miles east of Ojitos where they remained until early evening to allow the horses to graze. They traveled all that night and marched to an American-owned ranch, Santos de Ojos, southwest of Espia. To their surprise they found two black Americans, one of whom was the ranch foreman. There was little to eat, so they made do with the flour, corn, and molasses they took from the ranch storehouse. They also took four horses, three saddles, and the foreman, whom they pressed into their service as a guide. The foreman was given to Fernandez's detachment, as that was the unit that was generally in the lead. In the course of the night five men deserted. They were quickly captured by Cervantes' men and execution immediately followed their return to camp. Their horses, saddles, arms, and equipment were issued to men who were in need.

Camp was broken that evening because Villa had decided that night marches had become necessary. The desertions of the previous evening had shaken him, and he believed that night marches would discourage men from leaving. Movement at night would also make it easier to conceal his column and its intentions. The men marched all night to an American-owned ranch called Bocas Grandes, where they arrived the following day at mid-morning, Tuesday, March 7. The trek had been an easy one across flat country and because of the darkness fear of detection was minimal. When the main body arrived at Bocas Grandes ranch they found about twenty horses and mules; they were confiscated to replace bad mounts. The Villista columns remained at Bocas Grandes the remainder of the day.

On the morning of March 8 they left shortly after sunrise and followed the river road for about two hours, then took a cross-country route in a northerly direction until they arrived at an arroyo, covered from the direction of Columbus, NM, by a small hill. It was about two o'clock in the morning, and they quickly took advantage of the abundant grass and water to feed and rest their horses. They unsaddled their mounts for what appeared to them to be a long halt. The unit leaders sent word back that Columbus, NM, was plainly visible from the hill to the north and was not more than four miles distant. There was no longer any doubt that an attack was imminent, but there was doubt about whether they were already on American soil.

Soon after their arrival at this arroyo, Villa, Cervantes, Nicolas Fernandez, and Carmen Ortiz were observed engaged in animated conversation. Presently they mounted and rode in the direction of the commanding hill, from which they would make a final reconnaissance. The reconnaissance party returned to the arroyo and engaged in another animated conversation. From later testimony given to Expedition intelligence officers, it appeared that Villa had changed his views with respect to the object of the march, an attack on Columbus, New Mexico. His position was almost entirely at variance with the others. He said, in effect, that there was no need of sacrificing the lives necessary to take an unimportant town like Columbus; that the garrison there was very large; and that better chances of success were to be had in fighting the Carrancistas. The cause for this change of view was not known. Cervantes on the other hand, as spokesman for the opposition, said that reliable information indicated that the American strength at Columbus was not more than fifty soldiers and that two hours' fighting should bring a decision in the Villistas' favor. A heated discussion continued for about two hours. Finally Villa was pressed for a decision, and he consented to attack. He issued orders that the attack on Columbus would be undertaken on the following morning.

Much of the story of the Villa's plan of attack later emerged from a series of interviews of Villista prisoners held in the State Penitentiary at Santa Fe, New Mexico. The interviews were conducted by Santa Fe attorney A. B. Renehan, who was preparing petitions for pardon to be presented to New Mexico's Governor Octaviano Larrazolo. One of the prisoners, a "Captain" Rodriguez as he called himself in the Penitentiary, was interviewed several times and provided an interesting account. There was no Captain Rodriguez listed in Expedition intelligence reports, only a General Rodriguez in Pedrosa's detachment and a Private José Rodriguez who was captured at Columbus. "Private" Rodriguez was tried for murder along with six others, found guilty with the others, and was sentenced with the others to death by hanging. The sentences were reviewed by Governor McDonald, and the Captain's sentence was commuted to life in prison (the other six were hanged in Deming, New Mexico, in June 1916).

The account given by José from his Penitentiary cell to Governor Larazollo's attorney was essentially as follows. Villa had given the spies precise orders. They were to enter Columbus, pose as Villista deserters if questioned, and locate the commercial properties of the merchant Samuel Ravel as well as where he lived and slept. A map was to be made of the town that would indicate the railroad station and above all the military encampment. They were to learn which military units were in Columbus, the positions of the guards, where the horses were stabled, and the schedule of when the guards were relieved in the morning. Captain Rodriguez was charged with drawing a map, which was to be used by Villa and his generals in determining the disposition of men during the attack.

The group arrived at Palomas on the evening of March 3 and left their horses with Miguel Nevárez, Hernandez's brother-in-law. They had been told to go to the Salon Palomas Bar and enter one by one and seek out the woman who owned the establishment. They mingled with the many patrons and spent the evening in the town's red light district. The next day they went to Columbus with the proprietress and several other women. One of the women was quite familiar with the town and showed Rodriguez what he was looking for. They took many walks and shopped. He spent the nights with the girl in the Salon Bar, and noted that Palomas had a Carrancista garrison of seventy-five men under the command of Major Alfredo Melsose. An additional one hundred men were billeted in a nearby hacienda. In this manner Rodriguez and his comrades spent several days gathering information and making a map. On the evening of the March 7 they went to where their horses were stabled, departed for Boca Grande, and made their report to Villa.

Two

FRANCISCO'S FOLLY: THE ATTACK
ON COLUMBUS, NEW MEXICO

President Wilson's recognition of Venustiano Carranza on October 19, 1915, followed by an end to the embargo on arms shipments to Carrancistas seemed to signal a new era of good relations between the beleaguered governments. On October 18 a Gulf Coast Railroad train was attacked on the outskirts of Brownsville, Texas, by Mexican bandits led by Luis de la Rosa. One soldier and two civilians were killed in the attack, and the cry for punishment was immediately raised. Carranza muffled the outcries, however, when he dispatched troops to the area and entered into an agreement with American military commanders in the Brownsville area, which provided for the mutual pursuit of bandits on either side of the border by American and Mexican troops. With Villa's defeat at Agua Prieta on November 1–2, followed by subsequent Villa losses in Juarez, Chihuahua, Hermosillo, and Nogales, Carranza's forces appeared to be in control in the north of Mexico.

Convinced that his policy of watchful waiting had triumphed, President Wilson, in his Annual Message to Congress on December 7, claimed that his administration had been put to the test in Mexico and had won. He was even more confident in a private talk with members of the Democratic National Committee the following day. He told his listeners that he believed that a people had the right to do with their government what they pleased, and if the Mexicans wanted to raise hell with theirs it was acceptable to him. He went on to say that after they had raised enough hell and had gotten their bellies full of it, they would develop a government that would be stable. These confident words of his steadfast belief in a peoples' right to revolution without interference would soon be put to the test when he and the nation learned of the fate of eighteen American mining managers at the hands of Villista bandits.

On January 10, 1916, a train bearing eighteen American employees of the American-owned La Cusi Mining Company of Cusihuriáchic, Chihuahua, was stopped at Santa Ysabel by a group of Villistas commanded by Pablo López, one of Villa's closest lieutenants. The Americans were taken from the train, robbed, stripped, and shot in cold blood by men shouting "Viva Villa!" One man, Thomas B. Holmes, was shot but survived by feigning death. A Mexican eyewitness, José Maria Sanchez, told an El Paso correspondent that Pablo Lopez had advised the passengers that if they wanted to see some fun they could watch him and his men kill the Americans. Those who had not been shot in the railcar were herded out to the side of the track, lined up, and shot by rifle fire. Lopez ordered that each be given a "mercy shot" and his orders were enthusiastically carried out. The bodies were stripped of clothing and shoes. When news of the outrage reached the United States two days later, the Wilsonian belief that *if the Mexicans want to raise hell, let them raise hell* was sorely tested. From one end of the country to the other, Congressional and editorial voices were raised in a chorus calling for action.

Both the Senate and the House were divided between those who wanted intervention and those who wanted to wait to see how the new Carranza government would handle the situation. Senator Borah of Idaho seemed to typify the dilemma when he said that America did not want Mexican territory; they did not want to impeach Mexican sovereignty; they wanted the Mexican people, as the President had said, to settle their own troubles. On the other hand, he continued, Americans did want and were entitled to have the protection of American citizenship. To the applause of both sides of the aisle in the House, James L. Slayden called for the apprehension and execution of those responsible for the outrage but cautioned against rash action before the Carranza government had time to bring the guilty parties to account. Others professed the belief that involvement in Mexican affairs could mean war, something the United States was not prepared for and something in which the American people had no interest. Congress was, at least for the moment, willing to accept Wilson's watchful waiting.

The nation's editorial voices reflected those in Congress and in state and local governments. On the one hand the Cincinnati *Enquirer* demanded the application of bayonets, artillery, and naval gunfire to guarantee the citizens' safety; on the other hand the San Antonio *Express* pointed to the reasonableness of the American people who realized that Carranza had not been in power long enough to gain control of all situations in Mexico. While expressing indignation over the incident and stressing that something must be done, moderation prevailed. The demand for immediate intervention was blunted by the realization that the murdered men had taken a terrible risk by entering an area in which their safety could not have been guaranteed. The American reading public was reminded of Carranza's June 30, 1915, announcement that the foreign investor must accept both the good and the bad fortune of the country in which he has settled and was consequently willing to question the wisdom of foreign involvement to protect business enterprises. The Mexican Ambassador to Washington reassured the American people that every action necessary to bring the killers to justice was being taken, and the Mexican Consul-General in New York City declared that the Government of General Carranza would be diligent and work actively to bring the guilty to justice and punish them as they deserve. When news of Villa's attack on Columbus reached the nation, however, the moderation and wariness so much in evidence in the weeks following the murders dissolved.

THE ATTACK

At about 8:00 PM on March 8, 1916, Villa's force left its hiding place near Sierra Prieta, Chihuahua, and marched slowly and quietly across the country in a northerly direction. They retained the same formation as on the march except that there was no distance between detachments. They crossed the railroad track about three miles west of Columbus and continued their march until they reached an arroyo two miles farther north. It was about 3:00 AM and they saw a train eastbound but ignored it. They remained there for about half an hour while Villa and his staff discussed the plan of attack. At 3:30 AM they countermarched, crossed the railroad track nearer to town, and halted at a point about one and one-half mile west of the Columbus knoll, Cootes Hill, just west of the town and south of the railroad tracks.

At this time Villa assembled his leaders and gave his orders for the attack Cervantes with 40 of Villa's mounted Dorados, for a total of 120 men, was to advance in line of skirmishers with his left side on the small knoll, Cootes Hill; Pablo Lopez (40 men) was to form his men in a line of skirmishers on Cervantes' left and guide the center of his force on the railroad track; Fernandez (60 men) was to form his men facing east on the left of Lopez and attack the town from the north; Beltran's force (125 men) formed on the left of Fernandez and attacked from the north with the goal of enveloping the American troopers. Pedrosa and his forty men remained with Villa, the horses, and the other half of Villa's escort near the reserve position, approximately seven

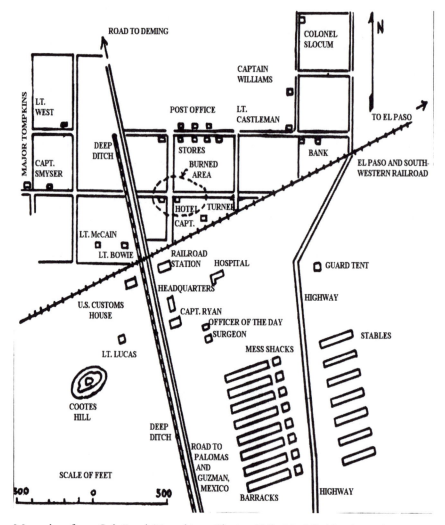

Map taken from Col. Frank Tompkins, *Chasing Villa*. Modified by the author.

hundred meters southwest from the center of Columbus. This small force of eighty men made up the attackers' rear guard. Colonel Nicolas Fernandez's promotion to the grade of General was announced after the order to attack had been given at 4:00 AM. The command had formed in lines of skirmishers, and with Villa's "Go ahead, boys!" and the countersign "Viva Mexico!" the attackers advanced.

The number of men involved in the attack is open to speculation. Villa's men fought as mounted infantry, not as cavalry. Horses were too valuable to be risked in the modern battle environment of barbed wire, machine guns, entrenchments, and accurate high-powered rifles. The horse became, therefore,

a means of transportation to the site of battle where designated horse holders secured the horses as their riders proceeded afoot. The number of horses
held by each holder determined the number of men who were then available
to fight. It is reasonable to assume that one man could hold the reins of two
horses in each hand, thus freeing three others to fight.

Applied to Villa's deployment of his forces, the numbers would have been
as follows. In the reserve position, 500 meters southwest of Cootes Hill, were
Villa, 40 *Dorados*, and the 40 men of Pedrosa's command with their own 81
horses. The horses of Cervantes' command (80) and the horses of Lopez's
command (100) could have been held by the 80 men in reserve with Villa.
The 40 *Dorados* who went with Cervantes were mounted. This would have
been in accord with Villa's earlier statement to his command that he would
be in the reserve with the horses. For Fernandez, some 600 meters north of
the reserve, and for Beltran, some 900–1,000 meters north of the reserve, it
was a matter of using delegated holders from their ranks. This meant 15 horse
holders and 45 fighters for Fernandez, and 30 horse holders and 95 fighters
for Beltran.

North of the railroad, in the heart of Columbus, the Villistas attacked with
140 men in two columns. South of the center of town 100 attackers were
divided on either side of the railroad tracks. South of the railroad tracks in
the center of the Army's establishment in Columbus 120 Villistas, forty of
them mounted Dorados, struck the barracks, the kitchens, and the stables.
The total attack force was 380. This number is of course an approximation; it
might have been slightly larger but was probably not significantly smaller.

Columbus was a small town, and as described by Lieutenant John P. Lucas,
recently stationed in the Philippines, did not present an attractive appearance.
There were a few adobe houses, a hotel, a few stores, and sandy streets. The
scenery consisted of cacti, mesquite, and rattlesnakes; the surrounding desert
was treeless. It was garrisoned with 553 men of the Headquarters and Machine Gun Troops and 7 Rifle Troops of the 13th Cavalry, Colonel Herbert
J. Slocum commanding. The troops were deployed in an area some 65 miles
along the border: 67 at the border gate (3 miles south of Columbus), 158 at
the Gibson's Line Ranch (14 miles west of Columbus), and 274 in Columbus.
The relatively small number of troops in the town may have been responsible
for the misconceptions of Villa's scouts. Colonel Slocum would later testify
that he had 266 fighting men with which to meet Villa's assault.

The entire Army force present in the camp at the time of the attack consisted of 12 officers and 341 men, most of whom were asleep. The Officer
of the Day, Lieutenant James P. Castleman, had three one-man guard posts
in camp: one each at the guard house, the stables, and near the regimental

headquarters (see Map: "Camp at Columbus"). Four men per cavalry troop (F, H, K, and M) slept in the stables of each troop. As may be seen by looking at the map, Columbus was divided into four sections by the El Paso and Southern Railroad (which ran in an east-west direction and the Deming-Guzman road), which ran in a north-south direction. The military establishment was located for the most part in the southeast quarter of town. The exception was officers' housing, which was almost exclusively private and scattered throughout the town on the north side of the railroad tracks.

The attack developed as a five-pronged action. South of the railroad tracks the men in Cervantes' command divided in two, and the larger portion rushed toward the stables while the smaller portion moved past the north side of the barracks. It was the presence among Cervantes' men of the mounted Dorados with their distinctive medallion-marked sombreros that gave rise to the mistaken notion that Villa was personally present in the attacking forces. The attackers with Lopez moved along the tracks toward the Customs House and the railroad station. The men with Fernandez moved east parallel to Broadway Street before they turned toward the commercial center of town and the men with Beltran circled to the north and struck farther east toward the bank and the Hoover Hotel. The plan of attack was tactically sound, but the faulty intelligence Villa had received from his scouts regarding the number of soldiers in Columbus proved fatal to any hope of success.

The camp was alerted when the sentinel near the headquarters issued a challenge and was shot by an attacking Villista. The Officer of the Day, Lt. Castleman, organized the men of F Troop, already out of the barracks, and led them toward the center of town where the fighting was heaviest They took up position on the main street near the bank, but Columbus had no streetlights and the only illumination was the occasional muzzle-flash of fired rifles. The darkness made it virtually impossible to see individual attackers, and the defending troopers were hampered by the muzzle-flashes of their own rifles. When the Commercial Hotel burst into flames, however, the illuminated attackers made relatively easy targets, and the American defenders were for the most part concealed in the surrounding darkness. The situation really began to deteriorate for the Villistas when Lt. Lucas got the machine gun troop into action.

Lt. Lucas had returned from El Paso, where he had been playing in a polo tournament for a week, aboard the midnight "Drunkard Special." He retired to his adobe near the base of Cootes' Hill, and was awakened by the sound of horsemen near his open window. When firing broke out he rushed to the guard tent to open the lockers in which the machineguns and ammunition were stored. The guns were kept under lock and key because in the clandestine

gunrunning trade along the border functioning machine guns were in constant demand. The current black market price was between $500 and $600
in Mexico. The first gun put into action jammed, but soon others arrived and
were deployed near the railroad at a crossing that went into town. The gun was
the Benèt-Mercier, an old gun of questionable design, with a reputation for
jamming and general unreliability. Its complicated design meant that conditions had to be perfect for it to function consistently, circumstances that were
rarely found in combat. The rigid feeding device further complicated the situation: if bent, it refused to feed properly and only a skilled gunner could clear
the jam.

Lt. Lucas managed to get three machineguns and thirty riflemen stationed
along the railroad tracks about the time the Villistas set fire to the hotel. A
fourth machinegun was deployed against the attackers near the barracks and
stables. Illuminated by the flames from the hotel and caught in crossfire from
the rifles and machineguns of the men of Lucas and Castleman, the Villistas'
resolve wilted and they began to fall back. The "Benny," as the weapon was
generally identified by the soldiers, was scornfully dubbed the "daylight gun"
due to the difficulty of operating it at night: assembly was difficult, repair was
next to impossible, and ammunition clips could be loaded upside down thus
jamming the gun. Broken firing pins and extractors were common in cold-
weather operation, and the failure of either part under combat conditions
meant that the gun was effectively neutralized. The fact that Lt. Lucas' gunners fired their guns as effectively as they did is high tribute to their training,
leadership, and determination.

The Army was later criticized in both Congress and the press for its adop-
tion of such an unreliable weapon as well as for having had the machineguns
locked up and not immediately available. Lt. Lucas' reply to his critics was
simple: He claimed as a matter of fact that the four guns used up about 5,000
rounds *apiece* in the hour and a half they were in action, which was much
more efficiency than the most sanguine had ever expected them to display.
Major Tompkins later came to the defense of Lieutenant Lucas by stating
that the Benny had always jammed, even in target practice, but in spite of the
jamming Lucas' men fired close to 20,000 rounds. Furthermore, Tompkins
claimed that the machineguns had caused the greater number of enemy casualties and kept down the accuracy and power of their rifles, while the defenders
organized for the counterattack with but few casualties.

Five of the machinegun troopers became casualties and one, Sergeant Mark
A. Dobbs, though shot through the liver refused to abandon his gun. He fired
until he died from loss of blood; he was the only fatality among the machinegun troopers. Lt. Lucas recommended Dobbs for the Medal of Honor and

later for the Distinguished Service Cross but never heard from either recommendation. Lucas was also recommended for both medals but received neither. The absence of awards may be a result of the fact that the Army was in the process of reviewing Medal of Honor (MOH) awards. On June 3, 1916, Congress passed *Section 122 of the National Defense Act*, which called for a review of all previous MOH awards. A board of five retired Army Generals was appointed to review each of the 2,625 MOH awards. Presided over by Lieutenant-General Nelson Miles (himself a MOH recipient and past commander of the MOH Legion), the Board sat from October 16, 1916 to January 17, 1917. It rescinded 911 previously awarded medals and ordered the return of the medals from those recipients still alive. An outgrowth of the Board's work was the creation of a "Pyramid of Honor," which established a hierarchy of awards for the various degrees of bravery above and beyond the call of duty. The recommendations for men at Columbus either fell through the bureaucratic cracks or were most likely ignored.

It should be noted that the Army was embarrassed by the Columbus raid, and it was taking a great deal of criticism from Congress, the newspaper reports, and the states of the Southwest. Much was made in the press and elsewhere of the successful element of surprise in the attack. Colonel Herbert J. Slocum, Commander 13th Cavalry came in for the bulk of the criticism, and the Army held an investigation. The results went up the chain of command from General Pershing, through General Funston (Commander Southern District), General Garlington (Inspector General), General Tasker Bliss (Assistant Chief of Staff), General Scott (Chief of Staff), to Secretary of War, Newton Baker. At each level, Colonel Slocum was exonerated from any blame. The fact that recommendations for medals were ignored would seem to indicate that the Army was in no mood to honor those who were involved in what so many individuals in places of power believed was a fiasco.

The figure of 20,000 rounds that the troopers were said to have fired has been a matter of much debate. The Benét-Mercie fired the M1906 (.30-06) cartridge. Its gas-operated mechanism fired at the rate of 400 rounds a minute. The mechanism was fed by metal strips (each of which held 30 cartridges) and the ammunition was transported in wood boxes, which held ten loaded strips, or 300 rounds. The rate of fire of seven rounds a second, or four or five seconds to fire one strip of thirty rounds, generated such heat that the weapon's capability of sustained fire was open to question. For this reason each gun was equipped with interchangeable barrels, but it was soon realized that the "Benny" would never be capable of the sustained fire of a water-cooled weapon. Furthermore, in cold weather the Benny had a tendency to break firing pins and extractors (in a cold-weather test at the Colt factory where the guns were being manufactured, firing pins and extractors were broken as fast they could be replaced). This was a weapon with obvious limitations.

In the hour and a half that Lt. Lucas reported that his gunners were in action, it is certainly *theoretically* possible that they fired close to 5,000 rounds each. In *theory* one strip (30 rounds) fired in seven seconds with perhaps three to five seconds to reload another strip would have produced 180 rounds per *minute* or 10,800 rounds per *hour*. In theory, therefore, the numbers match the weapon's mechanical potential; in practice, however, the numbers defy credibility. Certainly the raiders made inviting targets silhouetted against the burning buildings, but they were not targets of constant and unending presence. As they ran through the fire-illuminated streets they were targets of opportunity to machine gunners and riflemen alike, but they were neither so numerous nor so obvious that a constant hoselike spraying of bullets would have been practical or possible. The number of rounds reported as fired would have been reasonable had the gunners been firing at waves of massed infantry in frontal assault. Given the limitations of the weapon itself and the conditions of combat in the streets of Columbus, however, it seems unreasonable that 20,000 rounds of ammunition were fired.

When the Villistas fled from the center of Columbus, it was possible for the officers who had been isolated during the initial fighting to find their commands and organize pursuit Colonel Slocum authorized Major Tompkins to take the offensive with whomever he could organize, and he gathered thirty-two mounted troopers with whom he began the pursuit of the fleeing Villistas. This small command was reinforced to the total of fifty-six men. They crossed the international border, and attacked Villa's rear guard with deadly effectiveness. The brisk engagement of charge and countercharge continued until Tompkins ordered a return to Columbus. The return was made because in Tompkins' judgment ammunition was running dangerously low, both men and horses were fatigued from several hours' hard riding and fighting without food or water, and they were at least fifteen miles into Mexico. Upon his return to Columbus, Tompkins noted that his command had been mounted and moving for seven and a half hours, covered between twenty-five and thirty miles, and fought four engagements without the loss of a single man.

The civilian population did not fare quite as well. Ten civilians were killed, four of them murdered at the Commercial Hotel: William T. Ritchie, hotel proprietor, was taken from his room and shot; J. W. Walker, who was an overnight guest with his bride, was forced from his room, taken downstairs and shot; Dr. H. M. Hart, veterinarian from El Paso, was shot in the street; and Charles DeWitt Miller, New Mexico State Engineer, was shot in front of the hotel while trying to start his car. The others were J. J. Moore, merchant;

C.C. Miller, druggist; James T. Dean, grocer; Mrs. Milton James, wife of an El Paso and Southwestern Railroad employee; Harry Davis, railroad worker; and W. A. Davidson, occupation unknown. The grocery store was set on fire, and the flames spread to the Commercial Hotel. Stores and homes were looted, horses were stolen, and even bolts of cloth were carried away by the looting bandits. For all the violence, mayhem, and murder the raiders visited upon Columbus, they received precious little in return.

The Villistas had absorbed dreadful punishment. At the first light of morning they could see that their intelligence reports regarding the size of the garrison had been badly mistaken; the number of American soldiers greatly exceeded the number reported. The retreat was sounded and the able assisted the wounded where possible. The main body of Villistas, which had been directed against the town, simply collapsed. The chaos of their retreat was compounded by the fact that their horse-holders had themselves retreated one half mile or farther west of their assigned stations. Without horses the task of saving the wounded became more difficult, and a few were abandoned.

THE RETREAT

One of the raiders later captured in Mexico told the story of the disorderly retreat. At 6:30 AM the first driblets of bandits arrived at the reserve area where Villa awaited them. By about 7:00 AM all the attackers who had not been killed, seriously wounded, or captured, had rejoined, and each chief took charge of the wounded from his detachment. The wounded were tied to their mounts, and the retreat began in great disorder. The men were so demoralized that despite the officers' best efforts, no orderly formation in the retreat was possible. The threats of Villa, who had remained with the horses during the entire action, could not stem the tide of retreat. He then occupied a ridge about three and a half miles southeast of town with an escort of thirty men in order to cover the retreat of those units that had been delayed. The retreat continued until the survivors halted at an arroyo near Bocas Grande at approximately 11:00 AM.

Ordered to unsaddle and rest their horses, the raiders posted a rear guard and at 1:00 PM made an effort to check their horses. The roll call, made by Villa himself, indicated that about one hundred men were unaccounted for and were listed as killed, wounded and not present, or missing. Both General Pablo Lopez and Lt. Colonel Cruz Chavez had been seriously wounded and were placed on litters. It was here as they gathered by the side of the wounded Cruz Chavez that a conversation between Villa, Cervantes, and Nicolas Fernandez was overheard. It was a bitter Villa who berated his chiefs: they had misled him, he claimed, and had led his men into a disaster. The chiefs began to rebuke each other, and Colonel Martin Lopez was heard to say that the whole affair had been a futile effort for a few dollars believed to be in the Columbus bank. Major Carmen Ortiz, who believed that there was a considerable amount of money in the bank, was killed by the bank door as he and his men tried to break it down. With little organization left and with more stragglers coming in, they began the painful march south toward Ascencion.

The march took the remainder of the day and through the night, and the weary detachments reached Ascension at noon on March 10. That afternoon Cruz Chavez died, and it was obvious that Pablo Lopez was in a critical condition. Forage for the horses and food for the men were confiscated, and it was decided to leave several of the wounded until transport of some sort could be found. When the retreat continued it was hastened by reports that Carrancista troops were in the vicinity and looking for the Columbus attackers.

The Villistas left Ascension at 8:00 AM and marched to Vuelta de Los Alamos where they arrived about 4:00 PM. There they learned that there were indeed Carrancista troops in the area and precautions were taken. Villa dispatched Cervantes and Fernandez with twenty men to go to the Corralitos Ranch to seize wagons to transport the wounded and to get fresh horses to replace the rapidly deteriorating stock at hand. The wagons taken from the ranch were sent to Ascencion for the wounded, and the following morning, March 12, the mass of stragglers left for the Corralitos Ranch. Villa had preceded them, and when they arrived at 11:00 AM they learned that five members of the Palanca family had been shot at the express order of Villa because of their refusal to produce fresh mounts and their general indifference to render required assistance. The wagons returned with the twenty-six wounded, and a buggy was taken for the use of General Pablo Lopez whose condition had deteriorated alarmingly.

Villa used the day spent at the ranch to reorganize his detachments and to communicate with the Carrancista commander at Casas Grandes. He informed the commander that he would be passing the commander's area during the night on his way to the district of Guerrero and was not looking for a fight, and that the only ambition he had left was to kill Americans. It was generally believed that the Carrancista commander and Villa conversed on the telephone. While Villa was busy assuaging the commander's anxieties, a final count of casualties was completed and the reorganization has taken place. The total number of casualties (killed, wounded, or missing) was set at 105. This represented 22 per cent of the attacking force of 485 men. Candelario Cervantes' detachment of 80 men had suffered 30 casualties, the largest number of any detachment (and over one-third of his command). The Villistas numbered 380 men divided into an advance guard (50 men), five units of the main body (320 men), and a rear guard of ten *Dorados*.

On the night march past Nueva Casas Grandes toward Galeana the Villistas did not use the road; the only group that used the road was the wounded and wheeled transport guarded by *Dorados*. The trail passed near the Dublan railroad station and came within one mile of the Casas Grandes barracks, which housed 400 Carrancista troops. At dawn on March 13, the marchers paused to water and rest their horses before proceeding to El Vado del los Chinos to camp. Scouts had rustled cattle, which were slaughtered to provide both breakfast and a noon meal before the march to Galeana was resumed. That afternoon the march was resumed, and in the evening they reached the town. The detachments were housed in whatever shelter could be found, and Villa ordered the town's chairman to assemble the people at the plaza at 7:00 AM the following day.

Early on the morning of Tuesday, March 14, the people began to gather, and by the time Villa appeared several thousand had gathered. They appeared eager to hear what he had to say about his venture in the United States. Villa spoke from a window facing the plaza and told those gathered that he had attempted to enter the United States but had been stopped on the line and was compelled to fight a large force of American soldiers. He pledged that he would never again direct violence toward his Mexican brothers, but would save all his ammunition to use against the Americans. He asked the people to prepare themselves for the struggles to come and to assist him in caring for his wounded men. The people of Galeana reacted by offering what assistance they could to the wounded, and by 9:00 AM presented Villa with a wagonload of food and clothing. Money was also given, and the people of Galeana were rewarded by having five of their young men pressed into Villa's service.

Prior to departure it had been decided that fresh mounts were badly needed and if not procured large segments of the detachments would be afoot. The districts of Namiquipa and Cruces had been so thoroughly picked over that it was decided to try new areas to rustle. Fernandez and twenty men were, therefore, dispatched to Rubio by way of the La Cantara-Las Animas-Santa Clara-La Quemada trail. For three days Fernandez and his detachment collected horses until they had nearly fifty. On Friday, March 17, they prepared to return with the horses when they were attacked by a Carrancista force. Fernandez was routed but made good his escape with most of the horses and began to make his way back to Guerrero to rendezvous with Villa.

In the meantime Villa, the transport bearing the wounded, and the rest of the detachments arrived at El Valle in the early evening. The wounded were taken to the schoolhouse and turned over to the care of Señor Vega, the schoolteacher. The wounded were in bad shape as the only care they had had since March 9 was from Francisco Beltran, who had received some training in the dressing of wounds. No medicine of any kind had been available, and the suffering of the wounded had been appalling. Villa ordered the community leaders to gather the people of the pueblo at 4:00 PM on March 15 as he wished to talk to them. He then set about with selected men to collect all the horses, provisions, and cattle available.

The address given the following day was brief and to the point. The Americans were on their way to Mexico to make war on the Mexican people; war had already been declared and the brave people of El Valle must join him to repel the invaders; he will never again take up arms against his fellow Mexicans; all his efforts will henceforth be directed against the invaders. He took advantage of the gathering of the pueblo's men folk to impress about forty of them into his service. He further repaid the pueblo's hospitality, or so it was believed among his men, by raping two daughters of Señor Gonzales. The reason he gave for the outrage was that Gonzales resided in the United States and was a traitor; someone, therefore, had to pay the price for his infamy.

During the night, Villa learned that Cervantes' scouts reported that a large Carrancista force under Colonel Cano, perhaps 500, was marching to El Valle. Concern for the welfare of Pablo Lopez prompted Villa to order his evacuation with an escort of ten men and an officer. The escort was directed to take Lopez to Animas and make contact with Fernandez who was expected to be there with fresh horses. The entire detachment left El Valle at 6:00 PM in order to avoid the Carrancistas. Despite the fact that the Carrancista advance guard and then their entire force could be seen not two miles distant, the Villistas made their way safely and unmolested to their camp at El Arco.

The next two days found the Villistas moving to Cruces, where they seized one Manuel Madrid and charged him with furnishing Carranza officials with the names of local Villistas who had joined Villa in the attack upon Columbus, and then they moved on to Namiquipa. Since many of Cervantes' detachment were native to the pueblo, they remained there for the night while Villa and his *Dorados* marched to El Molino. On Sunday, March 19, Villa received word that the Carrancistas were moving toward Namiquipa, and he ordered the town to be evacuated. The last detachment cleared the town's limits at 9:00 AM only to find the Carrancista force had arrived and was pushing hard to attack. Villa had maneuvered for days to avoid the Carranza force and now it seemed that a fight was inevitable. When he saw that the pursuers numbered perhaps 150 while his own force numbered over 400, he gave the order to turn to meet the Carrancista advance.

Shortly after 10:00 AM, near Los Cerritos, the government force attacked. The engagement lasted less than two hours and the Villistas routed their opponents, captured one hundred rifles, two machineguns, one hundred horses with equipment, and about sixty prisoners. The retreating Carrancistas were pursued almost to Cruces, and with the end of the engagement most of the prisoners were released. Villa hoped now to consolidate his forces by reuniting with General Jesus Maria Rios, who was near Bachineva, and with Fernandez who was at Las Animas. He anticipated that reunion with Rios and Fernandez would replenish both his food stores and the badly needed horses. By March 24 reunion had been affected, and Villa learned that Pablo Lopez had been left in a cave in the Santa Clara Mountains with a small guard. His force now numbered 450 men who were restocked and rested. The evening of March 26 found Villa and his men at Aguas Calientes, where they rested for two hours before they marched to the railroad track two miles north of San Ysidro. At midnight Villa assembled his leaders and gave orders for simultaneous attacks on Guerrero, Minaca, and San Ysidro.

General Beltran and Colonel Martin Lopez with 200 men (among whom were those men recently impressed at El Valle) were ordered to attack the Carranza garrison, estimated at 80 men, before dawn. Colonel Rios and Captain Pedrito, with 80 men, were ordered to attack the Carrancista garrison at San Ysidro, estimated at 50 men, before dawn (the real strength of the garrison was 250). Cervantes and Pedrosa, with 110 men, were ordered to attack Guerrero where the Carrancista garrison was estimated at 100. Villa stated that he would be with the horse-holders and his escort in the graveyard on the mesa in the vicinity of Guerrero.

When the Villistas struck Guerrero at 3:00 AM they found the garrison asleep. A sympathetic farmer had informed them that the command post contained three machine guns and some ammunition, and the guns were captured without waking the sleeping Carrancistas. During the five-hour gun battle that followed, the machine guns were put to deadly use by the Villistas and the garrison finally surrendered. The Minaca business proved to be a nonevent; the garrison surrendered immediately when confronted with the superior Villista force. San Ysidro proved to be a different matter altogether, as Villa's intelligence-gathering proved once again to be faulty.

The Carrancistas at San Ysidro were commanded by General Cavasos and had no difficulty in driving back the smaller Villista force. They retreated toward Guerrero where they knew Villa was waiting with his escort and found an arroyo that proved to be a natural trench within which to receive the Carrancista charge. The stiff resistance of the entrenched Villistas, reinforced by Villa and his men, brought the Carrancistas to a halt just as Beltran's and

Lopez's detachments returned from Minaca. They rode to the sound of the guns and directed their fire into the rear of the Carrancistas. In the melee that followed, Villa was wounded in the left leg just below the knee, probably about 6:00 AM. The concern over his wound and the effect it had upon the Villistas' morale probably prevented the immediate execution of the captured Carrancista officers; eighty of the captured privates volunteered to join the Villistas. Villa insisted that only his officers could see the wound, and under his orders the privates were told that a horse had thrown him and the injury was a minor inconvenience.

Villa was taken to a private home near the town plaza in a litter as it was evident he could not walk and riding a horse was out of the question. The wound was dressed by a doctor about 10:00 AM, and Villa left Guerrero on the evening of March 27–28 in a carriage accompanied by a small number of his *Dorados*. The commander of Villa's escort, Colonel Tarango, had been killed in the battle and command had devolved to Colonel Julian Cardenas, whose twenty men were added to the *Dorados*. Villa's disabling wound, however, left no one strong enough in acknowledged leadership to assume command. His immediate concern was concealment long enough for his wound to heal, and he realized that if he remained in close contact with his forces sooner or later his location would be revealed. Desertions had long been a problem and would accelerate once it was realized that he was no longer in direct command. He therefore decided to lose contact temporarily with everyone except the close relatives taking care of him and to remain at a place or places known only to them. Information gathered later from Villista officers taken prisoner indicated that Villa would not if possible remain in any pueblo overnight, and that his main concern was to lead his pursuers in a direction other than the one he had chosen for himself. Disinformation to both Carrancistas and Americans had now become second only to concerns for personal concealment.

The plan was for a continued move southward away from the Guerrero area, as Villa apparently feared that an attack by superior Carrancista or American forces might come at any time. On the evening of March 28–29, 130 men under command of Colonel Nicolas Fernandez left Guerrero as a guard for the wounded, who were transported in three carriages. The same evening saw the remainder of Villa's command deployed at Guerrero and San Ysidro. A total of 230 men under the command of Candelario Cervantes were at Guerrero with Julio Acosta and Martin Lopes; 150 men who were commanded by Francisco Beltran were with Jesus Rio at nearby San Ysidro. Before these detachments could begin the southward march as previously planned, Cervantes' detachment was attacked by American troops of the 7th Cavalry.

REASONS FOR THE COLUMBUS ATTACK

Virtually everything connected to Villa's life and times has engendered controversy, and the reasons for his attack on Columbus, New Mexico, on March 9, 1916, are no exception: they remain a point of contention among historians, biographers, journalists, students, and southwest Border buffs. Villa was not kind enough to tell the world precisely why he launched his attack, thus leaving the field clear for any number of suggestions ranging from the scholarly on the one hand to the speculative on the other. Five broad categories of motivation for Villa's actions have been suggested, not necessarily in order of significance: revenge, the hope to provoke American intervention, intrigue by German agents, the need for supplies, and the sinister manipulations of American business interests.

The revenge motive is the broadest, having as it does several different facets. Villa had had a number of business dealings with the Ravel brothers, merchants with a hardware store and other properties in Columbus. The brothers had served Villa as fences for stolen and smuggled property; they had supposedly cheated him in an arms and ammunition deal, and then insulted him when they told one of his emissaries that they no longer did business with bandits. The burning of the Ravels' properties (hotel, home, and business) by the Villistas is offered as reinforcement for the personal element in the revenge argument. It was also rumored that Villa had substantial money deposits in the bank in Columbus but was refused access to it by the manager who, as the story has it, was perhaps thinking of keeping it for himself. The raid has also been seen as Villa's revenge for Wilson's recognition of Carranza and the subsequent defeat of Villa's forces at Agua Prieta. Wilson's arms embargo has also been seen as an element in the revenge thesis, as Villa was almost always short on reliable weapons and ammunition.

Villa's latest biographer presents him as a patriot who believed that Carranza had entered into a corrupt bargain with Wilson in which Carranza exchanged Mexican sovereignty for recognition. Villa's attack was an attempt to sabotage the agreement by forcing American intervention that in turn would rally the people of Mexico to his patriotic cause. There was no such agreement, but it has been suggested that a plot along similar lines had, in fact, been developed by a senior U.S. State Department official, Mexican conservatives, and American businessmen. The plotters had purportedly first approached Villa with their scheme and were rebuffed. When the plan, so it is said, was aired at a cabinet meeting in Washington, both President Woodrow Wilson and Secretary of State Williams Jennings Bryan rejected it. There is, however, no evidence of such a plot.

Despite the absence of evidence, conspiracy theories continue with lives of their own. Congressman Meyer London, Socialist from New York City, claimed from the floor of the House of Representatives that Pancho Villa was nothing more than the tool of powerful interests of the bankers and industrialists of Wall Street who callously plotted the murder of American citizens and soldiers in order to force intervention and thereby protect their Mexican investments. One Southwest history buff offered a tale of intrigue in which Villa was paid a large sum in gold ($80,000) by the United States government to attack Columbus. The story is complete with the comings and goings in Columbus of mysterious strangers, rented cars, and clandestine meetings near Lake Guzman to deliver the gold to Villa. A variation on this story has a group of traitorous Army officers and soldiers detailed to take the gold to El Paso by train only to steal the gold. They fled to Mexico, were captured, relieved of the gold, and had their throats slit in the bargain! And somehow they were buried in Columbus just west of the town between the Catholic and Presbyterian cemeteries.

The question of Germany's influence behind Villa's attack continues to be debated. It has been asserted that German foreign policy as carried out by Germany's military was partially responsible for the Columbus raid. Following the raid Villa supposedly received increased German aid and through his agent, Felix Summerfeld, was in contact with German Secret Service agents. Summerfeld was, according to this account, busy buying arms for Villa. Because increased desertions and defections had cost him so dearly, he was desperate to regain lost power and prestige. General Felipe Angeles had retired, General Luis Herrera had defected to Carranza, General Tomás Urbina was dead at Villa's own hand, and the trusted "Butcher" Rodolpho Fierro had drowned. In addition to the loss of this leadership, scores, if not hundreds, of soldiers had either gone home or joined the Carrancistas. Villa needed to prove that he was a force to be reckoned with.

A combination of German intrigue and revenge is offered in another suggestion that the origin of Villa's decision to attack Columbus seems to have been a quarrel with one of the town's banks. Villa had apparently maintained an account in the Columbus State Bank and when he attempted a withdrawal through a written request he was informed that his account lacked sufficient funds. Connected to this incident were Dr. Lyman B. Rauschbaum, Villa's personal physician and bookkeeper, and Felix A. Sommerfeld. Both were looking for a way to precipitate a war between Mexico and the United States. Rauschbaum, who was Villa's connection to the bank in Columbus and through whom Villa became convinced that the banker was a cheat, was willing to help Sommerfeld create the subterfuge necessary to secure Villa's attack on the United States. Between them they sought to maneuver Villa into creating an incident that would precipitate a war between the United States and Mexico. Deception, they believed, would be necessary to influence the Mexican guerilla, and this deception would be the hypothetical misdealing of the Columbus State Bank.

The need-for-supplies theory has its persuasive adherents, and it has been argued that the raid may be explained simply as guerilla foraging. One of the driving passions of the Villistas was *need*—the unremitting need for money, clothes, arms, ammunition, and, as mainstay of their profession, horseflesh. Money and clothes from men like rich Sam Ravel, and military arms, ammunition, and horses would go far to replenish the usual scarcity of bandit life. Villa had instructed his scouts to find where the horses were, and the location of the stables was clearly indicated on Captain Rodriguez's map. Loot had always been part of the anticipation of reward among Villa's rank and file, and Columbus proved to be no exception. Moreover, the burden imposed on Villa by the United States' arms embargo meant that supplies had become a critical problem, and there seems little doubt that the prime object was to pick up guns, horses, money, and as much incidental loot as possible. Others have echoed the argument of necessity, and have emphasized the effectiveness of the arms embargo coupled with closer military surveillance of potential smuggling centers. Arms had become almost impossible to obtain legally in the open market, and a large repository of military weapons just across the border was a strong attraction.

His anger at the Wilson Administration over its recognition of Carranza made him prone to thoughts of retaliation, and he saw in this the opportunity to make himself a hero by striking across the border. Such a strike would become an embarrassment to President Wilson and might result in a retaliatory strike by the American army. Such an incursion would cause problems for Carranza and might redirect Mexican loyalties to the Villista cause. The raid was followed by the Punitive Expedition, Villa's evasiveness was an embarrassment to Wilson, and through the continued American presence the United States and Mexico came close to war. In the final analysis, however, what must be kept in mind in any consideration of Villa's motives for the attack is *complexity*. He was a complicated man who was quick to repay both kindness and faithlessness, and he had a long memory for both. His temperament was capricious, and more than once in his life he was the personification of the old adage, "Act in haste and repent at leisure."

Three

AMERICAN REACTION TO VILLA'S RAID

An editorial in *The Independent* on March 20, 1916, went far to sum up the attitude of the American people: "We Can Wait No Longer: The murderous raid upon the town of Columbus in New Mexico by the organized and lawless crew of Francisco Villa, the Mexican desperado, was the last straw." Carranza was proven impotent by the course of events, the editor concluded, Villa was a murderer, and it was the task of the United States Army to seek out the Columbus raiders and put them to death. The Army must follow the trail wherever it leads, and it must use whatever means are necessary to bring the guilty to justice. "Our armed invasion of Mexico was intended to preclude the possibility of intervention in Mexico's internal affairs," proclaimed the *Literary Digest*, and the editor looked forward to Carranza's cooperation. The New York *World* declared that America was united and a murderous assault upon Americans, in one locality at least, was resented by the entire body of our citizenship. Other papers across the country spoke of Wilson's fitness for the tasks ahead, of the wisdom of the policy of reciprocal rights and mutual cooperation, and of the possibility for a speedy resolution to banditry along the border. The general mood of optimism was, however, to be short-lived.

Prior to Villa's attack on Columbus, Wilson's major concerns in 1916 were the war in Europe and the upcoming November presidential election. Since the outbreak of the European war in 1914 Wilson had pursued a policy of neutrality, a policy widely accepted by the American people. He hoped that America as a nation and he as an individual would ultimately have a pivotal role to play in bringing a war-ravaged Europe to a peace settlement, a just and lasting peace in his words. The precarious course of neutrality that he had charted was threatened by Germany's reinstatement of her abandoned policy of unrestricted submarine warfare, a policy that Germany saw as her only hope for victory if not survival, but a policy that most Americans abhorred. Wilson also realized that an abandonment of neutrality would alienate two large groups within his Democrat Party: Americans whose family roots were in Germany and in Ireland. Americans of German descent were not eager to wage war against a nation wherein resided their relatives; Americans of Irish origin were concerned that Ireland's independence from Britain would be compromised by Allied victory, and they showed no enthusiasm for Britain's plight should German submarines establish a stranglehold about the island.

Wilson realized, moreover, that he was only the second Democrat to occupy the White House in fifty-six years; his political position was nothing if not precarious. He was determined to maintain his grip on the presidency in order to fulfill what he had come to see as his destiny: nothing less than that of peacemaker to a war-weary world. His party had decided to run on a strong policy of neutrality and had adopted the slogan "He Kept Us Out of War!" as the centerpiece of its campaign. Following Villa's attack on Columbus, Wilson was virtually driven to a policy of action by the explosion of indignation and outrage that rolled across America. In an election year he entered into a military "expedition" without calling it war, and he sent troops into a neighboring sovereign state while denying intervention. His order to General Pershing on March 10, 1916, was designed to disguise both invasion and intervention.

Relatively little attention has been given to precedents for Pershing's expedition into Mexico, despite a rather long and usually acrimonious history of such enterprises. While international boundaries have been sources of contention since earliest times, the case of the United States and Mexico has been particularly contentious. Faced with filibusters, bandits, cattle rustlers, horse thieves, and marauding Indians the military and police forces of the two nations had not often been able effectively to cooperate. Not only governments at the Federal level but also local jurisdictions had from time to time sent troops and armed posses across the Rio Grande River, usually without the consent and even in the face of protest on the part of the Mexican government. The antecedents of the Pershing Expedition went back to the occupation of Nacogdoches in 1836 (an episode in the Texan Revolution of that year) and came forward some three-quarters of a century.

In 1855 following a series of attacks by Indians who lived in Mexico, three companies of Texan volunteers under command of one J. H. Callahan and following orders of the Governor of Texas crossed into Mexico and were driven back by a combined force of Mexicans and Indians. In the course of their retreat they pillaged and burned the town of Piedras Negras (October 6) before crossing back into the United States. This depredation was settled by a Joint Claims Commission in 1868 under which several thousand dollars were awarded to the town and citizens of Piedras Negras. Two precedents were thereby established. The Secretary of State, W. L. Marcy stated that if Mexican Indians, whom Mexico was duty bound to restrain, were permitted to cross its border and commit depredations in the United States, the marauders may be chased across the border and there punished. Marcy also determined that the right was reciprocal insofar as the Mexican forces refrained from injuring persons and property of citizens of the United States.

In 1858 President Buchanan asked Congress for permission to assume a temporary protectorate over the northern portions of Chihuahua and Sonora and to there establish military posts in order to offer protection for Americans residing in Arizona, New Mexico, and northwest Texas, who were plagued by bandits and by Indian raids. The occupation was to end as soon as the Mexican government could itself maintain law and order in its northern areas. Congress refused to grant permission, and it would do so again in 1859 and in 1860. The outbreak of the Civil War in 1861 drew American attention from the Mexican border, and all its difficulties were submerged by the bloody national conflict of 1861–1865. A resurgence of Indian unrest in the southwest during the Civil War plunged much of the area into near chaos, and the period from the close of the war until roughly 1880 was arguably the most restless and violent in the boundary's long history of bloodshed and mayhem.

With the advent of Porfirio Díaz in 1876 and his recognition by the United States on April 9, 1878, the situation began to change. By the beginning of 1880 President Díaz had both the willingness and the ability to devote government resources to border problems. A new and unforeseen difficulty arose, however, and it was the direct result of the United States government's policy of Indian relocation in New Mexico and Arizona. The Apache tribes' resistance to the policy plunged Sonora, Chihuahua, Arizona, and New Mexico into near chaos. By July 1882 Mexico and the United States had entered into an agreement that regular Federal troops of the two Republics could cross the boundary line reciprocally when they were in close pursuit of a band of marauding Indians. During the period of Apache unrest, the United States made a number of armed military incursions into Sonora and Chihuahua in pursuit of hostiles. With the surrender of Geronimo in Skeleton Canyon, Arizona, on September 3, 1886, the Indian wars of the southwest came to an end.

The practice of "hot pursuit," as it came to be known, was renewed several times during the period 1890–1896 as a result of the depredations of the outlaw Apache Kid, whose bands of renegades preyed upon the frontier regions from Sonora to New Mexico. In the years following the disappearance of the Kid, to the revolt against the Díaz regime in 1910, the border was relatively quiet, but the practice of border crossings in "hot pursuit" of lawless elements remained as part of the national memories of both countries. In Mexico the policy was generally, if not always, regarded with great suspicion; in the United States the policy came to be looked upon as just another means to be used to guarantee the stability and safety of southwestern communities. In 1916 the policy once again became a source of acrimony, and with its usual misunderstandings led the two nations to the threshold of war.

Under normal circumstances, Villa's violation of American sovereignty and his outrages perpetrated upon American citizens would have been presented to the Mexican government with a request that the violation be disavowed, that reparations be made, and that the perpetrators be apprehended and punished. Under normal circumstances, sending American troops across the border would have been a violation of Mexican sovereignty just as Villa's invasion had been a violation of American sovereignty. The revolutionary situation in Mexico, however, precluded normality. International law had long recognized the principle of *abating a nuisance in adjoining jurisdiction*, and as long as Villa roamed the north of Mexico freely and presented the possibility of another invasion of American territory he could with good reason be seen as a real and present nuisance. From the perspective of both the United States government and its citizens, Carranza's de facto government possessed neither the means nor the will to rid Sonora and Chihuahua of Villa and his bands of outlaws.

On March 6, 1916, Wilson had announced the appointment of Newton D. Baker as Secretary of War and it was Baker, on the recommendation of his advisors, who appointed Brigadier General John J. Pershing to lead the Expedition into Mexico. At his March 10 Cabinet meeting Wilson told the members that an adequate force would be sent after Villa with the single object of capturing him and putting an end to his outrages. This wording was preserved for the press release that followed the Cabinet meeting, and thus he hoped to gain the benefits of action without the sacrifices of war. The State Department was, furthermore, greatly concerned that the expedition should not seem to be directed at Carranza's government. Newspaper reporters came away with the impression that the purpose of the expedition was to capture Villa, which led to the colorful and spectacular headlines of "Catch Villa" and "Villa: Dead or Alive!" The order, on the other hand, directed Pershing to pursue and break up Villa's band; supplies and assistance were to be provided to meet the needs of the expedition to carry out its orders. Unfortunately, newspapers across the country posted variations on the New York *American's* powerful headline: "FUNSTON TOLD TO GET VILLA DEAD OR ALIVE."

On the same day Major General Frederick R. Funston, Commanding General of the Southern Division at San Antonio, Texas received the order promptly to organize a force adequate to facilitate the pursuit of the Mexican bandits who had attacked the town of Columbus, New Mexico. These troops were to be withdrawn to American territory as soon as the Carranza government proved itself willing and capable of the pursuit and punishment of the Columbus raiders. The work of the assembled American forces was to be regarded as finished *as soon as Villa's band or bands are known to be broken up.* Thus began in the minds of the American people the confusion over the Punitive Expedition's mission that has persisted to this day. On March 13, to assure that no confusion should exist over the orders already given, a telegram was dispatched by the War Department, which indicated that President Wilson reaffirmed his determination that the expedition into Mexico was limited to the purposes stated in the orders, namely, *the pursuit and dispersion of the band or bands that attacked Columbus, New Mexico.*

Wilson's anxiety about the role of the Expedition was produced by his desire for friendly relations with the newly recognized de facto government of Carranza and by his concern over his reelection slogan, "He Kept Us Out of War!" He was beleaguered throughout the campaign of 1916 by critics who on the one hand questioned the validity of his slogan (given the presence of American troops in Mexico), and by those on the other hand who called for a more aggressive approach to bringing the bandits to justice. The balancing act between his policy of intervention and his desire for limited military action caused Wilson a great deal of difficulty and goes far to explain the public's later perception of the failure on the part of Pershing and the Punitive Expedition.

In addition to his desire to have some influence in the course of the Mexican Revolution and his determination to protect the Southwest border of the United States from incursion by bandits, Wilson had other reasons for intervention in Mexico. Despite his disappointment with America's actions in Veracruz in April 1914, he was convinced that the Punitive Expedition could have constructive results. In a recent reassessment of Wilson and the Expedition, a number of reasons have been suggested for Wilson's actions:

he needed an American commitment to military preparedness and a stronger army because the United States might find itself in the European war and its military was inadequate; action in Mexico might make the public more aware of the dangers of military weakness and this in turn could open the door for legislation he wanted; the Expedition would provide training for the military forces should they be needed in Europe; and the border areas might be cleared of bandits, thus alleviating both anxieties and political pressures in the border states (a definite benefit to Wilson and the Democrats in an election year). After the attack on Columbus, a broad consensus developed across the United States among the citizenry, in the editorial comments of daily papers and weekly magazines of commentary, and in Congress: *something must be done.*

Wilson's policy seemed, therefore, both necessary and correct to most of the American public, and Secretary of War Newton Baker's statement that the Expedition's purpose was not in reality punitive but defensive was widely accepted: the real purpose was to extend American power into Mexico only as a means of controlling those lawless elements in Mexico that the Mexican government was unable to control. By confronting those lawless elements in Mexico it was hoped that they would not need to be confronted in the United States. Unfortunately, the de facto government of First Chief Carranza did not see it that way. The day following the Villa raid, March 10, Carranza had proposed a reinstatement of the 1880–1884 policy of reciprocal pursuit if the Columbus incident should *be repeated* at any other point of the frontier line. On March 12, 1916, Secretary of State Robert Lansing was given a telegram from Carranza, which plainly stated that any movement of American troops into Mexico would be seen as an unjustified invasion and a possible cause for war between the United States and Mexico. Secretary Lansing and President Wilson conferred on March 13, decided that Carranza's warning had been for domestic consumption, and interpreted the March 10 proposal as if it applied to Villa. In a note to Carranza, gratification was expressed for his cooperation with the United States in apprehending the outlaws who had attacked Columbus and stated that the United States would exercise the privilege of crossing the border granted by the *de facto* Government of Mexico in the hope that by their mutual efforts lawlessness would be eradicated and peace and order maintained in the territories of the United States and Mexico contiguous to the international boundary. Behind this screen of diplomatic logorrhea, the West Column of the Punitive Expedition crossed into Mexico from Culberson's Ranch in the New Mexico boot heel at about 12:20 AM on March 16. It was followed shortly by the East Column, which crossed the border at Palomas, Mexico.

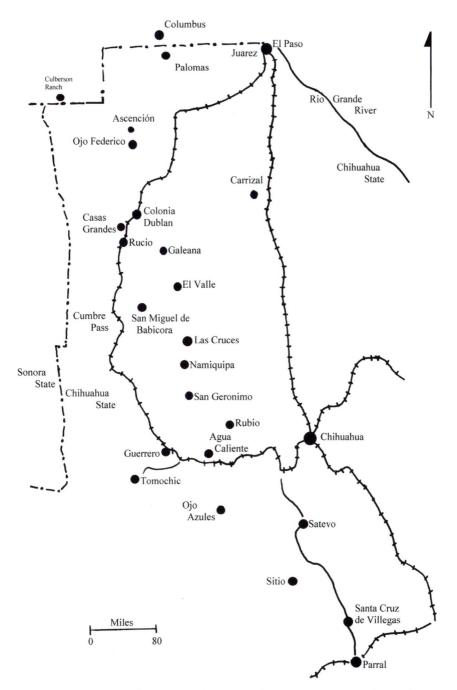

The Expedition's Area of Operations [Map taken from Col. Frank Tompkins, *Chasing Villa*. Modified by the author.].

COMMAND, ORGANIZATION, AND DEPARTURE

Command of the Punitive Expedition was given to General John J. Pershing, then fifty-five years old and resented by his senior colleagues for his meteoric rise to the Army's hierarchy. He faced not only resentment among the "Old Guard," but also had recently suffered a personal tragedy that would have crushed a lesser man. Assigned in April 1914 to move the Army's Eighth Brigade from the Presidio in San Francisco to El Paso, Texas, and to take command of the troops in El Paso and at Fort Bliss, Pershing was made responsible for the defense of the American border from Columbus, New Mexico to Sierra Blanco, Texas. He had hoped to move his family from their home in the Presidio, but his new duties kept him so busy he had not taken the time to make the arrangements. On the evening of August 26, 1915, the Pershing's house caught fire and became an inferno in minutes. Francis Pershing and her three daughters died of smoke inhalation; only the son, Warren, survived. When notified, a distraught Pershing cried, "Oh, my God! Can it be true? Can it be true?" Following the funeral and burials he returned to his command in El Paso, a man who carried a staggering burden of sorrow but managed to subsume it to his duty.

When President Wilson decided to send the Army after the Villistas, he probably did not realize how incredibly unprepared the Army was. The United States Army did not possess one reliable, tested component capable of operating in Mexico. The logistics of transport, supply, equipment, and communication simply were not there. Major General Funston had been ordered to organize an adequate military force of troops under the command of Brigadier General Pershing to pursue the Columbus raiders and to consider their work done when the band or bands responsible were dispersed. Authorization was given to secure motor transportation and civilian support (drivers and mechanics) as needed; the airplanes at San Antonio were assigned to be used for observation; and guides and interpreters were to be employed where necessary. Funston was cautioned not to expect the use of Mexican railroads for purposes of supply; his preparations had to include plans to ship all supplies from the border.

By March 14, 1916, a provisional division called "Punitive Expedition, U.S. Army" was organized and consisted of a First and Second Provisional Cavalry Brigade, a First Provisional Infantry Brigade (with two companies of Engineers attached), an Ambulance Company with Field Hospital, a Signal Corps Detachment with the First Aero Squadron, and Wagon Companies 1 and 2. The force was organized into two columns, one centered at Hachita, New Mexico, and the other at Columbus. The plan of operation called for the two columns to proceed to Ascencion, evaluate the circumstances, and proceed from there. Because Villa's band was reported to be near Casas Grandes and moving south, it was decided to make Casas Grandes the first advanced base of operations. The western column was ordered to move from Hachita south to Culberson's Ranch and prepare for departure on the evening of March 15, upon General Pershing's arrival. The eastern column, 4,000 strong, departed Columbus and crossed the border at Palomas at noon on March 15; the western column, some 2,000 men, delayed by General Pershing's late arrival (he had been involved in an automobile accident), crossed the border at 12:30 AM on March 16.

The Culberson column, which had sent its wagon transportation to Columbus in favor of pack trains, was smaller and much faster than the eastern column. The Second Brigade marched twenty-five miles to Geronimo Rock the first night, and after a brief six-hour bivouac on the morning of March 16, the march resumed at noon and halted for the night at Ojitos, fifty miles from Culberson's ranch (all this in less than twenty-four hours). Early the next day the march began toward Casas Grandes, and Pershing's column marched a startling sixty-eight miles and arrived in camp half a mile north of Colonia Dublan on the Casas Grandes River at 7:30 PM. This march broke all previous records for speed and endurance. The Second Cavalry Brigade covered the longest distance ever recorded in the annals of the U.S. Cavalry. Despite the grueling march, Pershing did not rest: upon being informed by locals that Villa was sixty miles south at San Miguel de Babicora he acted immediately.

Three parallel cavalry columns, separate but in communication, were sent south in search of the Villistas. The object of the scout was to prevent Villa from moving to Sonora in the west, or toward the railroad in the east, while at the same time increasing the chances of cutting his trail before he could get into the mountains near Guerrero where it was believed he was headed. The first detachment, commanded by Colonel James B. Irwin, consisting of 29 officers and 647 men of the 7th Cavalry, departed Colonia Dublan on the evening of March 16–17 with orders to proceed to the eastern edge of the San Miguel plateau to intercept any possible eastward movement of the Villista force. The second detachment, 14 officers and 258 men of the Second Squadron, 10th Cavalry, commanded by Colonel W. C. Brown, were entrained to Rucio and from there proceeded to San Miguel. The third detachment, the First Squadron, 10th Cavalry, 8 officers and 204 men under Major E. W. Evans, proceeded by train to Las Varas near Madera to patrol the Babicora plateau and prevent the Villistas from moving southwest.

The two units of the 10th Cavalry were sent by train because they had departed Fort Huachuca, Arizona, on March 10 and had ridden to Colonia Dublan, Chihuahua, a distance of 252 miles. They had averaged thirty miles a day across some extremely rugged terrain, and the horses were in dire need of rest and nourishment. Using rail transport, Pershing believed, was a way to give both horses and men a rest and at the same time offer the possibility of getting closer to the swiftly fleeing Villistas. The El Paso Southern Railroad sent a train from Juarez, and it arrived at Colonia Dublan on March 19. The boxcars were in bad shape and the necessary repairs caused significant delay in the troops' departure. Problems with fuel and water were encountered en route, the railroad employees were uncooperative, and Colonel Brown's Second Squadron did not arrive at Rucio until 8:00 AM on March 20. The troops proceeded to San Miguel, arrived on the morning of the March 21, and learned that the Villistas had not been within miles of the area. Brown then led his squadron on March 23 to El Toro hoping for news of Villas' whereabouts.

The First Squadron had hit upon hard times as they continued beyond Rucio toward Madera. On a switchback near Cumbre Pass several of the old boxcars overturned, and one rolled down an embankment, which resulted in several serious injuries. Major Evans ordered the injured men, eleven in all, to be taken to Madera aboard what was left of the train, the horses injured in the accident were shot, and the squadron proceeded across the country to Babicora. The decision to use rail transport, which seemed an excellent one at the time, proved to be something of a disaster and went far to convince Pershing that any future reliance on trains would be a mistake. Unless the Army could guarantee itself total control of railroad management and supply, the hazards were too great: shortages of fuel and water for the locomotives, and the possibility of sabotage to rails, bridges, and rolling stock was too great a reality to be ignored.

Colonel George Dodd, just a few months shy of the compulsory retirement age of sixty-four, was dispatched to join the 7th Cavalry detachment under Colonel Irwin and to assume command of both regiments in order to coordinate the pursuit. On March 22 Dodd contacted Carrancista Colonel Salas, commander of the de facto forces at El Valle. Salas had fought the Villistas near Cruces on March 19 and had been driven back to El Valle. His men, demoralized from their loss and hasty retreat, had taken up defensive positions as they expected the Villistas to return. Assuming correctly that Villa would not return, Dodd proceeded south, crossed the Santa Maria River north of Cruces on March 23, and bivouacked some fifteen miles north of Namiquipa. The reports he received in regard to Villa's possible location were inconclusive and perplexing, due primarily to Villa's skill in concealing his intentions from even those closest to him. Deciding that anything was preferable to inaction, Dodd moved westward toward Santa Ana in the hope of crossing ahead of Villa's route. He arrived early on the morning of March 26 completely frustrated that the extremely dry weather had precluded tracking any movement in the area.

Pershing's frustration at his columns' inability to find the Villistas led him to conclude that (1) the Carrancista troops in the area intended to prevent the Americans from overtaking Villa; and (2) the Mexicans themselves did not accept the legitimacy of the Expedition's purpose or presence. His frustration was compounded by his belief that General Obregon's proclamation of March 13 should have settled the question of legitimacy. The proclamation stated that the Mexican government had entered into an agreement with the Americans: the troops of either nation were free to cross the border in pursuit of bandits. Mexican commanders along the border were directed to act in accord with American commanders in order to achieve the best results in the pursuit of these bandits. Copies of the proclamation were carried by the Expedition's columns and displayed locally as evidence of the agreement between President Carranza and the United States, but it seemed to have no effect on local attitudes. Pershing took some consolation in the belief that the proclamation prevented active hostilities against the Expedition by the local populations encountered.

Both Colonel Dodd and Colonel Brown reported that the local Carrancista commanders had made no effort to learn where Villa was located, nor had they tried to organize pursuit of Villa's rapidly fleeing units. Deserters from Villista ranks were returning home and because of this Pershing and his officers found it difficult to believe that the de facto commanders knew nothing of Villa's location. The area in which the American columns were operating, the "Pueblos de los Indios" along the banks of the Santa Maria River, was inhabited by Villista sympathizers who were, naturally enough, reluctant to give accurate information when questioned. This was the area from which many of the Columbus raiders came, and there was a great deal of resentment toward Pershing's troopers. Some Mexicans expressed the conviction that it would be a national disgrace for the Americans to capture Villa. Many foreigners, Americans with economic interests in Mexico included, hoped that the Expedition would fail to capture the bandit leader because they believed that success would mean withdrawal of American forces, and the presence of the soldiers was a source of reassurance. Only later, when his Intelligence operation began to develop useful information, would Pershing and his field officers begin to trust the information given by Mexican informants.

The Campaign of the Three Columns, as it has been called, was soon reinforced by the creation of four support detachments to be held in ready reserve to move quickly in any direction circumstances dictated. The first column, under Major Elmer Linsley, 13th Cavalry, consisted of 11 officers and 275 men and was directed on March 20 to proceed to Chuichupa to guard the trails leading west, should the fleeing Villistas decided to move in that direction. Since Villa continued to run south, this detachment continued to fill in the territory vacated by the pursuing 10th Cavalry and arrived at San José de Babicora on March 30. The second column, commanded by Major Tompkins, 13th Cavalry, consisted of 11 officers and 160 men. They departed Colonia Dublan on March 21 and moved up the Santa Maria River to be ready should his services be needed for pursuit. Tompkins proceeded to Namiquipa where he established camp on March 29. Two provisional squadrons were organized, both from the 11th Cavalry. The first was commanded by Major Robert L. Howze and consisted of 10 officers and 255 men. This column left Colonia Dublan on March 24 and encamped at Namiquipa on March 29. The second squadron, under Lt. Colonel H. T. Allen, 11th Cavalry, consisted of men from each troop supplemented with two machine gun detachments and totaled 10 officers and 292 men.

The Expedition's detachments had been moving steadily southward, their objective to deny the Villistas the opportunity to divide and move either east or west before they could be brought to bay. By March 29, with its headquarters at Dublan, the Expedition's fighting point, the 7th, 10th, and 13th Cavalry, was at San José de Babicora, Namiquipa, Guerrero, Potrillo Pass, Santa Ana, Quemada, and Rubio. Units of the 6th, 16th, and 24th Infantry detachments were at Dublan (more en route), Corralitos, Colonia Juarez, Boca Grande, El Valle, Galeana, Cruces, and Chocolate Pass. The First Aero Squadron was divided between Dublan and El Valle, and the Signal Corps units were distributed along the entire route of transportation as needed. The medical resources, Ambulance Company 7 and Field Hospital 7, were at Dublan, and the Engineers were with the various units that needed their services. The 1st Battalion, 4th Field Artillery, was at Dublan. Held in reserve in New Mexico were units of the 5th Cavalry at Gibson's Ranch and units of the 5th Cavalry, 20th and 24th Infantry at Columbus. The Expedition was, in Pershing's mind, now ready to carry out its orders.

VILLA'S CONTINUED FLIGHT AND GRADUAL RECOVERY

Dodd's detachment of the 7th Cavalry had bivouacked at Santa Maria and on March 27, as the wounded Villa and his followers divided their ranks and fled south, marched to Providencia. They resumed their march toward Bachineva the following morning. By this time these troopers and their horses had been on the march fourteen of fifteen days, had covered a distance of 400 miles, and were close to worn out. Convinced that Villa was headed to or already at Guerrero, Dodd refused to allow rest for man or beast. The animals and men in most need of care had been left at Santa Ana, and a brief rest was given to the rest of the command south of Bachineva, while the horses grazed and the men ate. The march resumed once again with a halt called at dark; at 11:00 PM a night march began, a march of about thirty-six miles over unknown mountain trails. Dodd's information had the Villista force at between 500 and 600 men; his own force comprised 25 officers and 345 enlisted men. The lack of reliable guides meant that Dodd's column literally groped its way with many halts and delays, during which the men would lie down on the ground, in spite of the bitter cold, and sleep holding the reins. At about 6:30 AM the column had reached a position from which it was believed that the town could be reached, but it was probably another hour to an hour and a half before an attack could be executed.

Before the arrival of the 7th Cavalry at Guerrero on March 29, Villa's forces were divided as follows: Colonel Cervantes and General Julio Acosta's detachment of 230 men were at Guerrero; General Francisco Beltran with General Rios and Colonel Martin Lopez with 170 men were at San Ysidro; and Villa's escort with Colonel Nicolas Fernandez, Colonel Julian Cardenas as escort chief, and 130 wounded men. Following the Guerrero fight the Villistas were scattered to all points of the compass. The Villistas at Guerrero and San Ysidro had been taken completely by surprise with the appearance of the 7th Cavalry and therefore had no plans established for retreat and later reunion. Cervantes escaped to the mountains in a running fight and fled to Arisiachic where he believed he and his men would be safe, while the situation was reexamined and new plans made. He and Acosta were both familiar with this area and would be among people sympathetic to their cause. A camp was established, cattle were rustled and slaughtered, and an observation point was established nearby from which it was possible, with the use of field glasses, to observe the movements of American troops between San Ysidro, Guerrero, and Minaca. Couriers arrived periodically with information about the Americans who, according to reports, numbered in the thousands and were marching south. On April 8 information was received that a Carrancista force was marching toward the camp, and the entire detachment of 200 men, guided by General Julio Acosta and Colonel Antonio Angel, left Arisiachic and began a three-day march to Tomochic.

Martin Lopez had become separated from Cervantes at Guerrero and with twenty of his men fled in the direction of San Ysidro to join Generals Beltran and Rios. Both men were completely surprised by Lopez's report of the arrival of the American troopers and as they had no idea of the number of Americans in the fight, their first thought was of escape. Since Rios was familiar with the mountains near Bachineva, it was decided to follow his lead to a safe area from which further operations could be planned. Lopez joined the detachment with his twenty men, and they made their way to safety unmolested. They marched to Arroyo de Bachineva where they made camp, and the next day, March 30, camped at a ranch house overlooking Bachineva. They entered the town the next day, supplied themselves with necessities, and departed for Agua Caliente where they camped for the night. The following day they were at the Hacienda de Agua Caliente, grazing their horses, when they were notified by local farmers that American cavalry was coming toward the ranch at a fast trot. The Villistas fled with the Americans in swift pursuit.

The main concern of the scattered Villista leaders in the days following Guerrero was to find Villa's location in order to affect a reunion of forces. While evidence indicated that these leaders did in fact receive communications from Villa, they were vague, contained no information about his whereabouts, and spoke only of future operation upon recovery. There is reason to believe that Villa was uneasy in regard to communications, fearing that they could be intercepted and his location revealed. He may, therefore, have used this time to spread the disinformation at which he was so skilled. It is possible, however, to reconstruct his flight from an itinerary given to officers in Pershing's Information Service by a captured officer who had been a member of Villa's escort.

On March 29 Villa's escort with the wounded traveled through the night and reorganized itself at daybreak. Colonel Cardenas, escort chief, was in charge of the advance guard of fifteen men. The main body consisted of (1) Villa's headquarters and staff; (2) a train of four carriages for the wounded: one each for Villa, General Pedrosa, Major Emilio Pedrosa, Alberto Camargo, Mauro Dominguez, and one for two officers whose names are unknown; (3) Villa's escort on the flanks of the train for the wounded; and (4) the detachments of General Pedrosa and Colonel Nicolas Fernandez. The entire assemblage numbered 125. It was not known if the column was followed, and it was, therefore, decided to march all night.

In the morning, a halt was called for breakfast at a small ranch house where Villa remained in his carriage. It was decided to remain at this location for the remainder of the day but at 4:00 PM it was decided to resume the march south.

Because of his wounds Mauro Dominguez was left at the ranch, and Alberto Camargo, who was found dead in his carriage, was buried there. The column traveled all night on the San Borja road, and orders were given that no lights were to be shown as they were passing by the outskirts of the pueblo of Cusi. A halt was called in the mountains near Cusi at dawn, and a short rest was taken.

The march was resumed early the next morning and they paused to replenish the water supply and to kill four cattle. Food had been scarce for the past several days, and after a hearty meal it was decided to remain in the area for a day's much-needed rest. In the late afternoon, the horses were saddled and after a brief march a halt was called for the evening. It was discovered that six men had deserted. On the last day of March the column left its night's camp at dawn and after about two hours' ride arrived at a small ranch. They remained there for the entire day and night, and made use of the time to rest. Litters were constructed for the wounded, and they left the ranch house in the early evening. They took every precaution to avoid the Carranza forces reported to be in the vicinity. A dry camp was made that night in the mountains.

The next morning Colonel Cardenas ordered the column to take up an increased gait toward San Borjas. The advance guard was ordered to capture one Nicolas Perez, an alleged Carranza informer, who was believed to be in the vicinity. Colonel Marcus Corral located Perez and when he tried to make the arrest Perez resisted and was shot and killed. His wife attempted to intercede for him and she, too, was shot, although accidentally. The column made camp at this hacienda for there was an abundance of corn, sugar, coffee, rice, and cheese. The road on this day had been unusually rough, and about two miles before reaching the Perez ranch, one of the wheels on the wagon in which Villa was carried broke and the wagon turned over.

Fortunately for Villa, his caretaker had anticipated the condition of the road and had decided to carry the wounded in the litters constructed the preceding day. His wound at this time was quite severe, and at times he cried like a child. He was drinking large quantities of gin, but it did not have the least effect toward relieving him of pain. On one occasion during the day he put two bichloride tablets in a quart bottle of gin and drank it. Those who saw him do it thought he would die, but they noticed later that the tablets had not been given enough time to dissolve. On occasion the pain was so severe that he asked to be shot; he literally lost his mind and in a fit of anger ordered that the driver of the wagon be shot. He revoked the order when he found out that the driver was his own relative (Juan Velasquez). On this day snow covered the ground and the road was quite slippery; movement was slow, hazardous, and uncomfortable, particularly for the wounded.

The next day the column left the Perez ranch and marched south by a ranch road to another ranch house and arrived shortly before noon. This was the ranch of José Rodriguez, the father of General José Rodriguez who was killed at Madera. Villa was being carried in a litter and there was concern that further travel might kill him. It was decided that he would remain at or near the ranch in order to look after his wound more closely. The area was considered a safe one, and Villa was desperately in need of rest. He was moved into the ranch house under the watchful eyes of several trusted aides, and the men were informed that he would remain there until he recovered.

After taking their leave of Villa at the Rodriguez ranch, a break occurred between Cardenas and Fernandez over the secrecy that Fernandez maintained regarding the movements and objectives of the march. Cardenas led his detachment northward toward the Rubio Mountains, and Fernandez continued on to Tres Hermanos with his detachment. The mental and physical strain of constant flight was beginning to manifest itself among the Villistas. Villa's announcement that he had decided to remain at the ranch was another of his skillful uses of disinformation to confuse his pursuers as well as his own men, because shortly after their departure he summoned Dolores Rodriguez and asked him to find a secure haven in which he could conceal himself until his wound healed. With Dolores as a guide and accompanied by about thirty *Dorados*, Villa, now forced to ride his horse, was taken to a watering place in the mountains about ten miles southeast of the pueblo of Santa Ana, called Ojito.

The next day an aggressive Carrancista General, José Cavasos, in command of 180 men engaged the small Villista detachment of Beltran and Lopez at Cienegitta and drove them toward Santa Ana. He continued his pursuit and arrived in Santa Ana on April 4 and, assisted by Esteban Carros, the mayor of the pueblo, conducted a house-to-house search for Villa, which proved fruitless. Before leaving that day for the north to continue his search, Cavasos offered Carros a reward of 10,000 pesos and a commission in the Carrancista army for any information that would lead to the capture of the bandit leader. Apparently prompted by information he received from Carros in regard to the location of Villa and the other wounded Villistas, Cavasos returned to Santa Ana on April 6 at the head of 300 cavalry. He promptly impressed an equal number of men from the surrounding pueblos and made plans to initiate a thorough search of the immediate area.

All of this hectic activity did not, however, escape the watchful eye of Dolores Rodriguez who undertook a night trip to reach Villa at Ojito and inform

Villa of the new threat. Villa left his haven as quickly as possible an
to endure the pain of riding over a jagged and treacherous mount:
group reached a camping spot near Al Aguaje, which was believed
time being, and a messenger was sent to Gorgorio Beltran at Sa
come for a conference. Upon arrival Beltran assured Villa that th
Santa Cruz offered a number of havens where he could rest and
wound, and Villa departed his camp on April 10.

Ever since Guerrero, Villa had made it a practice never to spend
pueblo; he found a place outside a town and made dry camp in the (
his most trusted *Dorados*. Desertions had damaged his confidence
and file followers, and despite the success of his disinformation et
mained a man whose caution came close to paranoia. Santa Cruz p
no exception, and in the final analysis it saved his life. He made his
side of town, and on the night of April 10–11, American troops s
the pueblo with the intention of searching it at dawn. When the sez
Villa was less than a kilometer from the houses that were searche
held, and he was undetected. He later remarked to one of Pershing'
were in his camp that it was the closest call to capture he had ever
life; he believed that he was actually in very great danger. Under
Gorgorio Beltran he remained undisturbed in a house near Santa
May 31. Beltran organized and supervised a local guard for Villa's p
and in addition he developed an espionage system through whicl
mation about Villa's location was spread with great success.

Villa was now concerned about regrouping his scattered forces w
to regaining his loss of influence in the course of Mexico's revolutionz
He therefore left Santa Cruz on June 1, and despite the fact that h
was still causing him a great deal of discomfort he could ride for
tances. Accompanied by thirty *Dorados* and led by Beltran, the mar
across the country and passed near the pueblo of Olives, then sou
the National Railroad terminus of Canutillo, and arrived at San Ju:
six miles north of Cerro Gordo, Durango, on June 12. Determined
ble and to reorganize his followers, he established his headquarters
sent letters of instruction to his scattered leaders. He moved to the l
de Torreon, about five miles northeast of Canutillo, on June 27 ar
the rebuilding program he hoped would launch him back into a pc
power. He had no way of knowing that in a matter of days his cam
be penetrated by two of General Pershing's spies.

Four

THE INTELLIGENCE SECTION AND AN ASSASSINATION PLOT

Intelligence, the gathering of information about enemies or possible enemies, and the creation of agencies to engage in gathering such information, has long been a concern of governments and their military institutions. The United States Intelligence records were not declassified until the early 1970s, and until then most records of the FBI, the Office of Naval Intelligence, Army Intelligence, National Security Agency/Central Security Service, the Secret Service, and the State Department's Secret Intelligence Bureau were closed and therefore not available to historians. As far as intelligence was concerned, the period prior to World War II was a closed book. Recently, however, this has changed. Historians have in recent years begun to examine the subject, and a central point has emerged: that as a direct response to the Mexican Revolution of 1910 there came into being for the first time an American Intelligence community.[1]

During the chaotic years of the Mexican Revolution of 1910, the United States was faced with an unparalleled situation as its southern neighbor plunged into the first of the Century of Revolution's great social upheavals. With massive investments in Mexico and facing hundreds of miles of an unfortified border, the American government needed information about what was taking place in Mexico. Revolutionary factions and émigrés infested the border regions of the states of Texas, New Mexico, Arizona, and California, and there was an urgent need to monitor their activities. In the forefront were the Bureau of Investigation (in 1935 this agency became the Federal Bureau of Investigation) and the Office of Naval Intelligence. The years after 1910 witnessed the development of these agencies and others into an Intelligence community, the growth of which was a direct result of the involvement of the United States in the Mexican Revolution.

General Pershing, who through field experience knew the value of intelligence, created his own Intelligence Section. The Section was headed by Major (later Brigadier General) James A. Ryan (13th Cavalry). Ryan was proficient in Spanish and had been professor of modern languages at the United States Military Academy for three years. He was assisted by 1st Lieutenant (later Colonel) Nicholas W. Campanole (6th Infantry), a native New Mexican and fluent in Spanish and Japanese. Campanole succeeded Ryan as Expedition Intelligence Officer on October 10, 1916, and held that post until the withdrawal of the Expedition in early February 1917. Others in the organization were Captain W. O. Reed (6th Cavalry), Captain William E. W. MacKinley (11th Cavalry), 2nd Lieutenant Walter F. Winton (6th Field Artillery), and 2nd Lieutenant James A. Ord (13th Cavalry). The officers were designated as being on "Special Service" with the Expedition, as was 1st Lieutenant George S. Patton, Aide-de-Camp to General Pershing, who also had some additional intelligence responsibilities. These officers not only directed the activities of a system of scouts, guides, and spies that at its height numbered perhaps sixty individuals, but they also had access to a slush fund of $20,000 with which to pay for the services of these men.

The Japanese proved to be the most effective agents, because they could move with a degree of impunity between the Carrancistas on the one hand and the Villistas on the other. They were dependable and carried out their missions faithfully, and the Intelligence Section recruited four agents from northern Chihuahua who were employed at the sum of $5 a day.[2] They were given the task of locating the elusive Villa, and posing as itinerant peddlers as they began their journey south. After a brush with a Carrancista patrol on June 9 and under suspicion of being Villistas, they were jailed in Chihuahua City. They were freed on June 15, possibly because they promised to spy on Villa for the Carrancistas, and they made their way south to the town of Jimenez. Fuzita and Suzuki remained behind to gather information, and Dyo and Sato traveled into the mountains in search of Villa.

They traveled until shortly after midnight to the vicinity of a ranch called Guadalupe. They thought it was not advisable to disturb the ranch people at that hour of the morning, so they made a dry camp only a short distance from the ranch. At dawn, while making coffee they observed a wagon and two Mexicans coming from the direction of their line of march, and when the wagon stopped at their camp Dyo casually asked the Mexicans where they were from and their destination according to Mexican custom. One of them replied that they came from San Juan, and when Dyo asked if Villa was still there, the reply was that Villa had left San Juan the day before yesterday and that they had heard he had gone to Torreón de Cañas, a ranch north of the Pueblo of Canutillo. The two left their camp early the next morning and followed the directions given to them by the Mexicans. They reached a high point on the road overlooking the Canutillo valley that afternoon and as luck would have it, they struck what proved to be Villa's outpost. They were halted by eight men under a sergeant, who told them that the post was about three kilometers from the Hacienda de Torreón de Cañas. The outguard commander questioned them as to their destination and the nature of their business. Dyo boldly replied that he was going to Torreón de Cañas and that his business was none of his affair. They were permitted to proceed to the Hacienda under a sentinel.

As the Hacienda de Torreón de Cañas came into view in the valley, the two men were impressed at the obvious prosperity of the settlement. It was somewhat larger than Dyo's place in San Geronimo, and an arroyo, which ran past the houses, appeared to contain an abundant supply of water for drinking and other purposes. Many large cottonwood trees furnished shade; everything on the level plain looked green and pleasant to the eye. As they approached the Hacienda among the first men they saw was Colonel Bonifacio Torres with whom they had became well-acquainted at San Geronimo. He asked what they were doing so far away from home; they replied that they had come to see Villa on business. Colonel Torres dismissed the sentinel and personally ushered them in the direction of the house he indicated was Villa's shelter.

The house was rather a pretentious residence, surrounded by a large porch and numerous shade trees; many varieties of flowers grew in profusion. As the men entered the house they saw Villa seated on an armchair, a totally changed man since they had last seen him in San Geronimo. His long untrimmed jet black beard attracted their attention; beside him were two crutches; he wore only one shoe, the right, and the swollen left foot was covered with a light woolen sock. Villa immediately asked them what they were doing so far from home, and Dyo replied that he had seen his wife, Luz Corrales, quite by accident at El Paso, Texas, and that she was considerably worried at hearing of his wound. She had asked him, he continued, to come and deliver bandages; Villa seemed to have little interest in Dyo's answer, and he immediately changed the subject and asked if the men had had anything to eat. They replied that they had not, and Villa ordered his cook to prepare food for them.

During the meal Villa grew inquisitive as to the relations between the United States and Mexico and asked numerous questions concerning the locations of the American forces. The men offered him what information they knew on the subject, and were surprised when he asked them point-blank: "What does the world think about me; what is the consensus of opinion as to whether I am dead or alive?" They replied that the consensus of opinion was that he was dead but that a large number did not believe it. As the two guests were finishing their dinner, they heard Villa telling the natives assembled at his headquarters that he was leaving that night to attack Parral. He then said that he would not leave Torreón de Cañas until his leg was dressed with the bandages his wife had sent him. When Dyo informed him that he had taken a course in first aid and knew the method of applying the bandages, Villa insisted that the wound be dressed.

This was the first opportunity to examine in detail the wound of which they had heard so many varied tales. The soiled calico bandage was removed from the left leg below the knee, and it was seen that it had secured two wild leaves against the flesh. As the leaves were removed, considerable pus oozed out from the open sore. The bullet had entered from the rear, penetrating the leg bone midway between the knee and heel and had come out in the corresponding part of the leg in front. The bullet hole in the rear was closed and to all appearance healed. The hole in front was also closed, but the pus hole was just above it and as Dyo touched the area he could feel the fragments of broken leg bone. The leg was considerably swollen from the knee to the toes so that Villa was unable to wear a shoe. For very short distances about the house he moved with the aid of crutches, and the wound pained him considerably when he tried to ride a horse. In order to cover any considerable distance he was forced to sit in a buggy.

While dressing the wound Villa told them the manner by which he had been wounded. He had underestimated the strength of the Carranza force garrison at San Ysidro, he said, the location of the main Carranza force was reported to have been at Guerrero; he sent his largest force to fight them there and he remained with his escort on the mesa between San Ysidro and Guerrero in the vicinity of the horse-holders of the detachment sent to attack Guerrero. At daylight he saw a large force of Carrancistas about to capture those horses and in order to save them he charged the superior forces of the Carrancistas with his fifty escorts. The Carrancistas were forced to retreat when pursued by the *Dorados* who had been reinforced by other troops.

He was, Villa continued, returning to his original post when a stray bullet struck him. He believed it must have been a ricochet shot as it did not penetrate the legging he was wearing at the time. When the legging was removed he saw the bullet drop. He went on to say that no one would ever know how much he has suffered with this. He was throughout his life, he wanted them to know, a total abstainer, but had fallen three times in his life: once when his mother died; the second time when his father passed away; and the third time when he was wounded at Guerrero. No amount of stimulant seemed to relieve his pain, and he stressed for all to hear that he owed his life to his true friends.

It was dusk when the wound was dressed, and Villa's buggy was driven up to the house. The advance guard was well under way and the main body about to pass the camp as it marched on the Parral road to the northwest when Villa took his seat in the buggy. Dyo rode with him, and the *Dorados* marched about 300 yards in front of them. After about one hour's march, with the Hacienda de Torreón de Cañas well in the rear of them, Villa gave orders to change direction. They marched cross-country with not even the shadow of a trail. The buggy found numerous places rather difficult to negotiate, and at the dangerous crossings Villa would leave the buggy and walk or for the longer detours ride his horse. While on the march Villa informed Dyo of his plan of action. His immediate objective was the pueblo of Jimenez. His aim was to reach unobserved the mountain range running north and south parallel to and to the east of the Jimenez-Villa Lopez-Rio Florido road; then follow the western slope of that mountain range to a point east of Jimenez and to take by surprise the garrison of the pueblo of Jimenez. His men needed ammunition and clothes and he believed that Jimenez had these in abundance. Orders were issued that no smoking or fires would be allowed.

They left their camp in the early morning and continued their march eastward across the country. Dyo's best estimate was that the total strength of Villa's force was 800 officers and men. Travel was difficult as the terrain was undulating and covered densely with mesquite trees. When they arrived in their new camp in an arroyo called La Parida, near a ranch of the same name at sunset, Villa informed his men of his objective. Dyo had taken advantage of the opportunity to meet the leaders of the various detachments during the day. The leaders, all Generals, were Gorgorio Beltran, Nicholas Fernandez, Banderio Urives, Francisco Beltran, Agustin Garcia, and José Xeza.

Just before supper Villa asked Dyo to dress his wound. Dyo could see no change for the better as a result of the application of the new bandage, and he suggested that an operation was in order to remove the fragments of bone in the leg. Villa replied that he never had any use for doctors and preferred to let nature take its course. As the condition of the wound was discussed, a messenger arrived with a letter for Nicholas Fernandez from General Ignacio Ramos who was stationed with Carranza forces at the town of Salaices. His force was estimated at 600 men. The letter stated in effect that the relations between the United States and Mexico had become critical and that war was inevitable; and that it was imperative that all factions bury their hatchets and combine as one force to resist the threatened invasion. Would he, Fernandez, consent to a conference for the purpose of discussing the conditions under which he with his men would join the Constitutional forces? After a moment of reflection Villa dictated to Fernandez the reply: It was impossible to make an immediate and satisfactory answer to the letter as their headquarters were at Zarco and that considerable time would be required to inform the chief of his inquiry. The letter was signed by Fernandez and carried to Ramos at Salaices by a messenger.

The detachment left their night's camp at La Parida only after additional orders of precaution to the leaders had been given that all ranch houses were to be avoided on this march. The column had scarcely cleared the camp when a courier arrived with information that Pablo Salinas and Elijio Reyes were in camp at San Ysidro, a ranch situated about eight miles south of the pueblo of Rio Florido with about 400 men. This detachment was part of Villa's force under command of Salinas, which Villa had expected would join him at the Hacienda de Torreón de Cañas. General Canuto Reyes until very recently had been its commander, and the detachment had refused to follow Canuto and to avail itself of the amnesty offered by the Carranza government and immediately selected Salinas as leader. Salinas was not familiar with this section of the country and had evidently mistaken a locality also called San Ysidro, at which place subsequent orders from Villa had designated as a junction point.

The object of Villa's secret march to Jimenez had now been defeated and after a short conference with his leaders it was decided to march to San Ysidro, due north. They arrived at San Ysidro in the early evening, and the newly constituted Villa command was now estimated at about 1,200 men. Soon after their arrival, the daily couriers arrived with information that General Ignacio Ramos with a force of about 600 Carrancistas was in camp at Conception, a small town, at a distance of about fifteen miles. Villa at once made a plan to attack the following morning at dawn. Several strong patrols of twenty men each were sent out to observe the enemy during the night, and they returned the same evening with the information that Ramos had retreated to a Hacienda called Corrales about fifteen miles north of Rio Florida. This made a change of plans necessary. Since San Ysidro was one of the Terrazas family haciendas, a family of Carranza supporters, Villa ordered it to be confiscated for the use of his forces. He then proceeded to partition it among the tenant farmers with the only reservation that they should furnish food to the detachments of his forces that happened to halt there on the march. In the meantime, patrols under the direction of Nicolas Fernandez had collected about one hundred recruits already armed and equipped. These were assigned to the Fernandez detachment.

When the Villista forces left San Ysidro they were close to 1,300 strong, and Fernandez was designated to lead them. Villa explained to Dyo that since knowledge of the terrain was a key to victory, he always selected as the advance guard commander that leader who was most familiar with the ground on the line of march. When the time for attack arrived, Villa explained, this leader was allowed to have a prominent part in the disposition of forces and if advisable he did not hesitate to place him in absolute command. Fernandez was thoroughly familiar with the country in which the operations were now being conducted, and Villa considered him a very competent leader. In fact, as Villa was recuperating for active work, Fernandez was the actual commander of the entire force.

They arrived at Rio Florido at noon and halted for dinner. Villa called the mayor to assemble the people of the pueblo at the plaza at about 1:00 PM and he delivered a short address in which he told the people that in 1915 he had been approached by an agent of the United States with an offer. If he would sell the United States Chihuahua and Sonora and cede the Tehuantepec-Salinas Railroad and further dispose of Magdalena Bay (by sale or cessation) to them, then all the assistance necessary financially and otherwise to conquer his adversary would be given. His first impulse, he said, was to kill the agent on the spot, but he succeeded in containing himself sufficiently to say that neither Chihuahua nor Sonora were salable articles; that they belonged to the people of Mexico; that the railroad was purely a Mexican enterprise and should rightfully be left so; and that the Magdalena Bay was a part of the Republic of Mexico of which no man could dispose. This same representative, Villa asserted, made identically the same overtures to Carranza and his reply to him was clearly indicated by the events that followed: his immediate recognition by President Wilson.

Carranza was denounced as a traitor to Mexico, and Villa urged the people to join his effort to overthrow this usurper of Mexican right and liberty. Then and only then would the people of Mexico be free to challenge the United States of North America and demonstrate to them that the Mexican people will not allow themselves to be bought and sold in bondage. Although the speech lasted for about ten minutes, Villa repeated the above statement several times in different words. He was not gifted in elocution and frequently words failed him. In this effort, such as it was, between fifty and one hundred more recruits of the Rio Florido flocked to his standard.

They left Rio Florido shortly after the speech and marched via the Rio Florido-Villa Lopez-Jimenez road to a campsite on the banks of the Rio Florido River, midway between the pueblo of the Rio Florido and Corrales. In an effort to lull General Ignacio Ramos, the Carrancista commander at Corrales, into a false sense of security, Villa directed Fernandez to send messengers with a letter misleadingly dated San Ysidro and signed by Fernandez. The letter stated that Fernandez had been authorized to use Villista forces against the common enemy, the United States of North America. The letter suggested a meeting between the leaders the following morning to devise plans of cooperation. The ruse, of course, was primarily to hold Ramos at Corrales overnight and to lure him to relax the vigilance of his outguard. Villa meantime was making preparations to surround Corrales during the night and to attack the Carrancistas at dawn.

The next day the entire Villa force left the campsite on the Rio Florido River at midnight and marched north in the direction of Corrales by the main road. The orders against smoking were repeated, and the march was conducted quietly and slowly. The order to halt was given about 1,000 yards south of where it was thought that the Carrancistas might have sentries. Here the leaders were assembled and orders given disposing of the entire detachment with a view to surround the Hacienda except the Fernandez detachment, which was taken off to hold the Corrales-Salaices road. The *Dorados* were held in reserve with Villa on a nearby hill. The leaders were instructed to enter the pueblo under cover of darkness and engage the enemy in a hand-to-hand combat. Villa expected that the Carrancistas would not stand the shock and would immediately retreat to Salaices on the Corrales-Salaices road, which Fernandez was to hold with his detachment of 300 men. As the leaders were directed to join their detachments, Villa cautioned them to save their ammunition.

The Carranza force at Corrales was estimated at 600, and the principal roads were covered by sentries located on commanding positions. Part of the garrison was located at the ranch house and part was in camp near the graveyard with adobe walls on four sides; the latter proved to be the principal stronghold. There was a ditch running north and south along the river, which was deep enough for standing cover. The Villistas were surprised to find the Carranza sentries on the alert and upon their approach were fired upon, which alarmed the entire Carranza camp. The ditch and graveyard were occupied at once and a heavy fire immediately opened up. At daybreak it seemed as though the Carrancistas were holding their own, and from the position occupied by Villa on the Zapata hill he could see them in the ditch facing east, and a large force under cover at the graveyard walls. The house was also occupied by what appeared to be reserves. It was obvious that Villa was apprehensive lest his ammunition gave way while the firefight was in progress he sent numerous messengers to the various leaders with instructions to save ammunition. That the Carrancistas resisted at all, Villa believed, was due to an underestimation of the number in the attacking force.

As the fight developed, however, they could see that the Villistas had superior forces. At midday it was observed that the ditch was evacuated and the Carrancistas retreated to the house about 300 yards to the rear. The firefight, however, continued throughout the afternoon until early evening, when the detachment under cover of the graveyard walls could be seen collecting for a sortie. The retreat was obviously under way and only a short time elapsed before the Carranza detachment began to force its way out of the Hacienda by the Corrales-Salaices road. A running fight ensued in which Fernandez pursued with comparatively fresh mounts. Ramos escaped to Salaices with only about 300 of his men. Villa learned later that the Carranza commander was wounded and died of his wounds at Salaices; the remainder of his detachment was either killed or captured. Fernandez pursued them energetically into the town of Salaices.

Villa, Dyo, and the *Dorados* drove into the hacienda in the early evening, and soon after his entry he announced that since the ranch belonged to Americans, all the buildings there would be set on fire. He was dissuaded in this however by Gorgorio Beltran on the ground that all the tenants were Mexicans and that burning the houses would be doing harm to his own people. The produce (such as wheat and corn) was all confiscated, and the portion not used by his troops was divided among the tenants. Of the 300 Carrancistas about 30 were killed outright and 60 wounded; the wounded were all killed whether severely wounded or not, as no facilities for their treatment were available. The coup de grace was very freely employed; all of the Carranza officers were shot on the spot. The total Carrancistas killed as a result of the engagement was estimated at 120. The prisoners (about 180) were released, but not, however, until a large number were branded. General Baldario, who was known as the "inventor" of the Villa forces, suggested the singular punishment for the prisoners of branding them was by cutting pieces of flesh from one or both ears so that if caught a second time in the service of the Carranza government their identification would be easy. Baldario produced shears, knives, and scythes from the farmhouses, which he handed to volunteer privates to carry the idea into effect. About fifty or sixty of the Carranza prisoners were abused or punished in this manner.

The Villista losses were six killed and forty wounded. The latter were sent to Rio Florido and other points south for treatment. From the prisoners captured at Corrales information was obtained that the Jimenez garrison

consisted of about 300 men and that about one half million rounds of ammunition was in storage there. Villa called a conference with his leaders and soon
after decided that the entire detachment would leave Corrales after supper
and the march to Jimenez. Pursuant to these orders the detachment cleared
camp at Corrales about 8:00 PM for the march northward. Villa, his bodyguard, and Dyo returned to the heights at Zapata and made camp there for the
night.

The following day the main body left Corrales and marched to Villa Lopez,
a distance of about eight miles, where the advance guard was fired upon. The
Carrancista force at Villa Lopez consisted of fifty men and constituted the
regular garrison of the pueblo. They fled quickly and the Villistas decided to
camp at Villa Lopez for that night. At dawn the march was resumed in the
direction of the town of Jimenez, and it was found deserted of Carrancistas.
The garrison had consisted of 300 men and was part of a small district command under Ignacio Ramos. Their withdrawal was made northward with all
their equipment. Villa had departed Zapata at daybreak and marched in the
direction of Jimenez; he rode in his buggy and Dyo accompanied him. Villa
Lopez was arrived at in the early evening, and as no report had reached Villa as
to the results at Jimenez, he seemed considerably worried. As soon as darkness
descended he decided, as was his custom, to leave the town and go to a ranch
about three miles farther north in the direction of Jimenez.

On the road Villa appeared anxious as to the success of his forces in the
capture of the one-half million rounds of ammunition reported at Jimenez.
He explained to Dyo that much depended upon its capture. He took the
opportunity to explain that what he sought was ammunition and popularity
and that he needed the former to ensure the latter. After Jimenez he would
attempt the capture of Parral, and after Parral he would go on and capture the
pueblo of Torreón. The capture of a large city, such as Torreón, was necessary
to success in restoring his prestige in the eyes of the people. His operations
thereafter would be governed by circumstances; the probability was that he
would undertake an expedition by rail northward to Ciudad Chihuahua. Villa
issued to Sato and Dyo rifles and fifty rounds of ammunition.

Early the following day, Villa left his camp north of Villa Lopez by buggy,
and rode in the direction of Jimenez. No information had as yet reached
him regarding the operations at Jimenez, and he was concerned about the
ammunition he so desperately needed. At Dolores, at a distance of about
six miles from camp, a courier from Banderio Urives, the commanding officer of the Villa forces at Jimenez, finally brought the information that
Jimenez had been captured at midmorning July 4, without firing a shot.
The ammunition that Villa needed badly had been removed northward to

Chihuahua the night before, and that Fernandez had joined a short time before the pueblo was taken. Upon receipt of this information Villa left Dolores and drove at top speed to the pueblo of Jimenez. Soon after the entry into Jimenez, the decision was made that all the stores should be looted, and that all the spoils be distributed to the farmers and dependent families. The families of the men who joined him were to receive double the allowance. That afternoon Villa made his usual short speech to the largest gathering he had seen since the last time he left Ciudad Chihuahua, December 22, 1915. Orders were issued for the entire command to leave Jimenez and march across the Rio Florida to an open camp about four miles distant.

An early morning departure from camp made it possible to eat the noon meal at San Felipe, a distance of about ten miles. After eating, a reorganization of the forces took place. About 250 recruits had joined Villa in the past several weeks and their assignments had not been formally made. The band's strength was now well over 1,500. When the reorganization was completed, Villa addressed his leaders and informed them that the opposition at Parral was estimated at 500 men. He planned to follow the national railroad and to destroy all bridges as he advanced. The wagons with the loot were placed in the center column with Villa, and the items in the wagons were distributed among the farmers as the column passed by.

Dyo and Sato accompanied the center detachment with Villa, and in the early evening they arrived at the Santa Ana ranch for camp. The ranch foreman was a Carranza supporter and therefore he was arrested, his hands were tied, and he was required to produce 500 pesos under threat of death. The foreman had no money but said that all he possessed in the ranch he gladly gave, if his life was spared. Every thing in the ranch was therefore taken and given to the soldiers, and the foreman was released before the Villistas departed. Villa, as usual, did not remain in the ranch for the night; when it became dark he had his escort march to a small arroyo and made a separate camp. Every precaution was taken to make the small camp immune to surprise. Villa did not remove either his shoes or his clothing and used his pistol for a pillow. His scant bedding and baggage were carried in the buggy, and only his closest friends or relatives were allowed nearby.

The next day's march was difficult, and Dyo and Sato both noted the extremely bad condition of the horses. The goal of the day's march was Valle Allende, a distance of fourteen miles, and a pause was made at Pueblito to feed the men and rest the horses. Villa ordered the mayor to assemble the men of the town as he wished to speak to them. The mayor failed to do this satisfactorily, and he explained that more of the men could be assembled if more time could be given as the men worked in the fields during the day.

Scarcely twenty men assembled to hear Villa. Upon seeing the small number he grew very indignant and told the mayor that it was quite obvious that the town was Carrancista and that he would not speak to them. The detachment left Pueblito shortly after eating and arrived at Valle in the early evening. The troops were billeted in the town, and Villa made camp in the outskirts in the company of a trusted few. When they had entered the town a countryman of Dyo's told him that one Fuzita was there, waiting for him. Dyo met Fuzita at the house of this countryman that night before supper and they discussed the situation and their future plans.

It was at this meeting on July 8 that Dyo was provided with three tubes of poison tablets that were said to have no smell or taste. A test of two tablets was made on a dog, and the results were satisfactory. For a man, however, it was decided that thirteen tablets would be necessary. The mission was to be accomplished by the middle of July. Fuzita and Suzuki departed immediately for the safety of the American lines, and Sato and Dyo carried on with their mission. They were to escape immediately following the poisoning by traveling at night and lying in concealment during the day until they reached San Geronimo and safety. The day of their arrival at San Geronimo was set at July 21, and if no report was received by July 29 it would be taken as an indication that the worst had happened to the men.

Valle was a town in which Villa was a popular man, and many of his admirers came to pay their respects to him. The mayor was directed to assemble the people that afternoon, as Villa wanted to speak to them. Here also, the stores of the rich had been ransacked under Villa's orders (as in other places) and distribution of the loot was made to the poor. The wagons laden with loot brought from Jimenez were all unloaded and the goods were also distributed. The empty wagons were returned to Jimenez about noon, and as soon as Villa finished delivering his customary address, the order to march was given. The column left Valle in the late afternoon, and marched to Talamante for camp, a distance of about seven miles.

During the period of Dyo's stay with Villa, he became his cook and assistant. Villa was very suspicious by nature and he carried his suspicion to the food he ate; he ate nothing unless the giver first sampled the food. The morning before his planned departure, July 9, Dyo got up early and made coffee into which he placed poison tablets. He gave Villa a cup of it, but only a small portion of the serving was consumed, perhaps one-eighth of the total. The Villistas left Talamante in the early morning, and Dyo and Sato marched with the troops in the direction of Durazno, situated at a distance of about seven miles northwest of Talamante. Before arriving at Durazno, however, under the pretense that Dyo's saddle was out of order, the two spies and would-be assassins were left behind, about two miles from the pueblo of Durazno. Following their successful return to the American lines, and unaware of what, if any, effect the poison had had on Villa, the men were debriefed and provided the information upon which the above paragraphs are based.

This shadowy episode did not, however, end with the return of Pershing's agents to safety. On August 25, 1916, an article appeared in the *El Paso Morning Times* based on an Associated Press wire story from Chihuahua City, Mexico dated August 24. The story told of a Japanese physician, a Doctor Nodko, who claimed to have killed Villa through the use of a slow poison administered under the pretext of medical treatment. Death allegedly came to the bandit leader following three months of "treatment," and it supposedly occurred shortly after his defeat at Parral. The origin of the letter is unknown, as is the real or imaginary "Dr. Nodko," but it may have been a cover story projected to account for Villa's intended death. On the other hand, this little conundrum presented something of a problem to the Office of Intelligence: a story of intrigue and assassination that was not intended to see the light of day had suddenly emerged, and the possibility of public embarrassment was more than General Pershing had bargained for.

In an effort to assess the real results of the plot, and to begin a program of damage control to neutralize any possible fallout, Dyo and Fuzita were on August 27 dispatched from Expedition headquarters on a new secret mission, this one to see if Villa had survived the poison. On August 30, accompanied by Suzuki, they went to the El Paso Immigration station because Suzuki was an alien and needed to register. While they were there they talked to the Japanese interpreter, Tom Hillworth, and Dyo foolishly told him the assassination story. When the Japanese departed to begin gathering information about Villa, they began by making discreet inquiries in the vicinity of El Paso and Juarez. No information turned up immediately, and by September 7, Fuzita was on his way to Villa's camp. The trip proved unnecessary, however, as the answer to Villa's condition was provided on September 16 when he and his reconstituted forces captured the city of Chihuahua.

In the meantime, Tom Hillworth phoned the El Paso Bureau of Investigation Agent, E. B. Stone, met with him the next day, and recounted Dyo's story. Stone in turn relayed the story to Washington in his next written report. The report eventually ended up on the desk of the Attorney General Thomas W. Gregory, who on September 22 included the "startling report" in a communication to the Secretary of War, Newton D. Baker. The cat was out of the bag, and an extremely delicate situation presented itself to General Pershing, the United States Army, and the Wilson Administration. The thought that the United States, her Army's officers and gentlemen, and perhaps even he President, would stoop so low as to poison an enemy leader was simply not to be countenanced. Something had to be done to deflect possible embarrassment, and that something was an "investigation."

On September 25 the Commanding Officer of the Southern Department was ordered by the Adjutant General to conduct a discreet investigation of the incident. The order was sent down to General Pershing on October 4 where it rested, perhaps in a desk drawer, for over three months. In the meantime, the Army and the Bureau of Investigation worked successfully to keep the story out of the newspapers. Major Ralph H. Van Deman, head of the Military Intelligence section of the Army War College and considered today the father of Army intelligence, branded the story a lie. He claimed that the story about the plot to poison Villa was absurd, simply a fantasy. On January 23, 1917, Pershing was sent a follow-up communication to the original October 4 order that demanded an answer. He hesitated until February 17, 1917, when he sent a carefully worded reply in which he assured Southern Department headquarters that no officer connected in any way to the Expedition's secret service section had any knowledge of or connection to any such plan as had been reported. It was possible, he went on, that the Japanese had some such plan of their own, but he was certain that none of his officers knew of it.

On the same say that General Pershing's report was submitted, Bureau of Investigation Agent Stone in El Paso sent an amended report to his original communication in which he stated that as of February 17 he had received no corroboration of the story originally given to Tom Hillworth by the Japanese. Given the absence of any reports, he continued, the story told to Hillworth should be regarded as false, "made of whole cloth," and the two aliens were no doubt looking for some kind of benefit to themselves in relating the tale. Stone also stated in a conversation with General Pershing that he did not believe that officers of the Expedition had been implicated in the alleged plot. As a result of all this, Secretary of War, Baker, wrote to Attorney General Gregory on February 29 that he was confident that no officer of the Expedition had either connection to or knowledge of any such plan as had been reported by the Japanese. The cover-up was complete; the damage control was successful.

NOTES

1. Charles H. Harris III and Louis R. Sadler, "Termination with Extreme Prejudice: The United States versus Pancho Villa," *The Border and the Revolution, Clandestine*

Activities of the Mexican Revolution: 1910–1920 (Silver City, NM: High Lonesome Books, 1990). See also the authors' *The Archaeologist Was a Spy* (Albuquerque, NM: University of New Mexico Press, 2003).

2 The agents were Tsutomo Dyo from the Hacienda of San Geronimo; K. Fuzita and A. Sato (both from Madera); and T. Suzuki from Pedernales.

.

Five

SCRAPS, FIGHTS, AND SKIRMISHES

Following Columbus, the first engagement between the Army and Villistas was at Guerrero, located along the west bank of the Guerrero River in the lower plain of the Guerrero Valley. On both east and west sides of the valley are steep bluffs cut deeply by arroyos, those on the east side virtually impassible. The arroyos are for all practical purposes undetectable from ground level and the terrain seems flat until the edge of an arroyo is reached. Many of the arroyos are partly wooded and may be traversed only with great difficulty. The valley is crisscrossed by roads to San Ysidro, which is above the valley floor and about four miles east of Guerrero, north to Casa Blanca, and south to Minaca; the Mexico Northwestern Railroad runs north past San Ysidro and south to La Junta. This is an area in which a surprise attack is difficult to initiate, as Dodd's command was to learn.

The Villistas at Guerrero with Cervantes on March 28–29 were a mix of men separated from their leaders in the recent battle, of Carrancistas who had "volunteered" to join, and of the men from Cruces and Namiquipa personally recruited by Cervantes. Even these men were of questionable loyalty; they were men who had joined for the adventure and romance of being a fighter for the great Francisco Villa and when the novelty wore off and the reality of battle set in, desertion became an attractive option. March 28 was spent stealing horses to provide mounts for the eighty Carrancistas and finding billets in the homes of private families who were sympathetic to Villa, to his men, and to *villismo*. The mood among the Villistas was perhaps best expressed in the words of one of their own, recorded later by American Intelligence Officers.

The celebration of their victory over the Carrancistas had continued for two days, and on the night of March 28 no precautions were taken against surprise because there seemed to be no need for them. The closest Carranza force was several days away, and the arrival of an American force in Mexico was unknown. Preparations had been made, however, to leave Guerrero in the morning and begin a march to the south. Villa had told them that he was going to Durango to recruit a force with which he could fight all the Americans in the United States. The townspeople were the first to take notice of a strange mounted force approaching from the south, perhaps two miles distant. Cervantes was notified at the command post and orders were given to saddle the horses and retreat. Arisiachic was designated as a rallying point for all whose escape was successful. Some of the Americans, the Second Squadron, Troops E, F, G, and H commanded by Captain Samuel F. Dallam, moved from the commanding hills west of town, and by the time the Villistas' horses were saddled they were just 150 yards away and closing in rapidly.

As they approached Guerrero from the south, the American plan of attack was to send one squadron across the river to the west side of the town in order to block any retreat in that direction. The main American unit was then to make its way along the eastern bluff above the town, trap the Villistas between the two forces, and envelop them. Captain Dallam's Second Squadron had little difficulty crossing the river and blocking access to the two major escape routes, the arroyos that led to the plain above. The main attack force to the east, however, was delayed by the deep arroyos and soon became aware of the fact that the Villistas had been alarmed and were running to the north and east toward the mountains. It was therefore necessary to open fire at long range, and the assault was opened with both rifles and machine guns.

Once firing began some Villistas carrying the Mexican flag made an orderly movement to the east without firing, apparently hoping that the Americans would be tricked into thinking they were Carrancistas. The ruse worked, and a large number of Villistas escaped. It did not work, however, for the second group that tried it; they were blocked by Dallam's column and took casualties, which included the death of General Elijio Hernandez. A number of Carrancista prisoners held by the bandits were liberated, two machine guns were found abandoned, and a store of small arms and ammunition was secured. The largest portion of the Villistas fled north and then east toward San Ysidro, and despite the fatigued condition of the horses, the pursuit of the bandits continued. The retreating groups made several stands, but were dispersed with dismounted rifle fire. A pistol charge was organized, but the horses could not sustain the rapid gait necessary for completion. The pursuit and running fights continued until the bandits reached the mountains to the east where they dispersed into small groups and disappeared. The condition of the horses precluded any further action, and by noon the regiment was reassembled. The troopers had ridden seventeen out of twenty-four hours, covered fifty-five miles, and fought for five hours.

Prior to its forced march to Guerrero, Colonel Dodd's column had been on the move and in the saddle continuously since March 23, and the campaign had been an extremely difficult one for both men and horses. They had marched 375 miles between March 16 and their arrival at Bachineva, the men had for all practical purposes lived off the land, and the horses had had little forage other than what was found during the march. At the time of his report, given shortly after the engagement, Dodd reported thirty Villistas were killed, about twenty Carrancista prisoners liberated, and two machineguns, a number of horses, saddles, and firearms captured. Four Americans were wounded, none seriously. The Carrancistas were in all likelihood from among the eighty men who had, following their defeat by Villa two days earlier, joined the Villistas and had been armed and equipped in time for the fight on the March 29. Dodd had no way of knowing who they were, took their word that they had not taken place in the engagement, and "liberated" them. The death of General Hernandez, who commanded the Villistas and was one of Villa's most trusted officers, was a serious loss. The surviving Villistas were scattered, the greater portion of them driven in a ten-mile running fight into the mountains northeast of the railroad. After brisk skirmishing, they separated into small bands and fled.

There were, of course, certain difficulties in reporting casualties, and field reports did not always agree with later official records. Officers in the field were aware that the mission of the Expedition was primarily to punish those Villistas who had taken part in the Columbus raid, and they tried to determine among the casualties those who had been with Villa during the raid as opposed to those who had joined Villista forces since the raid. A further difficulty arose in determining the number of Columbus raiders who were killed or captured by Carrancista forces at Las Animas, on March 17; at Namiquipa, on March 19; at Ciudad Guerrero, on March 27–28; at Cienegitta, on April 3; and those raiders who surrendered to the Carrancistas at Madera in April. As intelligence officers gathered information from informants, from spies, and from prisoner interrogations, numbers given in initial reports were revised. The number of casualties in Colonel Dodd's report was later revised: 5 Americans were wounded; and of the 380 engaged, 56 Villistas were killed and 35 wounded. The total Villista casualties reported included those stationed at

San Ysidro, and it was believed that the casualties reported were all Columbus raiders.

Since the mission assigned to the Expedition was primarily to punish those bandits who had participated in the attack on Columbus, the Army came to view as a measure of its success the casualties inflicted on those who in any form or manner took part in the attack. The difficulty in rendering an accurate statement of casualties due to recognized causes in any campaign should be fully realized: the dead on the field and the wounded who are captured make accurate statistics; the wounded that escape and either die later or recover to fight another day are usually not found in the casualty reports. Further difficulties in accurate accounting arose because (1) the Carrancista forces often concealed information regarding casualties in their encounters with Villistas; (2) Villa recruited from among Carrancistas whom he had defeated; and (3) new recruits to Villa's bands were added during the operations of the Expedition. For the determination of the number of casualties among the Columbus raiders, however, the Army saw it as immaterial whether the casualties arose as a result of encounters with U.S. troops or with Carrancista forces.

After the fight at Guerrero, the Villistas scattered to safety wherever they believed they could find it. When General Pershing received Dodd's report of the fight on March 30, he ordered a thorough search of the surrounding areas in the hope that more Villistas, perhaps Villa himself, might be found. Colonels Brown and Allen, Majors Evans, Howze, Lindsley, and Tompkins were alerted to rumors of potential hiding places and ordered to ignore no plausible information in their searches. In the belief that Villa's plan of retreat was a general movement south to Durango, Pershing again implemented a movement of parallel columns to converge near the Durango line in an effort to get ahead of Villa's forces. Colonel Brown took the road farthest east, Major Tompkins took the center, Major Howze took the farthest west position, and Colonel Dodd scouted and guarded the trails leading into the western mountains. It was Brown who unexpectedly flushed a band of Villistas.

Brown's 10th Cavalry, 14 officers and 258 men, had on April 1 crossed the continental divide in the early afternoon. As they approached Aguas Caliente, the advance guard and a Villista band, later estimated at 170, encountered each other at the same time and opened fire. As the 10th Cavalry charged the town, the Villistas retreated over a wooded hill pursued by Major Young and Troops G and H. Young's command pursued the Villistas six or seven miles east through the timbered range to El Mestemo, and abandoned the chase at nightfall. Two Villistas were killed; the number of wounded was unknown. The night was spent at Namipavechic, and the next day was spent in searching the trail of the fleeing Villistas with no success. Brown led the 10th Cavalry to San Antonio and there received a message from Carrancista General José Cavazos that American assistance in catching bandits was not wanted. Brown decided to await further developments and rest his command.

In the meantime, Major Tompkins had followed a Villista trail to Santa Maria on April 2, found nothing, and by April 5 was nearing the village of San Borja when he was given a note from General Cavasos. The note cautioned Tompkins that he was advancing in a direction that would put him in contact with Carrancista patrols and requested that the Americans stop before a conflict occurred. When he met Cavasos shortly after the note was delivered, Tompkins requested permission to continue south in pursuit of Villistas. He was told by the General that Villa was dead and buried. The situation was a tense one and rather than risk a confrontation Tompkins retired four miles to Cieneguita, where he camped for the night. It was here that Tompkins received news that Villa had passed through Santa Maria de Cuevas the day before, and the next day he marched his command to Santa Rosilia, where he ordered a halt to shoe the horses and rest the troopers.

Major Howze and the 11th Cavalry, 10 officers and 255 men, had stopped at San Geronimo for supplies at Cieneguita on April 7. There he received a confidential report that Villa was alive, though wounded, and with an escort of fifty men was moving down the Sierra Paras range to Durango. Howze launched an immediate pursuit, and en route to Los Estados and about ten miles south of San Borja, his column came upon General Cavazos and 300 men at midmorning on April 8. The General's advance platoon was reinforced with about fifty men, and they galloped toward the American column with rifles drawn. Howze anticipated a problem, deployed his men in an arroyo, which provided both excellent cover and a good field of fire, rode between his men and the advancing Mexicans, waved his hat, and called out in Spanish that they were Americans. A clash was averted, although the American officers believed that Cavazos was looking for a fight, and that only the strong defensive position that Howze had taken prevented one.

While camped at San José del Sitio on April 9, the troopers endured an ineffective but annoying sniper fire during the night, and the next day the march was continued south to Santa Cruz de Herrera with the purpose of intercepting Villa, should he come out of the mountains on his way to Durango. Late that afternoon the column was attacked near La Joya De Herrera by a band of forty Villistas who were dispersed after a brief exchange of rifle fire in which three Americans were wounded. The Villistas suffered seven dead, one of whom was their commander Captain Silva. On April 11, Howze surrounded Santa Cruz de Herrera in the hope of capturing Villistas who were reported as occupying the town, and an exchange of gunfire resulted in the deaths of one trooper and Villista Lieutenant Beltran, the son of General Beltran. Camp was made that night along the Belleza River and the following night at Heojolilan. The three columns were now south of any sizeable Villista force and ready to bring formidable strength to bear against Villa if left to their own devices. The situation was, however, soon to change.

Major Tompkins and his detachment of the 13th Cavalry, 8 officers and 120 troopers, had moved in a southerly direction from Santa Rosalia in a search for Villistas who were scattered from Santa Ana to San José del Sitio to Valle Zaragosa. He knew that Howze was on one flank and Brown was on the other, the former covering the San José del Sitio area and the latter covering the Satevo-Parral area, so he decided to head for Parral and secure much needed clothing and supplies for his men. The column reached Valle de Zaragosa on April 10 in time to find twenty-five Villistas looting a factory; Tompkins drove them off, recovered the stolen property, and returned it to the owners. He was able to purchase clothing, socks, and boots for his troopers, as most of them were literally in rags from the difficulties of the campaign. The men, for the most part bearded and gaunt, presented such an alarming appearance to the townsfolk that many panicked and ran away as the men rode in to get the needed supplies. Shortly before noon, a Carrancista Captain, Antonio Mesa, approached Tompkins' camp and informed the Major that he would be welcome in Parral and would be able to secure a campsite, food, pasture for the horses, and whatever supplies he needed. Captain Mesa spent the night there, took breakfast with Tompkins, and departed.

The following morning the 13th Cavalry moved out for the march to Parral, and following an uneventful day camped in the late afternoon near Santa Cruz de Villegas. They had covered thirty miles and welcomed the treelined stream where they spread their blankets for the night's rest. The weather had become mild and sunny and the nights were warmer, and both men and horses were spared the stinging cold they had faced in the higher altitudes. The government rations of hardtack, bacon, and coffee had been supplemented with what could be purchased from the locals: tomatoes, salmon, prunes, eggs, bread, flour, tortillas, frijoles, beef, and an occasional chicken. The water was good and plentiful, and while the change from oats to corn for the horses left many of them in a rather thinned down condition they were still serviceable. Rested, fed well, and in good spirits, the 13th Cavalry bedded down the evening of April 11 with no suspicion of what awaited them the following day at Parral.

Shortly after 7:00 AM the eighteen-mile march to Parral began, and just before noon Tompkins and his advance guard asked for and received permission to enter the town and confer with the Carrancista General Lozano. The

General professed no prior knowledge of Tompkins' visit, but agreed to secure a merchant for supplies and a campsite away from the town for the 13th Cavalry. While Lozano and Tompkins conferred, a crowd gathered in the plaza and cries of "Viva Villa!" and "Viva Mexico!" were heard. With Lozano and his staff and Tompkins in front, the advance guard made its way from the plaza to the outskirts of town with the crowd, increasingly vocal and angry, pressing close to the small column's rear. Firing broke out, apparently from the townspeople, and Lozano and his staff broke off and rode to the rear to stop the shooting. Tompkins' report to General Pershing stated that Lozano made an attempt to disperse the crowd with his saber, while one of his officers actually fired into the crowd with his sidearm.

As the firing continued, Tompkins located his rearguard to cover the retreat of his main force. When he observed that some of the Carrancista soldiers had moved to a position that threatened his flank, he sent out a squad to drive them away. The Carrancistas opened fire on the advancing Americans, and Tompkins ordered the fire be returned. With both the townsmen and the soldiers against him, he retreated some 16 miles followed by about 300 Carrancista soldiers. Tompkins decided to retreat from Parral to Santa Cruz de Villegas, a small fortress, which admitted of easy defense by a command the size of his. It was well stored with food for both the men and their animals.

The road permitted the 13th Cavalry to march in columns of twos over rolling fields separated by large, thick, stone walls. The civilian antagonists lost interest in pursuit as they were afoot, but the mounted Carrancista force continued on the flank of the retreating 13th Cavalry hoping to head, and perhaps surround, the Americans. The pursuers' plan was hindered by the presence of numerous stone walls and many became discouraged, while a few closed the distance and came within rifle range. Tompkins, Lieutenant Lininger, and eight troopers took position behind a stone wall and opened fire against the Carrancistas further discouraging them. The retreat continued as American rearguard riflemen who kept the pursuers at a distance, and the harried column made its way safely into Santa Cruz de Villegas. The horses were placed under cover and riflemen, chosen from among the experts and sharpshooters, were placed on strategically chosen rooftops. The Carrancistas made a cautious approach but a long-range rifle shot by Captain Aubrey Lippincott, estimated at 800 yards, toppled what appeared to have been a mounted officer. The Carrancista force moved back. This was followed by a note from General Lozano sent under a flag of truce in which he requested the immediate withdrawal of the American force northward.

Various writers have from time to time commented with skepticism on the casualty numbers submitted by the Army in it reports of the Expedition's engagements while in Mexico. The doubts expressed have generally been directed at the large number of Mexican casualties reported and the relatively small number of American casualties. In particular, Captain Lippincott's reported 800-yard hit on a Carrancista at Santa Cruz de Villegas has been called into question and, by implication, American marksmanship in general. Perhaps a few remarks about the men and their equipment will clarify the issue.

In 1903 the Army replaced its standard issue .30–40 Krag-Jorgensen bolt-action magazine rifle with the new U.S. Magazine Rifle, Caliber .30, Model of 1903, known to several subsequent generations of riflemen as the "Springfield '03," "Springfield," or simply, the "03." The Krag had proven no match for the German Mauser rifle in the Spanish-American War, and it is no accident that the Springfield's action was based on the Mauser design. In 1906 a new .30 caliber cartridge was adopted to replace the original and was designated the Model of 1906, soon and thereafter to be called simply the 30–06. This cartridge proved to be one of the most inherently accurate thirty-caliber cartridges in the world, and it is in widespread use to this day. The rifle quickly earned a reputation for fast, accurate fire in the hands of a trained shooter; it became one of the best-known and appreciated military rifles of its time. Prior to World War I, service-grade Springfields were used in Olympic and other international competitions with outstanding results.

With the advent of the new rifle, the Army was determined to train its men in such a way that the accuracy of the weapon would be put to most effective use. The program was described in the papers of General Pershing where he stated that the marksmanship of the Army rifleman was the result of a studied effort to bring shooting to the highest point of efficiency. Regular target practice on military reservations and bonuses paid to soldiers who demonstrated skill did much to achieve the Army's goals. Soldiers were put through physical training exercises designed to develop upper-body strength and endurance. They were then taught to set the sights of their rifles for proper elevation and wind adjustment, and these lessons were followed by two weeks of practical application. In these drills each man was graded by his shooting ability, from Expert, through Sharpshooter, to Marksman. The Expert received a $5 pay increase per month; the Sharpshooter received a $3 monthly increase; and the Marksman received an increase of $2 per month. Field practice was designed to simulate combat conditions, it was competitive, and each company was graded on its efficiency. Competition was keen; the results were dramatic. The training and monetary incentives seemed to have produced the desired results. In General Funston's Annual Report for the Southern District for 1916, for all units reporting, 88 per cent of the officers and 68 per cent of the enlisted men qualified as Expert, Sharpshooter, or Marksman with the 30–06 Springfield rifle.

If there is any doubt about the long-range accuracy of Mauser-type .30 caliber rifles, one only need look at the results of competitions, which are concerned exclusively with ranges of 800, 900, and 1,000 yards. In the modern Palma match, competitors fire at all three ranges mentioned, and shooters routinely shoot *perfect* scores on their targets in the first two ranges and score near-perfect, and sometimes perfect, scores in the 1,000-yard event. The Leech Cup, 20 shots at 1,000 yards with metallic sights, regularly produces scores of 200, and the match is then decided by the number of "X" hits (the "X" ring is a smaller ring inside the six-foot black bull's-eye). This shooting is done with metallic sights, and the 30–06 cartridge was dominant until the Army replaced it with the .308 Winchester (7.65 NATO). The Wimbledon Cup Match, 20 shots at 1,000 yards from the prone position with scope sights, is one of the more demanding courses of fire in competitive shooting. In 1921 at Camp Perry, Ohio, a civilian shooter, George R. Farr from Washington State, shot seventy consecutive bull's-eyes in a day-long competition using the 1903 Springfield 30–06 National Match rifle and ammunition issued free by the Army. This incredible feat of marksmanship, unmatched since, is today honored by the presentation of the Farr Trophy to the high score shooter in the Wimbledon Cup. At the time of his achievement, Mr. Farr was sixty-two years old. In view of the empirical data available regarding rifle accuracy, Captain Lippincott's reported shot at Santa Cruz de Villegas is not at all improbable. A man mounted on a horse makes an inviting target; a hit on the horse turns cavalry into infantry, and a hit on the man is not only a casualty but also inflicts a degree of discomfort on those who witness it that can, if repeated, demoralize.

Major Tompkins' reply said in effect that he would withdraw only under a guarantee of safe passage, and that if no such guarantee was forthcoming he would await the arrival of other American forces. Three troopers had been dispatched in an effort to find Colonel Brown's 10th Cavalry camp, which they located eight miles north of Tompkins' position. Brown, along with Major Young's squadron of Buffalo Soldiers, reached Santa Cruz de Villegas before sunset, and identified themselves through bugle calls before coming in. As they marched in and were seen by Lozano's command, the Carrancistas retreated to Parral. The 13th Cavalry suffered two men killed and seven men wounded, including Major Tompkins; one man was missing, seven horses were killed, and sixteen wounded. Forty Carrancistas were reported killed and an unknown number wounded.

Major Charles Young, 10th Cavalry [National Archives].

The news of the action at Parral infuriated General Pershing, who wrote in his report that the attack was unprovoked and outrageous and the involvement of the civil population aided by the Carrancista forces under their own field officers was the culmination of a long series of petty acts of hostility, which grew in number and viciousness as the American columns moved south. Pershing believed strongly in the legitimacy of the American presence in Mexico, and thoroughly distrusted First Chief Carranza's early assurances of cooperation with the Expedition. When he later learned of a poster signed by a Carrancista official on a wall in Parral, seen by Lieutenant Lininger of the

13th Cavalry, which stated American troops were in Mexico with the permission of the Mexican Government, and that they were not at war with Mexico but were in pursuit of the bandit Villa, and that people should remain calm, his distrust deepened. Throughout the remainder of the Expedition's time in Mexico, Pershing remained as suspicious of Carranza as he did of Villa, perhaps more so.

Pershing's report indicated that he was at first inclined to keep troops in the vicinity of Parral, but he came to believe that the strained relations between Mexico's de facto government and the Wilson administration brought about by the fight had moved the situation from the military to what he called the "sphere of diplomacy." He decided that it was best to withdraw, at least for the time being, in order to see what orders would be forthcoming from Washington. The four columns had united under Colonel Brown shortly after the fight, and while he was convinced that the command would be able to give a good account of itself under any circumstances likely to arise, he decided that it was best for the troops to return to San Antonio. His major concern was one of supply and communication. There was no forage or food in the area, the road was questionable, and there were no functional aircraft available to speed communication; but before ordering Brown to withdraw Pershing sent Colonel Cabell, Chief of Staff, to investigate the situation. Cabell decided that the situation warranted removal of the columns, and they were ordered to return to San Antonio. The active pursuit of the Columbus raiders was, for all practical purposes, halted.

On April 20, at the Verde River and Green Road a detachment of Dodd's 7th Cavalry, one officer and forty-five troopers, skirmished with a band of ten Villistas with the result that three Villistas were killed. It seemed evident at the time that the Villista bands were becoming smaller and more scattered, an observation that would be dispelled in two days at the village of Tomochic. Rumors had reached Colonel Dodd that a large band of Villistas had looted the town of Yoquivo and taken two hostages, an American and a Frenchman. Dodd's command, 10 officers and 145 men, reached Yoquivo on April 20 and hoped to surprise the Villistas the following morning, only to find that they had fled. At Yoquivo Dodd learned that the Villistas numbered about 140 men; that Cervantes was in command with Baca, Rios, and Dominiques as subordinates; and that the hostages had been freed. Since Tomochic seemed to be the band's destination, Dodd followed and arrived at the village at 5:00 PM. In his search for the Villistas he was not disappointed.

Tomochic was located along the banks of the Tomochic River, in a valley surrounded by craggy mountains at elevations of up to 9,000 feet. The town itself is at an elevation of 6,625 feet. According to General Pershing's report,

the command approached the town by a well-concealed trail from the southwest and when at the edge of town, it charged in at a gallop and occupied the
area. The Villistas, who had abandoned the town and occupied the heights
on the north and south sides, opened fire on the Americans. As described by
Colonel Dodd, those scattered on the hills north and south were dislodged
or killed, while others withdrew to the eastward mountains. From the first
point of observation, a large herd of horses and a column of troops were seen
in the distance. That suggested that the main body of bandits might be in
that direction, and two troops were sent with orders to attack any force found
there and to capture or kill the horses. At the same time a machine gun under
Sergeant H. H. Roberts, supported first by a platoon and later by the entire force of Troop L, was advanced to, where there was an abandoned adobe
house.

The firing on the part of the bandits diminished, but shortly thereafter the
Americans began to take heavy fire from the hills to the east. This proved to
be from the main body of Villistas who had retreated up to the top of the
mountain trail, about three miles away, and who had returned upon hearing
their rear guard under attack. They scattered themselves along the crest of
the mountain, extended from (northwest) to (southeast), and had a decided
advantage in position. There was no way the attacking Americans could hope
to get around them as daylight faded, and their only option was a fast, frontal
assault. Men of E Troop occupied the knoll and opened a brisk fire that caused
the Villistas slowly to withdraw. As darkness fell the Villistas scattered along
the several mountain trails, and pursuit was impossible.

Since a resumption of the fight was expected in the morning, Easter Sunday, April 23, the Americans reoccupied the town and chose defensive positions. Dawn showed the hills and ridges to be empty of bandits, however,
and the command spent the day in preparation for the return to its camp, San
Pedro, near Minaca. They had suffered two killed and three wounded; the Villista casualties were reported at thirty-two killed and twenty-five wounded. A
grisly story later told at Matachic reported that the Tarahumara Indians had
gathered up the wounded Villistas and, since they had no way of caring for
them, poured pitch over them and set them on fire. The Cervantes band was
thoroughly discouraged by the fight and began to disintegrate: according to
later testimony gathered by American intelligence officers, by April 27 desertions had reduced Cervantes' detachment to barely fifty men, by May 3
it was down to thirty-five, and by May 19 it was numbered at fifteen. In
recognition of the fact that Villa's bands were now scattered and demoralized, General Pershing decided that it was time for a reorganization of the
Expedition.

Following the movement of the three cavalry columns to San Antonio, infantry and artillery were moved closer to the front in case a new campaign of active pursuit was decided upon. Pershing's intelligence reports indicated that the Villistas, though scattered, were still in the State of Chihuahua and that Villa was in hiding in the mountains southeast of San Borja. The plan Pershing developed divided the territory into five districts, each patrolled by a regiment of cavalry, and most of the infantry and artillery close to the front should they be needed. On April 29 General Orders Number 28 were issued in which Pershing described the new reality faced by the Expedition. The soldiers no longer faced a cohesive force of considerable size, but were faced with isolated bands under subordinate leaders. The challenge to the Expedition was to hunt down these isolated bands over widely separated portions of the country. The territory to be covered under these circumstances was accordingly divided into districts and apportioned to organizations available for such duty.

Each commander was charged with developing his own intelligence-gathering units. Guides and interpreters were to be provided when and where possible. Intelligence gathered was to be reported to Pershing and also to be shared among district commanders. Each local commander was to be free to operate on his own initiative on any information that seemed likely to lead to the capture of any of the participants in the Columbus raid. Officers were reminded that they were operating within the boundaries of a friendly nation and that all due courtesy and consideration was to be accorded to the populace. They were, however, warned that they must not take any situation for granted and must always operate under the utmost awareness that seemingly friendly populations may turn out to be hostile. The lesson of Parral had not been lost on General Pershing. If faced with unprovoked hostility, Pershing ordered, the officer in command must without hesitation take the most vigorous measures at his disposal to administer severe punishment on the offenders, bearing in mind that any other course is likely to be construed as a confession of weakness. The districts established were Namiquipa (10th Cavalry, Major Evans); Bustillos (13th Cavalry, Colonel Slocum); Satevo (5th Cavalry, Colonel Wilder); San Borja (11th Cavalry, Colonel Lockett); and Guerrero (7th Cavalry, Colonel Dodd). The assignments were based upon the territory that each regiment had had the most service and with which the regiment's personnel were most familiar.

On the evening of May 4, Pershing learned that Julio Acosta and Cruz Dominiques were in the vicinity of Cusihuriáchic with over one hundred men and were threatening the town and the small Carrancista garrison there. Two representatives of the town, usually called Cusi, came to San Antonio and requested protection from the bandits. The bandits apparently had boasted that they had a 1,000 men and intended to attack the Americans at San Antonio, thus frightening the inhabitants of that town as well. Pershing decided that the time was right to teach the bandits a lesson, and he accordingly dispatched Major Howze with six troops and the Machine Gun Platoon of the 11th Cavalry (14 officers and 319 troopers) with twenty Apache scouts to Cusi with orders to move against the Villistas as circumstances warranted.

Howze and his command reached Cusi about midnight on May 4 and were informed that the Villistas were camped at Ojo Azules, thirty miles distant. The Carrancista garrison was encountered in a more or less intoxicated condition, and from them an account of the Villistas and of the day's battle was obtained. It appears that they fought desperately all day, with an hour for lunch and had both retired in good order at nightfall. The casualties were zero for both sides. Civilian guides were obtained as the Carrancistas refused to provide them, and at about 3:00 AM the column set out with the guides and the Apache scouts in the vanguard. At about daybreak, the Ojo Azules ranch was seen and the advance guard noticed a great deal of activity. Major Howze had previously given orders to attack upon sighting the Villistas, and the advance guard galloped to within a 1,000 yards of the ranch, deployed and advanced as skirmishers. The original plan was for the troops following the advance guard to move to the right and to the left, deploy from the column, and cut off any retreat forced by the initial contact. A barbed wire range fence on the right side of the road made this plan impossible to execute, however, and each troop commander entered the fight as best as he could bring his troopers to bear.

In his report to Pershing, Major Howze wrote that the Americans had surprised the Villistas, with Julio Acosta, Cruz Domingues, and Antonio Angel among them. In a running fight of two hours, the bandits were driven into the hills toward Cusi. Forty-two were killed and several were taken prisoner, along with fifty to seventy-five horses and mules. A Carrancista lieutenant and four soldiers were rescued just before they were to have been shot. The bandits who had retreated were estimated at 140, and the American troopers did not stop their pursuit until their horses were completely exhausted. The rout was so complete that those Villistas who escaped did so as individuals. The surprise and confusion among the bandits was so complete that although several 11th Cavalry troopers took bullets through their clothing not a single man was wounded.

The action was broken off at about 9:00 AM, and all the troopers returned to the ranch to search for arms and concealed Villistas. A few older rifles and outdated revolvers were found and destroyed, but it was impossible to differentiate between the farmers, villagers, and possible Villistas and therefore all were released. The Carrancistas who had been held for execution were liberated, and were so overjoyed at their deliverance that their officer volunteered personally to execute the Villista prisoners if someone would give him a pistol. His offer was politely declined. First Sergeant Chicken of the Apache Scouts summed it all up rather nicely: "Huli! Dam fine fight!" The official report recorded sixty-one Villista dead and possibly fifty wounded.

The newly organized districts had been staffed with their cavalry regiments and supporting infantry and artillery and the work of searching for the scattered Villista bands had begun, when on May 9 instructions were received from the Department Commander, which directed the withdrawal of the command to Colonia Dublan. Relations between Washington and the de facto government of Carranza had become so strained that the possibility of war seemed more than just likelihood, and the instructions that had been received for withdrawal and concentration were considered imperative. Rather than withdraw to Dublan it was decided that Namiquipa was to be the southern camp, and the troops that withdrew from the advance stations were deployed around Namiquipa with support groups at San Geronimo and Providencia. Troops were engaged in the pursuit of small bands of Villistas and in keeping track of Carrancista troop movements in the area when they unexpectedly flushed a real prize.

Colonel Cardenas, who was on Villa's staff, was reported active at Rubio and its vicinity, and Expedition troops had made several unsuccessful attempts to capture him. On May 14 Pershing had dispatched a member of his staff, Lieutenant George S. Patton, with fifteen men, five of whom were civilians, in three automobiles to purchase corn. Their convoy approached San Miguelito ranch near Rubio, where the only visible activity was four cowboys skinning a steer. As Patton and one of the civilians approached the house, however, three horsemen bolted through the arched entranceway and precipitated a gunfight. Patton returned fire and hit one rider in the arm, hit another's horse that came crashing down on its rider, and the third was killed as he attempted to flee. The wounded rider was killed by rifle fire as he attempted to flee the ranch compound. The melee was brief but lethal, and Patton had the three dead Villistas strapped over the hoods of the automobiles to be taken to camp for positive identification. They turned out to be Colonel Julián Cárdenas (an important figure in Villa's staff), Captain López, and Private Garza. The fight received a great deal of press attention in the United States where readers were eager to hear something positive about the Expedition's fortunes; correspondents provided Patton with a great deal of often lurid publicity and did much to begin the notoriety that followed Patton throughout his military career.

Lieutenant George S. Patton [National Archives].

On May 22, First Chief Carranza issued a brusque demand that Pershing's forces withdraw immediately from Mexico, and charged that the continued presence of the Expedition in Mexico had nothing to do with bandits and everything to do with President Wilson's reelection campaign. Wilson replied with an exceptionally long and blistering reply in which, among other things, he commented on the discourteous and intemperate tone taken by the First Chief. He went on to say that he was compelled by candor to add that the hostility of the military commanders of the de facto government toward the American troops engaged in the pursuit of Villa's bands was a menace to both the safety of the troops and to the peace of the borderlands. Wilson went on to inform Carranza that any use of de facto troops against Expeditionary forces would result in a total embargo on arms, ammunition, and the machinery for their manufacture. The diplomatic climate between the two governments, which had never been very warm, had chilled to brittleness, and Pershing was directed to rein in any offensive campaigns he might have in mind.

It was, oddly enough, under these tense diplomatic circumstances plus the fact that Pershing had for all practical purposes been immobilized, that the Expedition succeeded in bringing to justice one of the major Villistas involved in the Columbus raid, a raider second only to Villa himself, Colonel Candelario Cervantes. Along with perhaps twenty-five men, Cervantes had returned to the vicinity of Namiquipa and daringly preyed upon the local population. Small units of American cavalry were kept in the field near Namiquipa with the hope of flushing the brigands and finishing them off. On May 25 a small detachment made up of eight men of the 17th Infantry's Machine Gun Platoon, two men of the Corps of Engineers, and a Quartermaster under command of Lance Corporal Davis Marksbury were looking for cattle and sketching roads and trails when they were attacked by a small band of perhaps nine Villistas. By a strange quirk of fate, and unknown to the Americans, the man who had eluded all cavalry patrols and terrorized the area for weeks was about to be brought down by infantry: the Villistas who charged the mapmakers were led by Colonel Cervantes. In the exchange of gunfire, Lance Corporal Marksbury was killed and three other Americans wounded; Private George D. Hulett, 17th Infantry, shot from their saddles and killed two men galloping toward him who later proved to be Cervantes and José Bencome. General Pershing would report that the killing of Candelario Cervantes was particularly fortunate, as, next to Villa himself, he was the most able and the most desperate of Villa's band.

On May 31, General Pershing went from Namiquipa to Juarez for a meeting with General Gabriel Gavira, who commanded all Carrancista troops in that area. A formal meeting was held on June 1 to discuss possible cooperation between the military forces of the two nations, and an agreement was reached that limited the number of de facto troops along the railroad lines near American forces and that no de facto troops would occupy towns or villages along the American lines of communication. The agreement was tentative, contingent upon approval by both the American and Carranza administrations, and Pershing reported that nothing really came of it. At this time relations between the governments of the two nations had reached an all-time low, and Expedition intelligence reported de facto troops assembled along railroads both east and west, threatening American lines of communication. The de facto commandant at Ahumada had ordered his field commanders to be prepared for action against the Americans, 10,000 de facto troops were reported in that vicinity, and a large number of Carrancistas were reported in movement from Chihuahua City. It was widely accepted by the Mexican population that these troop movements were not for the purpose of attacking bandits, but rather to be used to drive the Americans from Mexico. It appeared to Pershing and his staff that preparations were indeed being made for a campaign against the Expedition.

Six

THE FIGHT AT CARRIZAL

On June 16 the de facto Commander at Chihuahua City, General J. B. Trevino, sent Pershing a telegram, which stated that orders had been given him to prevent the movement of American troops to the south, east, or west from the places they now occupied. Should American forces move in any direction but north, they would be attacked by forces of the Carranza government. Pershing replied that he had received no such orders from his government, and that he intended to pursue the bandits in whichever direction they led him, and that if the Mexican forces attacked his columns the responsibility and consequences would rest with the Mexican government. Informed verbally the same by the local de facto Commander that Carranza had issued orders for the Americans to begin movement north, Pershing replied that he did not take orders except from his own government. Against this background of flashpoint tensions, Pershing continued to send reconnoitering columns out to scout for Carrancista troop movements and concentrations. Reports of Carrancista troops massing near Villa Ahumada on the Mexican National Railroad meant that gathering information was critical, and the failure of the aircraft accompanying the Expedition forced Pershing to resort to perhaps the oldest source of intelligence gathering in the field, the cavalry.

The political situation had reached a point where President Wilson was apprehensive lest another clash occur, which could possibly precipitate a war. The use of cavalry for gathering intelligence, while as old as warfare itself,

Captain Charles T. Boyd [National Archives].

presented certain risks. Chief among them was the possibility of an armed clash, something that, given the tensions of the time, Wilson was anxious to avoid. Despite the risks, or perhaps because of them, two detachments were sent in the direction of Ahumada to scout the country and obtain whatever information about de facto troops could be found. The detachments found themselves, unfortunately, confronted by Carrancistas at the small town of Carrizal, a short distance from Villa Ahumada.

The scouts chosen for the reconnaissance were Troop C, 10th Cavalry, commanded by Captain Charles T. Boyd, recently arrived in Mexico. He was to be assisted by Lieutenant Henry R. Adair. An additional scout was ordered for Troop K, 10th Cavalry, commanded by Captain Lewis S. Morey, unassisted by another officer. The orders given to Capt. Boyd were verbal; Capt. Morey's orders were transmitted by telegraph. The written orders from General Pershing were in effect that the troops were to reconnoiter in the direction of Villa Ahumada and to obtain as much information as possible. Their mission was a reconnaissance only, and they were to avoid a fight if possible. If attacked they were to use their judgment as to a course of action, and they were above all else to have a regard for the safety of their command. Both officers departed on June 18: Boyd, Troop C, with sixty-three men from Dublan, about one hundred miles west by southwest of Villa Ahumada; and Morey, Troop K, with forty-six men and a Mexican boy from Ojo Federico, about one hundred miles northwest of Villa Ahumada.

Captain Boyd was accompanied by a Mexican boy named José and a Mormon scout from Colonia Dublan, one of several hired by General Pershing for use by the Expedition. Lemuel H. Spilsbury was fluent in Spanish and knew the land fairly well. When he asked Boyd what the purpose of the reconnaissance was, Boyd replied that they were going out there with a chip on their shoulder. If the Mexicans knocked it off, Boyd continued, Pershing was going to move and Funston was going to move as well. When Lieutenant Adair suggested that Mexican soldiers would not fight a tenacious charge of disciplined troops, the Mormon scout replied that Adair was wrong. He told Adair that the Mexicans were as brave as any Americans he had ever known, and they were also not afraid to die. Only Captain Morey, it seems, was wary of a frontal assault on several hundred entrenched soldiers equipped with at least one machine gun.

The mental outlook of Captain Boyd was assessed in the report of the investigation of the incident at Carrizal. The report concluded that Boyd felt that audacity was necessary; that a bold front would intimidate the Mexican defenders; and that any resistance would be easily brushed aside. Boyd also believed that if his force were attacked by the Mexican detachment a crisis would follow that would immediately bring into action all the forces of the United States. This belief was probably behind the remark that Boyd made to Captain Morey the evening before the encounter, something about "making history." Launched on a tide of overconfidence, which stemmed from a refusal to look reality in the eye, Boyd led his troops forth on the morning of June 21. He had a command of three officers and eighty-one men, including his two civilian guides.

At 4:00 AM on June 21, Boyd led his small force from the ranch toward Carrizal, a distance of about nine miles. He halted the column at an irrigation ditch just one mile from the town, giving time for the horses to be watered and the men the opportunity to check their rifles and pistols. It was 6:30 AM. A herd of horses grazed on the open plain between Boyd's force and the town, and through their binoculars the Americans saw Mexican troops (both mounted and on foot) being deployed among the cottonwood trees, which lined an irrigation ditch southwest of the town. Mexican cavalry also moved south along the ditch to present a force on the American's right flank. The watering of horses and loading of weapons completed, Captain Boyd deployed his troops athwart the road leading across the plain to Carrizal. Troop K (Morey in command) was on the right side and Troop C (Boyd in command assisted by Adair) was on the left side. Both were in platoon columns and their scouts were present, the Mexican boy José with Troop C and Spilsbury with Troop K.

Boyd sent José into town with a note requesting from the local mayor permission for his column to pass through town. While waiting for a reply, the Americans noticed further deployment of Mexican soldiers into defensive positions on both sides of the road. The first reply to the request was in the form of Major Genevo Rivas, who rode out to meet Lem Spilsbury. The scout thought Rivas was the commanding officer, and in keeping with Boyd's instructions, announced that the American troops were looking for a deserter and a group of Villistas. Rivas' attitude was brusque: he claimed that a deserter had been sent to El Paso and that there were no bandits in the area. He then told Spilsbury to take him to see Captain Boyd. Rivas and two soldiers rode with Spilsbury to where Boyd waited and informed Boyd through the scout that the Mexican troops were under orders to stop any American movement that was not north. Boyd repeated his request and Rivas replied that he was not in command, and that General Gómez was in bed. He dispatched a soldier to awaken the General and then rode back to town.

From their position along the road, about halfway between their first halt and the town, the Americans waited. The open flat plain on which they found themselves held no shelter; it was not terrain conducive to an assault by a small force against a well-entrenched, larger force with greater firepower. How this could have escaped an officer with Boyd's experience is difficult if not impossible to explain. A Mexican soldier approached with a message inviting the Americans into the village for a conference. With the Mexican troops deployed the way they were, Boyd feared that a trap had been set and the invitation was declined.

When about thirty minutes had passed General Felix U. Gómez rode toward them, and Boyd and his scout dismounted to meet him. He courteously explained to Boyd that he was under orders to stop any American troops from going *through* the town; that he would telegraph General Treviño in Chihuahua to see if permission could be obtained for the Americans to pass; and that if permission were not granted he was duty-bound to try to stop the Americans. Angered and sensing a delaying tactic perhaps to get reinforcements from nearby Villa Ahumada, Boyd asked Spilsbury for advice. The scout suggested returning with the command to General Pershing and giving the General the information he wanted. Boyd replied that he was not going to turn tail and run, to which Spilsbury replied that there was no need to run. They could get on their horses and try to go around the town. If the Mexicans opened fire on them, Spilsbury suggested, they would know what the situation was and could act accordingly. Boyd replied that he was going through the town, and while he looked at General Gomez he told Spilsbury to inform the General that he was going through the town. Spilsbury had been watching Gomez as Boyd spoke and concluded that the General understood enough English to know what had been said. It was then that Gomez replied that Boyd might get through the town, but that it would be over his dead body

The conferees returned to their horses. Boyd's group returned to the waiting troopers, and he addressed his men saying that the situation looked fine and that he was going to obey his orders to travel east to Villa Ahumada and was going to take the men through this town and not around it. His remarks were greeted with cheers, and as the columns moved forward they deployed in a line of foragers. The led horses were sent several hundred yards to the rear, and Captain Boyd rode to his right to Troop K with his final directions: troop K was to be moved more to the right (this because of the Mexican troops on the right front and to the south of the town) and that the men were to go in dismounted. Lieutenant Adair's platoon was to send a few men through the southeastern part of the town, and Troop K was to look out for the right flank. As an old cavalry expression proclaimed, "The ball was about to begin."

Accounts of battle by eyewitnesses vary, as each participant saw a relatively small portion of the greater picture while at the same time carrying out his mission as best as time and circumstances permitted. When the firing began, Captain Boyd and Lieutenant Adair led their 43 men across the open plain, 200 yards into the trees, dislodged the machine gun and forced the Mexicans back. He was killed soon after the first shots were fired. Lieutenant Adair was wounded early in the fight and mortally wounded as he rose from the irrigation ditch to fire with his pistol on advancing Mexicans, near the close of the fight. Troop K entered the action with one officer and thirty-six enlisted men, a total force of eighty-two.

On Troop K's left, Troop C had driven through the Mexican line near the cottonwoods, had overrun the machine gun, and had forced the Mexicans back toward the irrigation ditch. Four men of Adair's platoon and three men of Boyd's platoon actually reached and passed beyond the woods. Adair's death at the irrigation ditch left Troop C leaderless at the time that Troop K was being flanked on its right. Troop C's left flank was turned and its led horses were driven off as no guard had been posted with them. Corporal H. C. Houston of Troop K later wrote that they had only fifty men on the firing line, not enough to halt the Mexicans who turned the Americans' right flank. Houston judged that about and hour and a half had passed since the beginning of the fight and the withdrawal of the Troop. Captain Morey, wounded in the right shoulder, ordered the men closest to him to retreat. The men, some sixty or so, moved out singly and in groups of two or three, headed for any cover to be found. First Sergeant William Winrow of Troop C, fatally wounded and in shock, was last seen riding a Mexican pony off the field. He was never seen again.

Mexican cavalry charged the field shouting *"Rendirse, rendirse!"* (Surrender, surrender!) Those troopers who had been unable to make good their escape raised their hands and were taken prisoner. Twenty-four Americans were taken prisoners along with the guide, Lem Spilsbury. In addition to Captain Boyd and Lieutenant Adair the following men were killed: First Sergeant William Winrow, Sergeant Will Hines, Horse Shoer Lee Talbot, and Private Thomas Moses of Troop C; Private James E. Day, Private Charlie Matthews, and Private DeWitt Rucker of Troop K. Those not killed or captured made their way back to the American lines or were rescued by search parties. General Pershing, upon hearing of the fight, sent out Major Robert L. Howze, 11th Cavalry, who proceeded to the San Luis Ranch to search for survivors. It was there that Captain Morey, four troopers, foreman McCabe of the Santo Domingo Ranch, and a Chinese cook made their way to safety. Their statements provided the first information about Carrizal.

Reports of casualties differ only slightly: Colonel Frank Tompkins reported twelve killed, eleven wounded, twenty-three captured, total forty-six; the Garlington Report, the result of the Army's official inquiry, recorded nine killed, twelve wounded, four missing and twenty-four captured, total forty-nine; the War Department reported nine killed, ten wounded, twenty-four captured, total forty-three. Both troops suffered between 41 and 42 percent casualties. Mexican losses were by their own accounts twelve officers, including General Gomez, killed; thirty-three enlisted men killed and fifty-three wounded. Estimates of the size of the Mexican force suggest perhaps between 300 and 400.

The prisoners were taken into Carrizal and placed under guard. Since General Gomez had been killed in the fight, Major Rivas was in command. According to scout Spilsbury, Major Rivas ordered the prisoners lined up for execution and was dissuaded only when Spilsbury told him that if he shot the American prisoners who had surrendered to him, the American soldiers would never take another Mexican alive. Rivas had second thoughts and ordered the prisoners marched across the desert to Villa Ahumada where they were pelted with rocks by the townspeople. A guard of Mexican soldiers kept the crowd away, and under orders from General Treviño the prisoners were sent by rail to Chihuahua City. Once there the Americans were marched to the penitentiary, where they were held for a week until State Department demands secured their release. They were taken by rail to Ciudad Juarez and released to authorities in El Paso.

Evaluations of the Carrizal Affair include formal investigations made by the Army, memoirs of participants, articles by contemporary journalists, books and monographs by historians of the Mexican Revolution, and essays and articles by students of the Pershing Expedition. With perhaps one major exception, the evaluations have been highly critical of Captain Boyd's role in the affair. The foremost exception is Colonel Frank Tompkins whose criticism, one is inclined to say condemnation, is directed at Troop K. Tompkins took his cue from General Pershing's report, Captain Morey's statement to Major Howze, and foreman McCabe's statement to 1st Lieutenant S. M. Williams.

Pershing's report stated that Captain Boyd's men had pushed forward with a dash and carried the Mexican position, Lieutenant Adair leading. In Tompkins' view, Troop K, ordered to push forward and to guide on Troop C, did not obey its orders but instead took shelter in a slight depression and finally quit cold. It was always Tompkins' firm belief that if Troop K had shown the same mettle as Troop C, the Mexicans would have been routed. Morey's statement was that when Troop K began to take fire from one of the two Mexican machine guns, the men laid down in a road of very slight depression, and thus made it impossible to protect Troop C's flank. Troop C had advanced toward the ditch near the town and was then about 250 or 300 yards away. Tompkins concluded that Troop K quit the fight to save itself, and he remained convinced that the American defeat was best explained by this single moment.

The statement made by the foreman of the Santo Domingo Ranch, W. P. McCabe, added to Colonel Tompkins' belief that neglect of duty led to the fiasco. McCabe reported that at about eight or nine o'clock on the morning of June 21, five men rode into the ranch at a gallop and told him that the Mexicans had fired on the troops and massacred the bunch. There were two loose horses with these men and the troops' pack train came right behind them followed by two or three more troopers. According to McCabe, all these men had rifles and ammunition. Most of them were very much excited, said they wanted a guide, and that they were going for help. McCabe tried to stop them, but they insisted on going. He gave them a guide and reported that he never saw any of them again. He later described the intermittent chaos at the ranch as more troopers came in, all in various stages of apprehension that bordered on panic. Stragglers filtered in through most of the day, and at one time a group of fifteen or twenty troopers with horses returned from their flight. Most were armed and McCabe thought they were going to make a stand should the Mexicans appear. There were so many horses in the ranch yard that McCabe concluded that most of the horses of both troops were in the yard at this time.

Two men decided to head toward Carrizal and reconnoiter. Shortly thereafter the two men came back at a gallop and rode for the picket line. When McCabe asked what was happening, one of the returning troopers told him that they were going to get out, and that 1,500 Mexicans were coming. All the men present rode off at a trot, and McCabe was left with three or four Mexican laborers and two Chinese. He then left the ranch and hid in a place where he could watch the house.

He did not see a single Mexican soldier or any sign of any that day or night. He remained in hiding until four or five o'clock in the afternoon, and since he saw no sign of any one around the house he returned, had supper, and spent the night in the field about a quarter of a mile from the house. Early the next morning (June 22), he went back to the house, ate breakfast, and went down to the barn. There he found four American soldiers inside a locked enclosure. They said they came in afoot during the night. Two of these men were slightly wounded. He gave them breakfast, left them at the ranch, and went to the bushes to hide. At sundown he went back to the ranch, found the place deserted, and partially ransacked. Everything left there by the American soldiers had been hauled away. The following morning McCabe saw fifteen or twenty mounted Mexicans approaching the ranch, and he left accompanied by one of the Chinese. When the Mexicans entered the ranch he departed for Galeana, and while on the trail he came across four troopers and Captain Morey, who was wounded and in a very weak condition.

The Garlington Report offered the official Army evaluation, approved by the Secretary of War, and presented to President Wilson on October 9, 1916. The report discussed at some length the handling of the led horses and the subsequent conduct of the men in charge of them. When the troops dismounted to engage the Mexicans (the report observed) the led horses were assembled at a point only a short distance in the rear of the firing line, no guard was detailed for the led horses, and no competent noncommissioned officer was with them at any time. It was probable (the report continued) that a part of the initial Mexican rifle fire was directed at the led horses, and when a body of mounted Mexicans passed around the left of C Troop and either attacked or threatened to attack the led horses, the horse-holders, who testified that the horses stampeded at the first fire, themselves panicked. There was no reasonable room for doubting that this was the case. The same was said of the pack train—there were two Quartermaster Corps men in charge—which was with the led horses. Despite the horse-holders' testimony that they were pursued by a large body of Mexican Cavalry, it was observed by the board that practically all the horse-holders, including the Quartermaster Corps men, assembled safely at the

Santo Domingo Ranch from which they very soon departed for their respective camps.

The conduct of the horse-holders and the Quartermaster Corps men was branded as "reprehensible," but not sufficiently so to justify a trial. It was concluded that the men were placed in an untenable position without proper leadership, and that their difficulties were undoubtedly great. Moreover these men were practically the only witnesses to their own conduct and the difficulties were not minimized in their testimony. The mention of a trial, however, would seem to indicate that there was some belief in the Army that these men were possibly guilty of desertion or cowardice, or both.

An outline of the principal features of the affair concluded the report. The Mexicans had fired upon the Americans, but the conflict both should and could have been avoided. Captain Boyd committed a grave error in judgment, there was no justification whatsoever in the tactical conduct of the fight, no competent person was in charge of the led horses, there was neither cohesion nor coordination on the firing line, and with the loss of commissioned leadership the command disintegrated. Brigadier-General Garlington finished his report with the recommendation that no further action be taken, and Newton D. Baker, Secretary of War, agreed. On the other hand, according to Captain Daniel González, who had brought his 300 men to Carrizal from Hacienda El Carmen some fifty-four miles to the south, it was the Americans who attacked. General Gómez had sent troops to flank the attacking Americans and then opened fire with a machine gun.

The news of the debacle at Carrizal was greeted in the United States with dismay, confusion, and anger; in Mexico it was greeted with demonstrations of patriotic fervor in all major cities. General Gómez became a national hero. In Washington an angry President Wilson, who assumed that the Carrancistas were the aggressors, demanded that First Chief Carranza release the American prisoners immediately, and General Funston was ordered to seize all Rio Grande bridges in preparation for a full-scale invasion of Mexico. The intensity of Wilson's note and the increase of American military activity along the border tempered Carranza's belligerence, and the freed prisoners arrived in Juárez on June 29. American bellicosity was in turn dampened by the publication of Captain Morey's report that it was Boyd and not the Mexicans who started the fight. While tensions remained high for the remainder of June, Carranza's July 4 offer of negotiations in order to ease and eliminate tensions between the two countries was accepted by President Wilson.

10th Cavalry troopers captured at Carrizal [National Archives].

Carrizal ended the fighting phase of the Expedition's deployment in Mexico. Pershing took measures to assume an aggressive posture immediately following Carrizal: troops south of El Valle were ordered north immediately; truck trains were assembled for whatever need might arise; and the command as a whole was placed on high alert to be ready for immediate action. There would, however, be no use for high alerts and concentrations of forces because, in reality, the Expedition's mission was over. Ordered to disperse the band or bands that had attacked Columbus on March 9, 1916, the Expedition successfully completed its mission by June 9, when at Santa Clara Canyon twenty-one men of the 13th Cavalry killed two Villistas and scattered twenty-odd more in a skirmish that would prove to be the Expedition's last clash with Villista bandits.

In ten engagements with Villistas beginning with Guerrero, March 29, and ending at Santa Clara Canyon, June 9–10, Expedition forces killed 169 Villistas and wounded 65, while losing 6 (killed) and 19 were wounded. If the losses Villa suffered in his attack on Columbus are added to these figures, the total is much higher. In the two engagements with Carrancista forces, Parral and Carrizal, American losses were eleven killed, nineteen wounded, and three missing. The *total* casualties for the Expedition were 15 killed, 31 wounded, and 3 missing; the total casualties for enemy forces were 251 killed and 166 wounded.

The fight at Carrizal had, however, served to confirm the more pessimistic views of General Hugh L. Scott, Chief of Staff of the Army, and General Frederick Funston, in command of the Southern District. Both men realized that the entire Regular Army, with the exception of a regiment of Cavalry and the Coast Artillery, was either in Mexico with Pershing's Expedition or scattered along the border. The Expedition's position was a precarious one: it was deep in Chihuahua with a long line of supply and communication supported by relatively slow motor/truck transport and a secondary rail line. Because of their concern, Scott and Funston held a series of meetings in late April and early May with General Alvaro Obregón. In these meetings they assured the General that once the Mexicans could bring order to the borderlands and stop the raids on American territory, the withdrawal of the Expedition would proceed with all due haste. The tentative agreement that was reached with Obregón was forwarded to Carranza, and the First Chief refused to give it his support.

Both Scott and Funston concluded that Carranza's refusal was evidence that the hostility of Carrancista forces toward the Expedition was not just the attitude of local commanders in the field, but that it was the position of the Mexican government itself. If a situation arose in Mexico where Pershing's force needed strengthening, such a deployment of scarce resources would in effect leave the lower Rio Grande and Texas open to invasion. General Funston believed that he had convincing evidence of a plan to invade Texas and capture San Antonio, and he therefore asked that the Organized Militia, later the National Guard, be called out in those states that had complete divisions. On May 9, 1916, Secretary of War Newton D. Baker sent telegraphs to the Governors of Texas, New Mexico, and Arizona in which he called for the mobilization of the States' Organized Militia. On June 18, following a Cabinet meeting, a similar telegram was sent by Secretary Baker to all States' Governors. The reason given for the mobilization was the necessity for the proper protection of the frontier in view of the possibility of invasion from Mexico. The reports of Generals Scott and Funston had convinced President Wilson that the situation was potentially volatile.

The first unit to reach the border from the second call was the 1st Illinois Infantry, which arrived in San Antonio, Texas, on June 30. Less than a week later, there were 27,160 troops from 14 states on the border; these troops included men from California to Maine. By July 31, there were 110,957 officers and enlisted men on the border and another 40,139 in state mobilization camps.

Forty days after the fight at Carrizal there were 151,096 National Guardsmen in Federal service. By the end of August, there were 111,954 men stationed along the border, for the most part in four large camps at Brownsville, San Antonio, and El Paso (Texas) and Douglas (Arizona). The presence of so many soldiers, however poorly trained and equipped (43 percent were recruits), had a moderating influence on the potentially explosive situation, which followed the fight at Carrizal. The bellicosity on both sides of the border diminished, and the fight, which could have meant war between the United States and Mexico, gradually faded from the public's attention as the possibility of war with Germany became a grim reality.

Seven

ENTERING THE DOLDRUMS: IDLENESS, FRUSTRATION, AND WITHDRAWAL

In March, as the Expedition was moving south into Mexico, General Pershing's reports regarding the local populations he encountered were decidedly negative. He wrote of the distrust and hostility with which the Expedition was greeted and he despaired of establishing any kind of rapport with the Mexican farmers and townsfolk. In May, however, his reports were different. The common people, he wrote, have few opinions and rarely express themselves on any subject, but they now met the Americans with every indication of approval. On occasion, one was brave enough to express the hope that the Americans were there to stay.

Pershing's reports portrayed a population caught between the proverbial rock and a hard place, living in a state of anarchy where there was little if any difference between the Villista bandit and the Carrancista soldier. The rural population lived each day exploited by brigands who were different only in the uniform (or lack of one) that they wore. Shamefully treated by both sides, the country people lived in quiet desperation. The country was in wretchedness, its people were in rags and poverty, and they had few cattle and no horses or mules with which to cultivate the land. There was no incentive to attempt cultivation, as the only result was the theft of the results on their labor. After years of revolution, chaos, and mayhem, the farmer had learned that it was perhaps the wisest course simply to accept what could not be changed. He and his family lived in hopeless despair.

When American troops first entered a pueblo, Pershing reported that they were regarded with the same apprehension as if they had been bandits. But once the people understood that the goods the Americans needed would be paid for in coin, and at an honest price, the situation changed. Chickens, eggs, firewood, corn, and beans that had been hidden emerged to be sold. Unfortunately, in some areas the farmers had been so severely exploited that there was simply nothing left to sell. They gradually warmed to the Americans, however, and this was particularly true when they learned that when the Americans arrived the Villistas departed and did not return. The total cooperation of the local population was tempered, Pershing believed, by their realization that the Americans' stay in the area was temporary and that obvious and enthusiastic cooperation with them would mean vicious reprisal after they were gone.

The major obstacles to the success of the Expedition, Pershing believed, were threefold: (1) the territory in which the Army was operating was completely unknown; (2) it was almost impossible to secure the services of reliable native guides who, even if they were willing to assist the Americans, were afraid of Villista reprisal; and (3) the lack of cooperation from Carrancista forces. The Villistas, on the other hand, had every advantage: they knew the country in every detail; they were informed of Expedition movements by a network of sympathizers; they lived off the country, simply stealing what they needed; and when their horses gave out from hard riding they took new stock wherever they found it. Pershing was particularly disenchanted with the Carrancistas, whom he believed had failed miserably in any effort to apprehend the bandits. Their efforts to overtake Villa, he claimed, were half-hearted and unorganized. Their objections and protests succeeded only in delaying the Expedition's advance when speed was imperative. He retained his optimism, however, and was certain that if left to its own resources and given the necessary men, horses, and supplies, the Expedition would succeed.

The essence of his plan, which he had outlined at some length, was simple: a vigorous pursuit of any and all organized bands of Villistas until they were destroyed or rendered ineffective through physical or psychological exhaustion. It would therefore be necessary for the Army to occupy the key pueblos in Villista territory, to establish a network of friendly and dependable natives to assure that information gathered was reliable, to begin a program of reconnaissance and study of the countryside in which Expedition forces would be operating, to establish and maintain an adequate supply line through the mountainous countryside, and, finally, to maintain a sufficient number of men and horses to guarantee that the requirements of the plan were met. The

Mexican Village Militia [National Archives].

major obstacle to success, as Pershing saw it, was the possibility that the larger Villista bands might break apart into smaller groups and ultimately blend in with the local populations, thereby creating a more difficult situation.

The incident at Parral only served to convince Pershing that the strength of his command needed to be augmented. All regiments should be increased in size to their legal limits, and one more regiment of infantry and one more regiment of cavalry should be added to the Expedition. He recommended the seizure both of Chihuahua City and of the railroads in and out of the city in order to guarantee the dependability of his lines of communication with Columbus. While Pershing's recommendations made sense to many in the military, President Wilson, who was apprehensive over relations with Germany and the upcoming national election, was not interested is an escalation of animosities in Mexico. He rejected Army Chief of Staff Hugh L. Scott's recommendation to call up the National Guard for border patrol duty, despite Scott's reasonable argument that Guardsmen on duty in border communities would free up regular troops if needed in Mexico. As Pershing made plans to continue his campaign whenever orders came, President Wilson decided it was time for diplomacy.

Wilson's gambit in the new scheme of things was that the mission of the Expedition had changed, and Secretary of War Newton D. Baker explained to General Scott the thinking that was behind the new policy. The Expedition was no longer to focus its efforts on the Columbus raiders or Villa, but rather to draw in the outlying military parties and maintain an establishment in Mexico as a means of compelling the de facto Government to take up and pursue to an end the chase of Villa and the dispersing of whatever bands remain organized. Baker explained that the new policy still advocated punishment for Villa and the Columbus raiders, but Pershing was no longer expected to deliver the punishment. According to Baker, the Expedition now existed for the sole purpose of removing a menace to the common security and the friendly relations of the two Republics. So long as Villa remained at large and was able to mislead numbers of his fellow citizens into attacks like that at Columbus, the danger existed of American public opinion being irritated to the point of requiring general intervention. Both Baker and Wilson hoped that Pershing's continued presence in Mexico would force Carranza to take over the task of destroying the Villistas, and in doing so he would through his own actions guarantee the removal of the Expedition from Mexico. The Expedition had become a pawn in a new round of discussions between representatives of First Chief Carranza and President Wilson.

On this occasion, however, the talking was to be done by the military, and a conference between Generals Scott and Obregón was endorsed by both Carranza and Wilson. The conference may have been doomed from the beginning, unfortunately, as Carranza was suspicious of Obregón's ambitions and was decidedly cool to the prospect of being overshadowed by a subordinate. He had no recourse, however, as there was no viable alternative and Obregón was known to Scott and both men respected each other. On April 30 they met at the Hotel Aguana in Juarez with General Frederick Funston, Commander of the Southern Department, in attendance. From the beginning Obregón reflected Carranza's inflexible position: the Punitive Expedition must leave Mexico immediately and unconditionally. Scott was patient and diplomatic, but Funston was not: after an explosion of anger and table pounding he stormed out of the meeting. Amid rumors of Carrancista troop movements and talk of driving the Expedition out of Mexico, Scott expressed the need for further consultation with Washington and suspended the conference. He later, on May 3, met secretly with Obregón in El Paso at the Paso del Norte Hotel, and for over twelve hours the men negotiated. They finally worked out an agreement acceptable to the United States only to see it come to naught because of Carranza's objections.

On May 5, President Wilson's confidence in negotiation was shattered when Mexican raiders crossed the Rio Grande and attacked the small Texas towns of Glenn Springs and Boquillas. The 14th Cavalry maintained an outpost of eight men and a sergeant, and when the attack began the soldiers barricaded themselves in a small adobe hut, which the attackers then set afire. The soldiers, three of whom were killed, continued fighting from the surrounding brush while some of the raiders looted the general store, the storekeeper's house, and murdered his four-year-old son. They then rode to nearby Boquillas, looted the store there, kidnapped the owner, a store employee, and seven International Mining Company management personnel. These towns were so remote that it was two days before news of the attack reached General Funston in El Paso. He immediately sent two troops of the 8th Cavalry by rail to Marathon, Texas, with orders to pursue and apprehend or punish the raiders even if it meant crossing into Mexico.

The detachment reached Marathon on Sunday, May 7, and began the two-day ride to the Rio Grande where there were, of course, no bandits in sight. The commanding officer, Major George T. Langhorne, ordered his men to cross the river into Mexico, thus launching what has been called "The Punitive Expedition from Boquillas." The mining personnel, who had been taken by the raiders, including the manager, superintendent, and assayer, had overpowered their captors and returned to Boquillas with three captive bandits. Several volunteered to accompany the troopers into Mexico as guides. On the evening of May 11 what must have been one of the strangest detachments in American military history crossed into Mexico at San Vincente Ford: one hundred mounted cavalrymen, twenty led horses, one truck, one Ford automobile with two correspondents, a second Ford with a motion picture crew of two, and the commanding officer's chauffer-driven Cadillac. The following morning, May 12, at 8:00 AM this colorful, one is inclined to say bizarre, column set out in pursuit of the Boquillas raiders.

For the next several days the American column chased the bandits to ranches at Del Piño, Rosita, San Francisco, Cerro Blanco, Castillon, and Santa Anita. At Del Piño they liberated the Boquillas storekeeper Mr. Deemer and his employee, Payne. At Rosita they engaged fleeing bandits, chased them in the Cadillac and the two Fords, and fired at them as the cars bounced and careened across the desert landscape. Apparently, the only casualty here was one Ford, taken out of action with a broken axle. The bandits were usually warned of the Americans' approach and scattered, but at the Castillon Ranch and the Santa Anita well the Americans had better hunting. They managed to surprise a group of bandits watering their horses and in a running fight killed and wounded several, took two prisoners, rounded up seventeen horses and mules, a supply wagon, nine rifles, two swords, and numerous saddles, bridles, packs, and equipment. Other detachments had been searching the countryside without much success, and by May 19 it was decided to return to the border. Without any further incidents, the entire command gathered at Los Alamos on May 20 and the following morning crossed the Rio Grande River, delayed only by the desire of the motion picture crew to take some final pictures. On May 23 the command was ordered to return to Fort Bliss, on May 27 it was entrained at Marathon, Texas, and the next day it was home. They had been gone three weeks, had seen some rough, dangerous duty, and had lost neither a man nor a horse during the deployment.

In a note sent on May 22 Carranza protested this armed incursion into Mexico, which was affected again without the consent of the Mexican Government and gravely endangered the harmony and good relations between the two governments. He also claimed that the raid was the result of Mexican émigrés in the United States. While émigrés in the United States were in fact plotting against Carranza, the raid on Glen Springs and Boquillas came from Mexico, as did earlier raids that had caused so much consternation and conflict in the lower Rio Grande area. It is now clear that Carranza had orchestrated these raids in order to further his political goals: first, recognition by the United States and second, as a means of pressuring Wilson to withdraw the Punitive Expedition. When on October 19 Washington extended de facto recognition of his regime, the raids stopped. Carranza's strategy had succeeded in securing American assistance against Villa at Agua Prieta, Sonora (October 14, 1915), and de facto recognition of his regime, but the Glen Springs-Boquillas raid backfired.

In reaction to the Glen Springs-Boquillas attack and at the urging of Generals Scott and Funston, on May 10 President Wilson called out the Organized Militia. Prior to the National Defense Act of June 3, 1916, which established a National Guard that would be under Federal control in time of war and grave public emergency as decided by the President, the States had Organized Militia, at the call of their respective governors, and subject to mobilization into Federal service. While military literature of the late nineteenth and early twentieth centuries made frequent use of the phrase "Organized Militia," it is rarely, if ever, heard today. General Funston believed that the most encouraging feature of the new National Guard was the fact that company officers were to be paid $500 a year; a sum he believed would attract competent men.

The National Guard units of Arizona, New Mexico, and Texas were the first to be called. The mobilization points for the troops were Fort Sam Houston, Texas; Columbus, New Mexico; and Douglas, Arizona. On June 18 President Wilson sent telegrams to all state Governors except Arizona, New Mexico, and Texas, which informed them of his intention to call out the organized militia for the proper protection of the border between the United States and Mexico. This telegram set in motion a process that would in time see over 100,000 soldiers stretched along the border. For all the confusion and despite much criticism, by July 4 Guardsmen of fourteen states were at their stations along the border. The 1st Illinois Infantry was the first to arrive, and detrained at San Antonio, Texas, on June 30. By the end of July 112,000 Guardsmen had made it to their assigned assembly areas in San Antonio, Brownsville, El Paso, Texas, and (Douglas) Arizona.

It may have been the suddenness of Wilson's calling out the National Guard in response to the Glen Springs-Boquillas raids, it may have been the sobering list of Mexican casualties at Carrizal, or it may have been the National Democratic Platform for the impending presidential election in November. The Platform contained a special plank on Mexico, which reaffirmed the Monroe Doctrine and the independence of all national states in the Americas, but noted that the absence of a stable government in Mexico capable of suppressing bandit gangs had made it necessary for the United States to occupy a portion of that friendly state. Until such time as the causes of the occupation were eliminated, the Platform continued, it would be necessary for the occupation forces to remain. In July Carranza suggested, in a note delivered by his agent in Washington (Elisio Arrendondo) that a conference of mediation be set up to discuss the volatile situation. A note was received in Washington dated July 12, in which Carranza proposed a conference of six commissioners, three from each government, to meet at a mutually acceptable location to discuss the removal of American forces in Mexico and to establish a protocol in regard to reciprocal crossing of the frontier by forces of both nations.

President Wilson's reply was delivered to Arrendondo on July 27, and agreed to a meeting as suggested by Carranza to discuss evacuation of American forces in Mexico and to develop a protocol in regard to reciprocal border crossings, and also to determine the origin of the incursions to date from Mexico into the United States. Wilson was particularly concerned to fix the responsibility for the recent raids on American border communities. Carranza, on the other hand, had no interest in fixing responsibility for the raids as he already knew who was responsible. His only interest was in getting the Expedition out of Mexico. The diplomatic communications between the two governments were, however, amiable, and Carranza appointed Luis Cabrera, Ignacio Bonillas, and Alberto Pani to represent the de facto government; Wilson chose Secretary of the Interior Franklin K. Lane, Reverend John R. Mott, and Judge George Grey. New London, Connecticut, was chosen as the site for the conferences, and on September 6, 1916, the first meeting of the Joint High Commission was held.

As the course of the negotiations would demonstrate, Carranza would not allow his delegates to the conference to discuss anything of substance until Wilson agreed to the complete and unconditional withdrawal of American forces. Since Wilson was in the midst of a difficult election campaign and could not afford to risk an impression of weakness in the minds of the American people, he instructed Lane and the other commissioners to insist on the border-crossing protocol and on the determination of responsibility for the raids in the lower Rio Grande valley. He was determined to make an impression of strength in the face of election-year criticism that became more strident as time passed and Villa was still at large.

The Commission's work was interrupted by news from Mexico that Villa had come out of hiding and successfully attacked, dispersed, and inflicted hundreds of casualties on Carrancista garrisons at Satevó and Santa Isabel. In the early morning hours of September 16, Villa and his followers stormed into Chihuahua City, seized the penitentiary, and released the prisoners who immediately added their numbers to the Villista force. The Carrancista commander, Colonel Treviño, was faced with widespread defection and desertion among his troops, and Villa, after making a grandiose speech from the balcony of the Governor's Palace, departed with hundreds of captured rifles, crates of ammunition, and artillery pieces conveniently manned by Treviño's deserters. It was a public relations coup for Villa and his followers; it was a nightmare for Carranza who had been insisting that Villa was dead and who now claimed that the attacks had been carried out by Huerta sympathizers disguised as Villistas, a claim shortly challenged by both Treviño and General Cavazos. As the borderland braced for a new outbreak of Villista violence, Carranza and Obregón insisted Satevó, Santa Isabel, and Chihuahua City were momentary aberrations in an otherwise tranquil Mexico.

The Joint High Commission reconvened October 2 in Atlantic City, and once again the Carrancista delegates insisted that there was no crisis in northern Mexico and that there was nothing to talk about until Pershing's forces were withdrawn across the Rio Grande. The American commissioners returned to their earlier position that at least three, and possibly four questions, needed to be discussed: (1) protection of life and property of foreigners in Mexico; (2) establishment of a claims commission; (3) religious toleration; and (4) prevention of causes likely to lead to friction between the two nations. The Mexican response was in the form of a three-point Program of Work. The first point was the withdrawal of the American forces from Mexican territory; the second point called for safeguarding and patrolling of the border; and the third point called for an agreement in regard to the pursuit of outlaws at the border. The American commissioners, faced daily with the Mexican declaration of "Take your troops out and then we will talk," suggested to Wilson that he threaten Carranza with a withdrawal of American recognition, a step Wilson was unwilling even to consider on the eve of the national election.

As the commissioners went through their diplomatic minuet, Generals Funston and Pershing became increasingly wary of the small yet boisterous Villista resurgence. Villa, his wound now healed and confident that Pershing's inactivity meant that the Expedition had been diplomatically neutralized, was emboldened as he had not been since his fight with the Carrancistas at Guerrero in late March. Earlier, on August 16, General Funston had recommended to the War Department that the Expedition be withdrawn because it seemed certain that Villa's bands had been broken up. The American forces had been withdrawn to Dublán and El Valle and were simply there without any visible prospect of further operations. Following Villa's mid-September successes, however, both he and Pershing discussed the possibility of capturing Chihuahua City, followed by an active campaign to rid the areas of Villistas.

General Bliss and Secretary of War, Baker, discussed the idea of reviving the active campaign against the Villistas, and Baker brought the idea before President Wilson. The reaction from Wilson, on September 25, was that before he could authorize such a plan, he wanted to have complete assurances that such an expedition had the full approval and concurrence of those in control of the de facto Government in Mexico. Wilson's concern was twofold: (1) that the de facto government of Mexico might at first give assent to a renewal of Expedition activity and then withdraw it; and (2) that the recent disturbances in Chihuahua might involve the general pacification of northern Mexico, something that in the President's view was not to be considered. Finally on October 27 the War Department decided that there would be no change in Pershing's orders, which were that he was not to move south or east except to maintain protective patrols. Furthermore he was not to attack Chihuahua City even if Villa captured it again, and while he was authorized to do anything necessary to defend his force, he was not to change the situation by any movement on his own initiative. Any hope Pershing might have had for a resumption of active engagement with the Villistas was at an end.

On November 24, the persistence of the American commissioners finally succeeded in producing a protocol for the mutual pursuit of bandits within a hundred mile zone on either side of the border, and further stipulated that forty days following the acceptance of the protocol American troops would begin their withdrawal. The withdrawal was conditional upon a stable northern Mexico, free from Villista or other bandit threats. Wilson, secure in his reelection, waited hopefully for Carranza's reply. On December 28 he learned that the protocol was rejected out of hand, and that the Mexican commissioners were forbidden to engage in further diplomatic contact with their American counterparts unless or until the Expedition had departed Mexico. Despite Carranza's prohibition on further meetings, at the request of the Mexican Commissioners a final meeting was held in New York City on January 15. The American Commissioners reported to President Wilson that the continued presence of American troops in Mexico made it impossible to secure Carranza's agreement to anything. They suggested to the President that American-Mexican relations would best be served by an early and unconditional withdrawal of the Expedition. Diplomacy had affected nothing, and now Wilson was forced to find some means of withdrawing the Expedition that would satisfy both his friends and his enemies. In the meantime, Pershing and his men waited.

As the Expedition fell into a mode of watchful waiting, Pershing was reminded of the old adage that idle hands are the devil's workshop. Determined to preclude any possibility of problems in discipline and morale, he began a program of training to ensure physical fitness and operational preparedness. His cavalry mounts had recovered from the hardships of severe use and were well-grazed, grained, and sleek. The four regiments of cavalry found the terrain at Dublan was perfect for mounted exercises, offered hundreds of square miles of varied landscape, and almost limitless possibilities for training. By the end of July, troop, squadron, and regimental drills in fighting while mounted and dismounted were developed; scouting, signaling, and messenger service were soon added to the training exercises. As this training continued through August, it became evident to Pershing, ever the perfectionist, that a more systematic plan was needed. Consequently, on August 31, he issued an order assigning periods of work to be devoted progressively to special training.

It was through observation of the infantry training exercises that cavalry officers, particularly Lieutenant Patton, became aware that in a number of areas the cavalry was woefully deficient: fire tactics, fire direction, fire control and discipline, designation of targets, and signaling all needed both introduction and reinforcement. The recently adopted pistol, Colt Model 1911, Caliber .45 ACP (Automatic Colt Pistol) was in the eyes of many cavalrymen a radical and unwelcome departure from the traditional revolver. This resistance to change in the most tradition-bound of Army combat units was reflected in both poor marksmanship and resentment at being forced to use a weapon in

Interior of adobe hut, Troop K, 7th Cavalry, Camp Dublan, Mexico [National Archives].

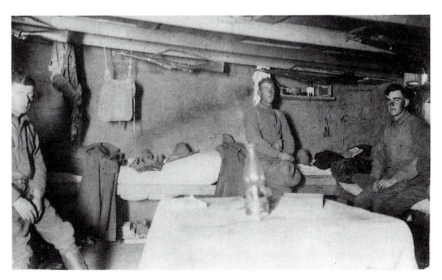

Quarters of Medical Department Personnel, 10th Cavalry, Camp Dublan, Mexico. Walls of adobe bricks with tent fly for roof [National Archives].

which many men had no confidence. A combination of training and combat experience, however, soon convinced troopers that the new pistol was a useful addition to their fighting equipment.

Pershing was quick to notice another deficiency in his cavalry: that of fire tactics dismounted. On September 23 he issued orders for a new series of marksmanship, or musketry, exercises. Between September 26 and October 25, the cavalry practiced range-estimation, sight-setting, target designation, shifting of fire and fire distribution, and simulated fire at the enemy at ranges from 200 to 1,200 yards. Other exercises were held in reinforcing the firing line and ammunition supply and distribution. Lieutenant Patton reported that a great interest was shown in all the exercises. Following the drills, General Pershing addressed his assembled officers and concluded his remarks by saying that if the cavalry were to maintain its important place in the Army it must become proficient in dismounted fighting. The idea was anathema to the older cavalry officers, who believed that the only place for a true cavalryman to fight from was the back of a horse. As October turned to November, despite some grumbling from the old hands, Pershing had every reason to believe that his cavalry met or exceeded those expectations.

At Colonia Dublan, the off duty activities of the men concerned Pershing as much as their battle readiness; he knew that monotony and tedium were enemies of good morale. There were no service organizations to provide diversions, no stores to shop in, no bars in which to relax, and no touring song-and-dance groups to provide diversion. One of the more obvious pastimes was hunting, and Lieutenant Colonel Charles S. Farnsworth, 16th Infantry, recorded in his diary how he and other officers supplemented their mess with ducks, once shotguns and shells arrived from El Paso, Texas. Captain James A. Shannon, 11th Cavalry, reported that those hunters fortunate enough to have the company of an Apache scout or two always returned with deer. The Apaches were perfect hunters. They trailed and found game so quietly that it appeared they were just riding around aimlessly. It took Captain Shannon a while to realize that instead of finding the game by following its tracks, they used their knowledge of the game and its habits to tell them where the game was going. Shannon told of the day an officer went out with the Apaches and came back with seven deer. A few days later the same officer and men from his detachment went out without Apaches and came back empty-handed. The same group went out several days later to the same area, but this time with two Indians; they returned with four deer. It amused Shannon that the soldiers did not seem to realize that the presence of the Indians had anything to do with finding of the deer.

In addition to hunting, baseball leagues were formed in each camp, the games were played with great enthusiasm, and the race for the pennant was hotly contested. When the weather turned colder, football was taken up, each regiment organized a team, and play was so enthusiastic that the medical personnel were kept busy, but fortunately injuries were for the most part minor. Polo associations were organized at both Colonia Dublan and El Valle, and

The "Blanket Toss" was a popular diversion [National Archives].

games were held twice weekly. When the El Paso district champion, the 1st Philadelphia Troop, visited Colonia Dublan during Christmas week they were decisively beaten in both games. Another popular diversion was gambling. The soldiers were paid in hard currency; there was no place to spend it and with no way regularly to send it home, the troopers became avid card and dice players. Pershing decided that as long as no problems in discipline arose he would look the other way and instructed his officers accordingly. In the middle of September both of the big camps, El Valle and Colonia Dublan, had received equipment for showing motion pictures, which were shown nightly. The funding for the equipment and the films was taken care of by organizations established by the Chaplains.

Chinese refugees from Villa's persecution had been accepted in both camps and brought with them both a blessing and a curse. In Colonia Dublan General Pershing allocated an area for their use where their shops, restaurants, and laundries appeared with almost miraculous speed. While their entrepreneurial spirit provided much-needed service for the men, the access to prostitutes the Chinese (and some Mexicans) provided brought a disturbing increase in the venereal disease rate. The months of July through September, the initial months of military inactivity, accounted for 41 percent of all cases reported. Pershing was quick to grasp the connection between the increase in cases of VD and camp life and his solution to the problem was typically direct: he would permit supervised and controlled prostitution. The solution was not new, as Pershing had instituted a similar plan in Columbus, New Mexico,

Boxing matches between units were a source of intense rivalry [National Archives].

several months earlier. Unlike Columbus, however, in Colonia Dublan he had no civilian authorities to deal with, and he simply contracted with a Chinese builder to construct a compound inside the camp at El Valle. Only Mexican women were allowed to work there, and they were regularly inspected and treated as were the men who made use of their services: each man was required to present a document certifying that he was disease-free before being admitted to the compound. No alcohol was permitted and each customer was restricted to thirty minutes, no exceptions allowed. Pershing's policy was successful in lowering the VD rate dramatically: the Expedition's VD rate was one-third less than the Army as a whole and its rate of men rendered inoperative was less than half the rate of the Army as a whole.

Not all of General Pershing's officers saw the presence of whorehouses near Army camps as salubrious. Major William R. Eastman of the Army's Medical Corps had some decidedly skeptical observations about the presence of prostitutes. Major Eastman had been dispatched from Fort Sam Houston, Texas, to Hachita, New Mexico, to accompany the 7th Cavalry into Mexico. By the time he reached Hachita the 7th Cavalry had departed, and he was attached to the 11th Cavalry on its march south. Eastman reached the 7th Cavalry shortly after its engagement at Guerrero and found much work to do. After much arduous campaigning with the 7th Cavalry, he was ordered to the Field Hospital at El Valle and it was there he took notice of a house of prostitution. The house had been established during Eastman's absence, and he was so disconcerted by its presence that he made it part of his final report.

In the Archives this photo is labeled "Recreation Center." In reality it was one of the establishments that upset Major Eastman of the Army's Medical Corps [National Archives].

It was, Eastman noted, a stone's throw from the hospital and directly windward for the prevailing winds. Some of the men grumbled that the wind covered them with "whore dust" and were not pleased. Particularly disturbing was the obligation for members of the Medical Department to administer prophylaxis. Even worse, in Eastman's mind, was the official sanction given to a whorehouse and to the women who worked there. The men on guard duty were thrown in with these activities with no regard to whether they liked it or not, and the medical personnel found it demoralizing and a shame to the Expedition. Eastman concluded his remarks by pointing out that all the medical officers were not only generally opposed to it, but had written letters of protest in regard to the presence of the house. Apparently no attention was given to their communications.

As November gave way to December, plans were formulated for celebration of Christmas in which no man would be overlooked. Every man in the Expedition, from Major General to mule driver received a Christmas present on this 285th day of their deployment in Mexico. It was General Pershing's wish that the day never be forgotten by the men who had been through unimaginable hardship in the pursuit of the Columbus raiders from one end of Chihuahua to the other. At every outpost and waterhole where troops were stationed, gifts were presented and the day was observed in true holiday fashion. More than 10,000 packages were distributed, each valued at between $2 and $3.

The most elaborate ceremony was held at Field Headquarters where the vast majority of troops were camped. From early morning when the troops were awakened by Christmas carols instead of the traditional call of Reveille to the evening when Taps was sounded, there was not a moment when the men lacked for amusements. The daylight hours were given over to athletic events and the troops, who had been free from duties since Saturday, gathered to watch polo matches, football games, pony express runs, mule races, foot races, and a greased pig run. The cooks had labored for several days to prepare a meal that was in truth a feast.

The day's climax came just before seven that evening as the men began to gather around the huge sixty-five-foot Christmas tree. The regiments marched to preassigned stations to await the signal that would begin the ceremony. The silence was broken only by the muted commands necessary to move the thousands of men to their stations. The only lights were the stars that seemed to snap in the cold, clear air. A sudden explosion shattered the silence, and the camp was illuminated by a huge ball of fire which fell from the sky as the trench flare made its way to earth. This was the signal for the troops to march to positions on the points of the Star of Bethlehem that surrounded the tree. When all had reached their places, the flares faded and the tree itself came to life with hundreds of incandescent lamps. Twenty feet above the tree's apex an American flag flew, illuminated by the headlights of trucks which had been posted in advantageous positions.

The tree, standing in the center of a six-pointed star and outlined by a hedge of fir branches, was an example of the much-heralded Yankee ingenuity. There were no large trees anywhere near camp, but one sixty-five foot fir in the center of six smaller ones made an impressive tree, with cone-like proportions. The trees were hauled thirty-five miles from canyons west of camp in eighteen trucks. Bridges had to be constructed, arroyos filled, and brush cleared to make passage possible. A smaller tree, also illuminated, stood at each point of the star. The program began when the chorus of 400 and the massed regimental bands, which had been practicing for weeks, assembled and were given the signal to begin.

The ceremony opened with the band playing and the chorus singing "Joy to the World." Chaplain John M. Moore, 7th Cavalry, offered a soldierly prayer, and the concourse, led by the band and chorus, chanted the Lord's Prayer, the 7,500 voices rising and falling in a great diapason of sound. All voices joined in singing "Battle Hymn of the Republic" and "America"; the music program concluded with the singing of "Pancho Villa," the Expedition's marching song. Two dozen Santa Clauses then escorted the biggest Saint Nick of all into the clear space under the tree, made their ways to the points of the star, and Sergeant Ole Larson of the 13th Cavalry, noted for the quality of his voice, presented the key of "Dobeville" to the patron saint of the ceremony. The distribution of gifts began immediately after Sergeant Larson's speech, and openings in the hedges forming the star were made at the six points and the soldiers filed through. Those doubters who had expected only a flimsy gift were pleasantly disappointed, for each of the 7,500 bags contained items that many at home would have been delighted to receive. The principal gift for most was one of the comfort bags sent by the various chapters of the Red Cross. In addition to what the Red Cross had provided, 41,000 cigars and 11,000 pounds of candy and assorted other sweets were received. Each officer received a book which, when read, was to be presented to his command. Presentation of the gifts brought the regular program to an end.

The troops were then ordered to fall out, and the various amusements that had been arranged got into full swing around the glowing pits of coals where two steers had been barbequed. Trucks with miniature stages mounted on their frames were stationed at other locations, each illuminated by the headlights of another truck. Some stages had comic dancers and others had vaudeville acts, and all were surrounded by thousands of soldiers who watched, sang, laughed, and bartered their gifts with others. Motion pictures were shown on makeshift screens, the massed bands played, and the barbeque was consumed to the last morsel. Only when everyone was exhausted from the night's celebration, and the lights on the great tree were turned off, did the curtain fall on what was the greatest celebration the American Army had ever held outside the borders of the United States.

December gave way rather quickly to January and on the recommendation of the American delegates to the American-Mexican Commission and in view of a probable war with Germany, President Wilson ordered the withdrawal of the Expedition from Mexico. On January 18 General Funston was notified to inform General Pershing of the government's intentions. On January 19, 1917, General Pershing received a telegram from Headquarters, Southern Division, which indicated that it was the intention of the government to withdraw his command from Mexico shortly. This information was to be kept in strictest confidence, and he was to report his recommendations for the withdrawal as soon as he had formulated them. Concern was expressed for the Mormon colonies, and Pershing was directed to contact them in order to accommodate their wishes regarding withdrawal from Mexico.

Pershing replied that the withdrawal should be made entirely by marching, which would avoid possible problems with the railroad and complications at Juarez. He reported that the Mormon Colonies had generally anticipated an early withdrawal and that probably one-half of the 600 men, women, and children would go with the Expedition to the United States. He planned to assemble at Palomas and march the entire command across the border together. Pershing's recommendations were approved, and all supplies and stores were sent to Columbus. The movement of supplies was regulated so that there would not be any large accumulation on hand to impair movement. Withdrawal plans were in accord with a schedule designed to assure that all troops arrived at Palomas on February 4 so that the entire Expedition could cross the border as an organized command. The greater portion of the command (9,813 men) departed from Colonia Dublan and was joined at Ojo, Hirsch's Hole, Twin Mills, and Vado by an additional 870 men, which brought the total assembled at Palomas to 10,690. In addition to the Expedition members, there were present 9,305 animals.

A major problem the Expedition faced in its withdrawal was the large number of refugees who believed that it was no longer safe for them to remain in Mexico. As word of withdrawal spread and then became a certainty, the Chinese who had established restaurants and laundries near the camps were among the first to decide on departure. For reasons not clearly understood, Villa had a murderous hatred for the Chinese. He believed they were not good citizens, that they had come to Mexico with nothing, and that they sent all their earnings home. When in November 1916 he had reoccupied Ciudad Chihuahua, his men engaged in a merciless and indiscriminate slaughter of the Chinese they found. Among the refugees was a large number of Mormons and numerous Mexicans, who for a variety of reasons decided they wanted to accompany the Expedition to the United States, and attached themselves to the several Expedition camps. Cavalry escorts for the assorted groups were organized, and in large columns the refugees were taken to the border. Their numbers, which included men, women, and children, were 2,030 Mexicans, 197 Americans, and 533 Chinese, for a total of 2,760. Three children were born during the withdrawal, and two were born in the refugee camp in Columbus.

On February 5, 1917, at Palomas, Mexico, the Expedition assembled in its entirety and, led by its Headquarters unit, crossed the border and marched in column to Columbus. A refugee camp was quickly established, and officers were assigned to look after shelter, security, and medical needs of the refugees. Fortunately there were no serious illnesses in the camp and most refugees seemed relieved to be away from the turmoil of uncertainty and revolution. Most Mexicans were released from camp by February 16, and through the efforts of the immigration authorities and the Army locations for settlement were found for all of them. The Chinese refugees were a different matter due to the laws against Chinese immigration. An appropriation of $40,000 was established by the Chinese government and the Chinese Relief Association, and the funds were used to provide for the repatriation either to China or to Mexico for those who wished to return. Some merchants remained in the United States with special permission under the law. The War Department took responsibility for the remaining Chinese, who were sent to Fort Sam Houston, Texas. The Chinese quickly made their way into the local economies wherever they went, as many of them were skilled cooks and craftsmen and all exhibited a keen sense for entrepreneurial activities.

The troopers of the Expedition were quickly sent to forts and posts throughout the United States, mostly along the Mexican-American border. By the summer of 1917 many of them would be in Europe fighting once again in unfamiliar territory, this time alongside the British and French. Their commanding officer was, however, a familiar one: John "Black Jack" Pershing. The base at Columbus was quickly dismantled, the heavy equipment shipped wherever the European war required it, and the trucks were taken to El Paso and San Antonio where they were repaired and rebuilt to meet the needs of the new army that was being assembled. In a short time the hustlers and whores, the bootleggers and smugglers, the people who had been attracted to Columbus because of the Army's presence drifted away to relocate wherever their seamy, shady occupations took them. Columbus became once again the sleepy, slow-paced border town it had been before Francisco's folly put it on the map for all to notice.

Eight

WINGS AND WHEELS: RECONNAISSANCE, OBSERVATION, AND TRANSPORTATION

Both the setting and the timing of the Punitive Expedition qualify it for the sobriquet, "Last of the Nineteenth and First of the Twentieth." The setting was in America's Old West; the timing was that of a dramatic, yet not clearly understood, transition in the nature of warfare. With the advent of the machinegun, the mainstay of the Expedition's strike force, the horse cavalry, was soon to go the way of the buggy whip. With the arrival of the 1st Aero Squadron, March 15, 1916, at Columbus, New Mexico, the future made its presence known. The squadron came from Fort Sam Houston, Texas by rail, and included ten trucks, eight airplanes, six motorcycles, eleven officers, eighty-two enlisted men, an aviation mechanic, and two Hospital Corps men. At Uvalde, Texas, one officer and fourteen enlisted men of the Engineers joined the train. Twenty armed guards were posted throughout the train, on the flatbed cars, and key rail junctions along the route were also guarded.

Shortly after the train arrived at Columbus the troops were assigned to barracks, which had been vacated by the 13th Cavalry, the trucks and planes were unloaded, and assembly of the planes began on a field east of town. The first airplane assembled was airplane #43, and Lt. Dargue took it for a test flight of twelve minutes.[1] The remaining seven planes were assembled on March 16. Over three hours were spent in fourteen test flights, and with Captain Dodd as pilot, and Captain Foulois as observer, airplane #44 made the first reconnaissance flight into Mexico. On March 18, twenty-seven Jeffery truck chassis for the Quartermaster Corps arrived in Columbus, and since the

Quartermasters had no men or tools to install the bodies on the truck chassis the Engineer Section of the Aero Squadron was assigned to the job. On March 19, while the machine shop section continued to work on the Jeffery trucks for the Quartermaster, the Aero Squadron received orders to report to General Pershing at Nueva Casas Grandes for immediate duty.

The Squadron left Columbus at 5:10 PM, March 19, minus one plane, because airplane #42, piloted by Lieutenant Kilner, experienced motor trouble and was forced to remain behind. The ground crew, under command of Lieutenant Arthur R. Christy, followed immediately in trucks. Due to the late departure time it became necessary for the Squadron to land at Ascencion at 6:30 PM, but only four planes landed. The other three, separated from the flight by darkness, landed individually at Ojo Caliente, Janos, and Pearson, Mexico. The plane that landed at Pearson was wrecked in the process, thus reducing the Squadron's strength to six planes within five days of arrival in New Mexico. Mounted patrols of the 11th Cavalry were sent out to search for the missing aircraft, but were unable to locate them.

The following day at 8:16 AM the four pilots who had landed at Ascension, Dodd (with Foulois as observer), Carberry, Bowen, and Chapman, flew south following the Casas Grande River and landed at Nueva Casas Grande at 9:35 AM without having sighted any of the missing planes. They reported for duty and learned that the pilot who had had motor trouble at Columbus and the pilot who had landed at Janos arrived at about the same time, while the pilot who had landed at Ojo Caliente reported in several days later. General Pershing's first orders were for reconnaissance flights south along the Mexican Northwestern railroad, with instructions to establish contact with the American troops who were moving south. This reconnaissance began from Dublan at 12:00 PM, March 20, with airplane #44 piloted by Lieutenant Willis and with Captain Foulois as observer. They had flown southward perhaps twenty-five miles when they found themselves unable to get enough altitude to get over the foothills of the Sierra Madre Mountains. The strong vertical air currents and the constant whirlwinds resulted in a struggle to control the underpowered machine, and Willis and Foulois were forced to return to camp at 1:00 PM to report their aborted mission to the Division Commander.

On this same afternoon Lieutenant Bowen in airplane #48 flew from Nueva Casas Grandes to Colonia Dublan, and in his attempt to land his machine he was caught in a whirlwind, stalled, and went into a nosedive. Bowen was able to regain partial control of the craft, but he was unable to recapture sufficient control to land and the plane was wrecked. While the machine was completely ruined in the crash, Bowen walked away with a broken nose and numerous scratches and bruises. The squadron was now left with five operational airplanes, and the growing realization that their machines were not mechanically sufficient for the terrain in which they were being ordered to operate.

Despite these early disappointments, on March 21 the Squadron was able to reach Colonel Irwin in the Galeana Valley at Galera Lopena. Captains Doss and Foulois left Dublan at 8:36 AM, landed their machine at Irwin's camp at 9:27 AM, delivered messages, received information for the Division Commander, returned to Dublan at 11:55 AM, and turned in their report to General Pershing. The distance traveled round trip was eighty-four miles, and valuable information had been delivered and received. As a result of the information from Colonel Irwin, six trucks loaded with much-needed supplies were dispatched to Galera Lopena. It was, however, the swiftness that impressed Pershing most: all of this had been accomplished in about three and one-half hours. No cavalry reconnaissance patrol could hope even to come close to such speed, and Pershing knew it. Near the end of the Expedition's time in Mexico, he openly declared that he would rather have a single airplane than a regiment of cavalry for reconnaissance work.

Unfortunately the limited reconnaissance successes of the Squadron were followed by several more failures, and Perishing questioned the wisdom of placing pilots' lives in danger simply to deliver messages. The major obstacle was elevation and the accompanying hazardous wind conditions. The base camp at Dublan was at an altitude of 5,200 feet; the Cumbre pass at the heart of the Sierra Madres was at 9,000 feet. To the east the passes to Casas Grandes and the Galeana Valley were from 6,000 to 7,000 feet, and the temperature variations were a further hazard: 28° Fahrenheit in the night to 78° Fahrenheit during the day. On March 24, the Squadron War Diary recorded that winds of forty miles per hour struck the area, dust storms raged through the night, and a snowstorm struck, which lasted several hours. Flying was impossible.

Captain Foulois wrote a memo to General Pershing in which he stated that the airplanes of the Squadron were not capable of meeting the present military service conditions and recommended ten new planes, two each from five different manufacturers in order to expedite delivery. These planes were to be furnished with the latest equipment and more powerful motors (125 to 160 horsepower, six-cylinder models) and were to be purchased for immediate express delivery. The newer, more powerful motors would assure that the planes could function in an environment where all operations began at 5,000 feet above sea level. It was further required that the airplanes possess a climbing ability of at least 18,000 feet while carrying a pilot, an observer, and four hours' fuel. The air disturbances in the Sierra Madres required that airplanes were sufficiently powerful to carry the necessary weight at least 5,000 feet above the highest peaks, thus assuring proper control of the machine. Then, and only then, could the pilots carry out the military missions assigned to them.

By the end of March, Foulois submitted another memorandum in which he set forth a detailed, multifaceted plan for the use of the five airplanes left in the Squadron. He pointed out to Pershing that the machines now in use had seen ten months' severe weather service in Oklahoma, Texas, and Mexico: rain, high winds, and brutally cold weather. As a result, all the machines were subjected to severe wear and tear. With the present extreme field service conditions every machine was liable, at any day, to be placed out of commission as unfit and too dangerous for further field service. That part of Foulois' plan accepted by Pershing, to be put into effect April 1, called for limitations to be placed on the use of available aircraft upon establishment of radio-telegraph communication between Namiquipa and Casas Grandes and a concentration of all aircraft at Namiquipa for the purpose of maintaining communication south of the base. Foulois was hoping to decrease the number of hours that airplanes would be required to fly, thus lowering both maintenance time and the risk of danger to the pilots. Radios and telegraphs, as well as motorcycles and automobiles, would take over most routine communiqués and the airplanes would be used primarily for vital mail and dispatches.

On the day the plan went into effect, the Squadron made nineteen flights by all five machines to Columbus, New Mexico, Dublan, Espindoleno, El Valle, Cruces, Namiquipa, San Geronimo, and Bachineva. Rain, snow, and hail forced several of the machines to land and wait until the weather had passed. Between April 1 and 6 the Squadron made fifty-four flights carrying mail and dispatches, all but one relatively uneventful. On April 6, however, airplane #44, piloted by Captain Dodd with Lieutenant Kilner as observer, was badly damaged when it landed at San Geronimo and ran into a ditch concealed by tall grass. All serviceable parts were salvaged, and the rest of the machine was destroyed. The Squadron was reduced to four serviceable airplanes, and its difficulties had been shaped by a combination of mechanical difficulties and the forces of nature. Contact with hostile human elements had not yet been encountered, but that was soon to change.

On Friday, April 7 two airplanes, both from Geronimo, took off with duplicate dispatches for the American Consul in Chihuahua City, a distance of 105 miles. Airplane #43, piloted by Lt. Dargue and with Capt. Foulois as observer, was ordered to land on the south side of the city; airplane #45, piloted by Lt. Carberry with Capt. Dodd as observer, was ordered to land on

Mexican Rural Constabulary (*Rurales*) [National Archives].

the north side of the city. Both machines arrived at 7:20 AM and caused great excitement among the inhabitants. Foulois then ordered Dargue to fly his machine to the north side of town to join Carberry and Dodd. As Foulois was walking into town and Dargue was taking off, four mounted *rurales* opened fire on the plane at a distance of about a half mile. Foulois made his way to the *rurales* and demanded that they stop firing at the airplane. They did so, but then arrested Foulois and took him to the city jail, followed by an excited crowd of several hundred men and boys. As the procession made its way to the jail, Foulois was able to speak to an American bystander and asked him to notify the American Consul of the arrival of the pilots and observers in the city. He also requested that the Consul provide protection for the aviators and both airplanes.

After considerable delay at the jail, Capt. Foulois was able to contact Colonel Miranda, Chief of Staff to General Gutierrez, Military Governor of Chihuahua State. Foulois was then taken to see General Gutierrez, who in a short time ordered both Foulois' release and guards for the two airplanes. The Captain then made his way to the landing site on the north side of town to locate the aviators and the two machines, but found only Lt. Dargue with airplane #43. Dargue explained that shortly after landing near airplane

#45, Capt. Dodd had departed to deliver his dispatches to the Consul in Chihuahua City. Upon his departure a large crowd of locals, along with Carrancista officers and soldiers, had gathered near his plane and began to act in a threatening manner. They made insulting remarks, burned holes in the fabric of the planes with cigarettes, slashed the cloth with knives, and began to remove nuts and bolts. The aviators with the machines, Lieutenants Carberry and Dargue, rather than risk the destruction of their crafts at the hands of the mob, decided to fly them to the American Smelter and Refining Company property, located about six miles southeast of Chihuahua City.

Carberry got away safely in airplane #45 and landed at the smelter without further difficulties. Dargue, in airplane #43, managed to get away in a storm of rocks thrown by the mob, but shortly thereafter the top section of the fuselage flew off and damaged the stabilizer, and he was forced to land immediately. While the landing was affected safely, Carberry soon found himself confronted by the same crowd. He managed to stand them off without further damage to the airplane or himself, probably by brandishing his sidearm. Fortunately, the arrival of the guard provided by General Gutierrez brought an end to any threat posed by the mob. Captains Foulois and Dodd spent the rest of the day with the Consul and arranged for supplies to be sent to the forward elements of the Expedition. Dargue and Carberry spent the remainder of their eventful day repairing the damage the mob had done to the two machines. The following day Capt. Foulois and Lt. Dargue flew dispatches from the American Consul to General Pershing at San Geronimo, and Capt. Dodd and Lt. Carberry returned to San Geronimo by way of Santa Ysabel and San Andres.

On April 8 the Squadron received orders to move its base to San Antonio, Mexico. The next several days were spent in reconnaissance flights and the delivery of mail and dispatches. On April 14 airplane #43, with Lt. Dargue as pilot and Lt. Gorrell as observer, made a reconnaissance flight from Columbus, New Mexico, to Boca Grande, Pulpit Pass, Oxaca Pass, Carretas, Janos, Ascension, and returned to Columbus, a distance of 315 miles. The purpose of the flight was to search for a large number Carrancista troops reported to have been moving east and threatening the Expeditions line of communication. No Carrancistas were sighted, but the reconnaissance set a new American record for nonstop flight with two men aboard. The same day the Squadron lost another plane when Lt. Rader, on reconnaissance in the vicinity of Parral, landed on rough ground in an attempt to reach Major Howze's command and damaged the aircraft beyond any immediate possibility of repair. The machine was abandoned and Rader joined Howze and his cavalry column.

The Squadron continued to lose aircraft in the following days, one (#42) because its fuselage was simply worn out, and another (#43) because of a serious crash that almost cost the Squadron the lives of Capt. Willis and Lt. Dargue. They had flown the venerable airplane #43 on a reconnaissance flight from San Antonio to Chihuahua City for purposes of photographing roads and approaches to the city. While west of the city their motor failed and they were forced to make a landing in the hills during which the airplane was completely wrecked. While Dargue escaped the crash unscathed, Willis was pinned beneath the wreckage and suffered a severe scalp wound along with lacerations and bruises on his legs and ankles. Since the machine was a total wreck it was set on fire, and the two men began the sixty-five mile walk to San Antonio. Carrying their personal equipment, and possessed of no food or water, the aviators made their way over mountains and through valleys accompanied only by a great deal of suffering. They finally reached the Squadron's base on the morning of April 21, completely exhausted. They had walked for just under forty-five hours.

With only two of the eight airplanes taken into Mexico in mid-March still in operation, and both in such condition that they were considered unsafe for further field use, the Squadron received orders on April 20 to return to Columbus, New Mexico, to test newly arrived machines. The two airplanes, #45 and #53, were flown back to Columbus: Lt. Carberry as pilot and Lt. Correll as observer flew airplane #45 from Namiquipa directly to Columbus, a distance of 230 miles; Lt. Chapman flew airplane #53 from Namiquipa to Dublan and thence to Columbus. Both machines were examined and condemned as having no further use. The remainder of the Squadron drove in trucks first to El Valle, then the next day to Dublan for gas and oil, and on to Corralitos that evening. On April 22, they reached Columbus at 7:00 PM where Lt. Carberry had to be hospitalized for severe asthma. The next day was Easter Sunday, and work was done in organizing the accumulated reports and correspondence. Four new aircraft from the Curtis Aeroplane Company awaited them, and the next day the tests began.

The four machines were tested extensively in the next several days, and the practical flight tests indicated that they were not suitable for field service in Mexico. They were rejected by the Army, and the Squadron received two new Curtis R-2 160 horsepower airplanes on May 1. By May 25 ten more were delivered to Columbus, and the months of May, June, and July were devoted to testing the new machines. The tests revealed defective motor parts, substandard construction, and most disturbing, unsound propellers. Manufactures from across the United States were contacted and propellers of every sort were sent to Columbus for testing. The Squadron constructed a stand upon which to test not only the propellers received but also the motors. The facilities at Columbus were not capable of accurate, sophisticated tests and the work proceeded very slowly. The Squadron was, however, able to determine with sufficient satisfaction the suitability of all propellers sent to them. Since virtually all of the propellers proved unserviceable, due primarily to climatic conditions, the decision was made to build them in Columbus. On June 29 three civilian employees of the Curtis Aeroplane Company arrived and began a task that was still in progress when Major Foulois submitted his "Report of Operations" on August 28, 1916.

The report was a detailed summary of Foulois' experiences and observations while with the Expedition in Mexico. His major concern was, as one would expect, the quality of the aircraft supplied to the Army's pilots. Airplanes intended for field use with the military should all be tested under as severe conditions of service as possible. The tests should take place at altitudes starting at 5,000 feet and where extreme weather conditions are to be expected. Foulois further recommended that an airplane testing station be established at Fort Bliss, Texas, or some other area along the Mexican border where the altitude above sea level and climatic conditions throughout the year are more closely related to maximum service conditions. The report concluded by noting that the Squadron was awaiting the delivery of eighteen new airplanes for assembly and testing, and that twelve new Lewis automatic machineguns and one hundred bombs had arrived at the base, and that instruction had commenced in the use of the new weapons. He provided no further elaboration on what was to become the future of the airplane in warfare: the armed fighter and the bomber.

Much has been made of the "failure" of the First Aero Squadron in Mexico, but much has also been ignored. The Squadron was attached to the Army's experimental branch, the Signal Corps, and its deployment to serve with the Expedition was precisely the type of trial and error endeavor at the heart of any practical experiment. No one could have foreseen that the old, underpowered machines given to the Squadron would fail in the environment into which they were sent. What is noteworthy, however, is what was accomplished by the Squadron in the more or less five months of its military service in Mexico. Five hundred and forty flights were made for a total of 19,553 miles. Critical dispatches were delivered to and from General Pershing and his staff, and communication was maintained with advanced units often considered to be lost and perhaps in difficulty. It was demonstrated that the airplane had no equal for purposes of observation, reconnaissance, mapmaking, and photography. While it had not yet evolved into a weapon, that aspect of the future was on the horizon: the United States Air Force was born in Chihuahua (Mexico) and Columbus (New Mexico).

Nine

LOGISTICS AND THE BASE OF SUPPLY

When the orders to pursue and punish the band or bands of Columbus raiders were first given to General Pershing, little or no thought had been given to the logistics of the pursuit. General Pershing had at first thought that the Mexican Northwestern Railroad would be his main artery of supply and transportation and made his plans accordingly. He was, however, warned by the Secretary of War that while his plans for pursuit were acceptable, he must not assume that any Mexican railroad would be open for his use. Pershing's belief that the rail-road would be open for American use was based on his assumption that since the United States had permitted Mexico's de facto government to transport its troops and supplies by rail to Agua Prieta through New Mexico and Arizona in 1915 (thus ensuring Villa's defeat at the subsequent battle fought there), an understanding of reciprocity existed. Unfortunately for Pershing's plans, Carranza saw the Expedition not as an arm in assisting the de facto govern-ment in ridding Mexico of Villista bandits, but as an invasion of Mexico and of a violation of her sovereignty. There would be no cooperation from the de facto government as far as Carranza was concerned, and the United States came to see his restrictions of the use of the railroad as one of several attempts to hinder the Expedition and force it to withdraw from Mexico.

Had the railroad been open for American use, El Paso (Texas) would have been the perfect supply center to send goods to the forward posts of San Antonio, Colonia Dublan, and Namiquipa, Chihuahua. Denied rail trans-port at the time, Pershing was forced to revise his logistical plans: he would now have to rely on truck convoys to deliver supplies. Without El Paso as a supply base Pershing's only viable choice left was Columbus, New Mexico, the closest American town along the Expedition's line of communication that had a railroad. It was, however, far from an ideal location; indeed, its close proximity to Fort Bliss and El Paso were its only real assets. There was nothing in the small border town of some 350 residents to sustain a sizeable military expedition, and Villa's raid had left the town in shambles. A single railroad track ran through Columbus, there were no warehouses for storage of supplies, no corrals for horses and other livestock, no motor vehicle maintenance facilities, no fuel storage facilities, no housing existed for the civilian workers that would be needed, and there were no facilities for the large number of additional military and civilian personnel soon to arrive.

Aside from the problems with the lack of infrastructure in Columbus, Pershing was faced with the realization that the entire United States Army had approximately 200 motor vehicles in its possession, ranging from heavy cargo trucks to passenger cars, and they were scattered among all the forts and border posts in the country. They were not, in any appreciable number, available for use by the Expedition. The only mechanized unit in the Army at this time was the First Aero Squadron, attached to the Signal Corps. When it arrived at Fort Bliss en route to Columbus, the squadron had eight trucks, one of which was a machine shop. It received two more trucks prior to its departure for Columbus, and it was from among these vehicles (and trucks from the Border Patrol at El Paso) that the first units of mechanized transport were put into service in Columbus.

Prior to mechanization, the standard Army method of supply in the field was either the pack mule (with a 200-pound cargo limit) or the escort wagon drawn by four mules and capable, under more or less ideal conditions, of carrying 3,000 pounds. The western column departed from Culbertson's Ranch, west and south of Columbus, on the night of March 14–15. Their supplies were carried by mules as they had sent their wagons on to Columbus. The first wagon companies that entered Mexico were Companies #1 and #2. A wagon company consisted of 27 wagons, 112 mules, 6 horses, and 36 soldiers (among who were a cook, a saddler, and a blacksmith). They accompanied the eastern column south on the morning of March 15 and carried four days' rations and two days' forage; in addition each man carried an additional two days' reserve rations and 120 rounds of ammunition. It took the wagon companies nearly five days to reach Colonia Dublan where their supplies were unloaded and distributed.

Two lessons were quickly learned in these early days: the countryside of Chihuahua could not provide either adequate supplies or the forage needed by the advancing columns, and the distances and terrain of Chihuahua made it impossible for animal transportation to reliably carry the necessary provisions to meet the Expedition's needs. While the obvious answer to the Expedition's transport needs was the truck, it was equally obvious that two serious obstacles stood in the way: the fact that the Army had nowhere near the necessary number of trucks, and the fact that roads suitable for sustained use by cargo laden trucks simply did not exist in Chihuahua's rugged countryside. There were not even enough trucks available to transport supplies within Columbus, and vehicles had to be borrowed from the First Aero Squadron just to unload the supply laden trains from El Paso.

Two problems were immediately apparent: the procurement of the necessary trucks, and the transformation of Columbus into an efficient base of communication and supply. The former was taken care of by Major General Hugh L. Scott, and the latter was handed to Major John F. Madden. General Scott, informed by the Quartermaster General (Brigadier General Henry G. Sharpe) that the Army did not possess the necessary trucks reliably to supply Pershing's columns from Columbus, took matters into his own hands. He personally authorized the purchase of the necessary vehicles without first securing the mandatory appropriation from Congress. In so doing, he knowingly committed a crime that was punishable by a prison sentence. When he informed Secretary of War Newton D. Baker of what he had done, Baker simply replied that if anyone would go to jail it would be he and not the General. The mechanization of the United States Army had begun and, curiously enough, it had begun as the result of an illegal act on the part of its commanding general.

Major Madden, designated the Quartermaster for the Expedition, arrived at Columbus on March 15 with a staff of three civilian clerks. Since the eastern column had departed the day before his arrival, he went to Palomas to receive his orders from the Expedition's Chief of Staff, Lieutenant Colonel DeRosey C. Cabell. His orders directed him to remain in Columbus until both the depot and the supply column were fully operational. He was to prepare to send forward as quickly as possible rations, grain, and any other stores called for by the units in the field. Madden's task was complicated by the need to build the depot at the same time that the newly purchased trucks and tons of supplies arrived in Columbus. It was necessary to add two spurs to the single railroad track that ran through the town in order to accommodate the growing rail traffic. The first spur was finished on March 20 and the second April 1. The new additions handled a total of fifty-eight boxcars and significantly reduced the railroad's congestion.

The lack of congestion did not, however, solve Madden's problems. Some trains arrived without bills of lading and no one knew what the boxcars contained. The contents of the cars were simply stacked on the ground until storage facilities were completed. In the meantime large numbers of laborers who had been hired in El Paso arrived, further complicating the completion of the depot. They brought nothing but themselves, and the need to feed and shelter them further exacerbated an already muddled situation. The arrival of civilian clerks and office personnel did nothing to help. The urgency to ship materiel south to Pershing's columns while at the same time construct storage facilities, office spaces, shops, corral space, a hospital, a veterinary hospital, and fuel storage tanks was a challenge no one had foreseen. Added to this challenge was the arrival, on March 18, of the first trucks, nearly all of which needed both assembly and modification.

In the rush to purchase and deliver trucks to the depot at Columbus, there had been little or no time to consider either standardization or maintenance requirements. Brigadier General Sharpe's purchasing agents fanned out across the country buying whatever was available for sale and immediate delivery. They began purchases on March 14 and before they were finished they secured 588 cargo trucks, 57 tank trucks, 12 machine-shop trucks, and 6 wreckers. All but twenty-three were sent to the Border, and in addition to these vehicles, seventy-three passenger cars were purchased and delivered.

The first shipment of twenty-seven Jefferey four-wheel-drive vehicles, or "Quads" as they were called, arrived with detached wagon bodies. There were, however, no tools with which to attach the bodies to the truck chassis. Fortunately, the First Aero Squadron's portable machine shop was capable of making the necessary modifications, and Truck Company 1, commanded by Captain Harry A. Hegeman, was organized on March 20. A day later Truck Company 2 organized, and within four months an additional fifteen new companies were organized. Each company was made up of two passenger cars and twenty-six trucks. Eventually the passenger cars were phased out and replaced with a truck outfitted to transport both supplies and maintenance equipment for the truck company.

An unforeseen problem immediately presented itself: there were few soldiers who could either drive or maintain the new motor vehicles. The only solution was to hire civilian drivers and mechanics until such time as soldiers were trained. Unfortunately, the civilians were not accustomed to the carefully regimented nature of Army life and they simply ignored the Army's rules, regulations, and attempts at discipline. The soldiers, moreover, were upset at the higher rate of pay the civilians received for the same work. This resulted in a number of confrontations that were not conducive to good order and morale. The $100 a month that the civilians were paid was another source of irritation to soldiers whose pay seldom exceeded $20, if that. The problems were ameliorated somewhat when the Adjutant General ruled that the civilians connected to the Expedition were subject to both military law and court-martial. They were then issued Army uniforms, along with rifles and pistols, although it was doubtful that many, if any, had had any training in how to use the firearms. Probably the only benefit of armed civilians was that they were useful in standing guard when the convoys paused for an evening's rest along the road. This at least gave the impression that they were facing the same hazards as the soldiers, but the friction continued and was only eased as most of the civilians were finally phased out. A handful of the best civilian drivers was retained, men who had proven themselves consistently reliable and hardworking.

There was no shortage of applicants for a job as truck driver. The sight of trucks bouncing along the road in relative ease and security aroused envy among the infantrymen, and even troopers were susceptible to the illusion of an easy job. The truth of the matter was a different story: driving a vehicle in a convoy over primitive and dusty roads for several days on end was a physically exhausting task, one that required both strength and stamina, to say nothing of determination. Many civilian drivers who had been attracted by the pay and the romance of the open road became first-rate drivers, but were soon found to be ill suited to the rugged outdoor life of the desert in Chihuahua. Mechanical and physical breakdowns were frequent (clogged fuel lines and broken springs were among the most common problems) and had to be attended to immediately. Routine maintenance and inspection was performed when a column camped for the night, regardless of how exhausted the drivers and mechanics were.

Gradually the number of convoys sent south increased, and an acceptable degree of regularity was achieved. As a result of this accomplishment (no mean feat in itself) the ugly law of unintended consequences reared its head: the regularization of traffic on a daily basis caused a rapid deterioration in the primitive roads that ran over the alkaline flats and the sandy plains of western Chihuahua. The mountain passes presented another and perhaps the most difficult challenge, particularly to the wheels and the suspension systems of the trucks. As General Pershing reported, in the dry season the heavy trucks cut deep ruts into the alkali soil and ground it to dust as fine as powder; in the rainy season the dust turned to a sludge that stuck to the wheels of the trucks up to the hubs and made progress virtually impossible. Only the sandy stretches were passable during the wet season. The Expedition's command quickly realized that the road problem was a job for Engineers, and not for the Infantry, the Cavalry, or the Quartermaster.

Major Lytle Brown was the Expedition's Engineer, and he commanded three companies of the 2nd Engineer Battalion. During the first several months progress was painfully slow, as the Engineers had neither the requisite experience in road building nor the equipment necessary to get the job done. Toward the end of May, the Quartermaster assigned three truck companies to the Engineer Battalion, and the authorization for the purchase of equipment provided the Engineers with eleven tractors, thirty-six dump trailers, six graders, three steamrollers, three tractor rollers, eighteen trailer water tanks, and numerous road drags. It was not until early July that the Engineers were fully ready to repair the older roads and scout and construct new routes. During the slightly more than six months left to the Expedition, the Engineers constructed 157 miles of new roads and repaired 225 miles of old roads. They also constructed two bridges, one at Vado Fusiles and one at El Valle. It is probably safe to say that without the Engineers' work the truck convoys could not have operated with the efficiency necessary to supply Pershing's command.

In the early weeks of the Expedition the supply trail went from Columbus southwest about fourteen miles to Gibson's Ranch, turned south into Mexico and progressed through Boca Grande, Espia, Ascension, Corralitos, and to Colonia Dublan. From there it turned south to Galeana, El Valle, Las Cruces, Namiquipa, San Geronimo, and San Antonio. In April, the original route was discontinued in favor of a shorter route via Palomas, Vado Fusiles, and Ascension. Dublan was reached through an alternate route through Ojo Federico. In May there was another route from Dublan to El Valle through San Joaquin. The trails were shown either by wheel ruts or by Signal Corps telegraph lines, but as the Engineers' proficiency in road building grew, the main route became so dependable that it was given the name Lincoln Junior Highway.

As the truck columns moved back and forth from Columbus to their destinations in the south, valuable lessons were learned in the new business of what was then called "motor trucking." Inefficient and incompetent personnel were quickly spotted and weeded out, and valuable modifications in vehicles were made. Each truck was fitted with a ten-gallon water container, and this freed the columns from dependency on water holes for camping and other necessary stops. The cooks quickly learned to function without cumbersome field kitchens; they took only the necessary cooking utensils. To prepare a meal, they simply dug a narrow trench, threw in firewood, placed a radiator guard across the trench, and put their pots and pans on the guard. Firewood was easily carried on the truck, and without the field kitchen there was no delay in movement as the men waited for the stove to cool off. Oatmeal cereal and cornmeal mush sometimes fried in bacon grease, while not exactly *haute cuisine*, provided both filling and nourishing breakfasts, and the truckers were well aware of the fact that they were better fed than the men in the front line columns.

An added lesson learned by the Quartermasters was the value of standardization of vehicles within each motor company. With truck companies made up of mixed vehicle types it was not always possible to transfer the cargo of a disabled vehicle to another, dissimilar truck. A disabled gasoline tank truck's cargo could not, for instance, be transferred except to another tanker. To Captain Francis H. Pope of the Quartermaster Corps, experience therefore dictated that it was better to carry gas in drums on a separate cargo truck and to use the tank trucks in regular supply trains.

As a result of the lessons learned and suggestions made, Major Madden as Chief Quartermaster of the Expedition recommended the following: that all truck and wagon companies be organized, trained, and maintained during time of peace for use in time of need; that this training was to be administered to selected officers and enlisted men in a School of Transportation; and that sufficient trained units were to be maintained to furnish all tactical units, each with its proscribed quota. General Pershing enthusiastically accepted the recommendations and gave unqualified approval.

One innovation connected to motor transport that was neither quickly realized nor promptly implemented was the value of moving infantry by truck. As the convoys made their way along the routes south, they often passed detachments of infantry. The trucks halted and took aboard those soldiers who were footsore or fatigued, as many as the trucks could accommodate. The idea of carrying combat troops in motor vehicles was not, however, widely accepted in the Army, as most infantry commanders believed that the practice would detract from discipline and morale. It was then widely believed that infantrymen needed to be hardened by marching, and truck transport would soften them and provide an attraction for malingerers. While it may be asserted that the Expedition pioneered the concept, mechanized infantry was an idea whose time had not yet come.

A further addition to mechanization that was pioneered by the Expedition was the motorcycle. Shortly after the Expedition began the Army purchased a number of motorcycles with sidecars, a combination that was just out of the experimental stage. Machineguns were mounted on the sidecars, and it was believed that the speed, mobility, and firepower of the vehicle would make it a formidable weapon. Unfortunately the rough desert terrain made the vehicle as designed impractical. The rough, rocky, and sometimes muddy terrain of Chihuahua proved too much: the sidecar was an unsatisfactory base for the machinegun and accuracy simply could not be obtained. The motorcycle proved to be of limited use in scouting and message carrying, but in either case the cavalry and telegraph proved to be more valuable.

Just as in the beginning of the Expedition, little or no thought had been given to logistics; little thought had been given to the question of ordnance, a service of the Army dealing with the procurement, distribution, and safe-keeping of weapons and ammunition. No one seemed to have thought of the necessity of keeping a steady flow of weapons and ammunition to the front, and no provisions had been made for either the quick replacement of ordnance or the repair of damaged weapons. General Pershing recognized that the strict adherence to regulations that were applicable to garrison service made it diffi-cult for troops either to obtain supplies or to keep those on hand in serviceable condition. Instead of following the cumbersome procedures developed dur-ing time of peace, orders were given that ordnance should be shipped to the front as needed, using slips of paper as requisitions if necessary.

This shortcut overcame the regulations that made it almost impossible for military units to obtain ordnance equipment in excess of the peacetime al-locations assigned to their commands. Pershing's General Order Number 25 directed that organization commanders who needed ordnance stores were to submit simple lists of the number and kind of articles needed to the proper supply point, Columbus, Dublan, or Namiquipa. The agent at the supply base then issued the supplies that were requested and received a simple receipt. Organization commanders were required to furnish the supply base agent from whom the supplies had been received with certificates of loss, destruc-tion, or damage setting forth the facts in each case. All receipts and certificates were required to be filed with the Officer of Ordnance at each base and to be made part of the permanent record of his office. These simple and reasonable changes resulted in a level of efficiency that made it possible for the Ordnance Department at Columbus to transact its business smoothly and effectively; a volume of business, incidentally, which exceeded that of every arsenal in the United States except for the one at Rock Island, Illinois.

An additional practical lesson the Expedition learned was that the succe-ssful maintenance of a large force in the field depended on a smoothly working base of communications. Unfortunately, just as little thought had been given to the logistics of the Expedition in its beginning, the Army's textbooks and regulations furnished little information on the organization and management of a base. Not only was it necessary for all supplies and replenishments to pass through the base, but newly arrived personnel of every description had to be fed, housed, and equipped during their stay. The lessons that were neither taught by the Army's texts nor covered in its regulations had to be learned by trial and error once the base had been established. The task of bringing the early efforts at Columbus up to the necessary level of efficiency fell to Lieutenant Colonel Charles S. Farnsworth, 16th Infantry, who received his orders from General Pershing on June 14, 1916.

On June 19 Farnsworth relieved base commander Major William R. Sample, 20th Infantry, and assumed command of the base. Present for duty were 61 officers and 1,070 enlisted men, not counting the 5 regimental bands on hand. Units represented were the 2nd Battalion, 17th Infantry; 1st Aero Squadron; 1st New Mexico Infantry; Base Ordnance Depot; Base Engineer Depot; Signal Corps Detachment; Base Quartermaster Depot; Bakery Company No. 2, and the bands of the 5th, 11th, and 13th Cavalry, and of the 17th and 24th Infantry. On July 2 the 2nd Massachusetts Infantry arrived with 52 officers and 921 enlisted men; by July 16 its enlisted ranks had grown to 1,442.

The 2nd Massachusetts Infantry reported for duty well-equipped, and with virtually no prodding from the Regular Army, its officers and men rapidly improved in efficiency. A schedule of training was established and covered those subjects deemed necessary to equip the Guardsmen for service along the border: practice marches, camping, drills, outpost details, field problems for both day and night, construction of semipermanent camps, and thorough target practice with rifles, machine guns, and the new Colt .45 pistol. A number of Guard officers and men were integrated into regular Army Staff Departments at the base in order to provide practical experience that otherwise the Guardsmen would have missed.

Lieutenant Colonel Farnsworth was aware of the friction that sometimes arose between Regulars and Militia when they were on active duty together, and he made every effort to forestall any conflicts that would be detrimental to discipline and morale. He realized, for instance, that the commanders of both National Guard regiments at Columbus were senior in rank to the Base Commander (both were full Colonels). All orders given to the Guard regiments by the Base Commander were therefore given by Farnsworth as the personal representative of the Commanding General. This end run around the chain of command was accepted by the Militia Colonels in what Farnsworth called true soldierly spirit, and a potentially disruptive situation was avoided.

The other National Guard regiment called to duty and ordered to Columbus, the 1st New Mexico Infantry, was a different story. Ordered to mobilize in May, the regiment had on June 19 only 9 officers and 196 enlisted men mustered into Regular service. A large number of the personnel in the regiment, 4 officers and 427 enlisted men, were rejected for active service because of physical defects. Efforts by recruiting parties were made across the state to secure the needed numbers, but it wasn't until July 14 that sufficient men were enlisted to permit the mustering of the regiment as a unit. The regiment was so poorly equipped and had had so little training that it was of no immediate value as a military component. It was therefore transferred to the New Mexico Border Patrol District on July 15 by order of the Commanding General of the Southern Department.

On October 3, the 1st New Mexico Infantry was placed once again under the command of the Base Commander at Columbus, and two companies were immediately ordered west to Hachita, New Mexico, for duty and patrol. A thorough plan of instruction was developed for this regiment, and it was effectively implemented until the departure of the 2nd Massachusetts Infantry from Columbus reduced the number of soldiers at the camp by some 1,500 men. The New Mexico regiment, never over 752 men active and present, replaced the 2nd Massachusetts for widespread outpost and guard duty at the base. The new assignment meant that the under-strength New Mexico guardsmen would be responsible for the work previously done by 1,500 men. This not only interfered dramatically with the plan of instruction established for the unit while it had been in Hachita, but also contributed to the regiment's rather sorry disciplinary record.

New Mexico's 1st Infantry as organized in Columbus was an undersized regiment of poorly trained recruits, and it predictably suffered from all the more or less petty infractions of rules and regulations found among men inexperienced in the manners and mores of the military. The February 5, 1917, report of the Expedition's Judge Advocate provided an almost picture perfect assessment of the 1st Infantry. The largest number of offences committed (21) came under the category of Offences by Guards: Leaving Post, Sleeping on Post, Quitting Guard, Sentinel Sitting Down on Post, and Sentinel Permitting Prisoner Escape. There were 17 unauthorized absences (absent without leave; failure to attend drill and/or roll call), 11 offences against military duty (hiring replacement to perform duty, sleeping on duty, malingering), 10 offences connected to intoxication liquors (drunk on duty; drunk in camp), and 10 offences against Constituted Authority (disobedience of standing orders, disrespect to a sentinel, disrespect to a noncommissioned officer). Of the total number of Summary Court trials held in Columbus in January 1917 (157) the total for New Mexico's 1st Infantry was 106.

The large number of Summary Court trials noted in the month of January 1917 was most likely the result of the realization that the Expedition was for all practical purpose over, and the resulting desire on the part of the guardsmen to be released. The picture that emerges from the sources is that of a regiment inadequately trained, bored with its duties, indifferent to the subtleties of military protocol, and too close to home to resist the temptations of an unauthorized visit to family and friends. The ban on alcohol and drugs in both the camp and the community, while enforced by the Provost Guard, was not totally effective and boredom and frustration sought release in both. The Provost Guard was commanded by 1st Lieutenant J. H. McHughes of the 1st New Mexico Infantry (in civilian life a member of New Mexico's Mounted Police), and his familiarity with the officers and men of the regiment made his job both easier and more effective. The construction of a Stockade made it possible to separate the troublemakers from the general population.

The Stockade as immediately structured had room for 190 in the Main Stockade, 50 in the Mexican Stockade, and 190 in the messing facilities. The general plan, aborted by the end of the Expedition, provided for separated areas for general prisoners, garrison prisoners serving sentences, garrison prisoners not sentenced, and prisoners of war. The idea of the Stockade's structure was to permit each group of prisoners access to the mess facilities without contact with or interference from the other inmates. Prisoners of war were to be given special housing and isolated from the general prison population, but no problem was encountered at Columbus as the number of Villista prisoners never exceeded twenty-two.

In addition to the facilities at the Base already described, the following were quickly organized: an Ordinance Depot, a Medical Group, an Engineer Depot, a Quartermaster Depot, a Remount Depot, a Property Storage Facility, a Mustering Office, an Intelligence Office, a Military Post Office, a United States Customs Service, a Western Union Telegraph Office, and a Young Men's Christian Association.

The YMCA established a branch in Columbus and with the assistance of the Base Commander soon had a large building completed. The Army personnel and civilian employees attended in large numbers and soon an addition was necessary. The entertainment facilities were improved, daily band concerts were held at the Base, and athletic activities were organized, all of which contributed much to the morale of both the troopers and the military's civilian employees. The number of civilians employed as mechanics, clerks, and laborers reached nearly 1,100 by late 1916. The men were away from their families, had little to do in the evenings, and were a source of concern for both the Army and the town authorities. Small wonder, then, that the YMCA was seen a something of a godsend.

The large and growing presence of the Army in Columbus attracted the usual assortment of social lowlifes: bootleggers, gamblers, drugpushers, pimps, and prostitutes. Prohibition of alcohol had earlier been voted for by the town's citizens, and the Army requested and was granted an ordinance, which forbade the sale of "near beers" and similar drinks. This did a great deal to reduce drunkenness and disorderly conduct, and since Columbus had no jail, arrangements were made for civilian offenders to be placed in the stockade until the cases were decided by the civil authorities. The town authorities and the Army's Provost Guard worked in close cooperation to obtain convictions against bootleggers, smugglers, drug dealers, and gamblers who were attracted to the area by the presence of so many soldiers and civilian workers.

The town government set aside designated lots outside of both the town limits and the base camp as designated areas for prostitution. Rather than attempt to eliminate the presence of prostitutes, it was deemed more practical to both contain and control the activities of the women. All prostitutes were required to live within the designated area in one of two separate sections; one section was for white prostitutes and the other was restricted to "colored" prostitutes. Existing whorehouses outside the district were closed, and the owners were forced to relocate within the district or get out of town. Medical supervision was maintained in the district, first by a civilian doctor under contract to the Army and later by an Army doctor and staff. The civilian doctor, it was found, took the money from the Army but was so negligent in his duties that instances of venereal disease threatened to become widespread. The doctor was fired, and the Army's medical team took over.

The local authorities and the Army were both under external pressure to do something about the ubiquitous prostitute and all the social ills associated with her. As the days of the frontier waned, prostitution came under closer scrutiny from reform-minded individuals and institutions. In 1913 the American Federation for Sex Hygiene and the National Vigilance Association merged to form the American Social Hygiene Association (ASHA), a blend of reformers and regulationists (the noun *activist* entered the English language shortly thereafter, in 1915). The basic division within the ASHA was between the abolitionists who demanded eradication of what they considered to be *the* great social evil and the sanitarians who wanted to regulate the health of prostitutes in order to curb the spread of venereal disease. The arguments within the ASHA over prostitution soon made their way into the discourse of the general public and within General Pershing's command, both in Mexico and in Columbus, action came down on the side of the sanitarians. Opinion within the Army itself was sharply divided, but as far as Pershing and the Base Commander at Columbus were concerned, the path of regulation, inspection, and control was the most effective program to follow in dealing with the question.

Under the careful supervision of the Base Intelligence Officer and the Provost Guard, the prostitutes were carefully interviewed and the information gathered was recorded and filed with the Base medical office. The individual profile contained the woman's name, her "sporting name" ("Dixie Lee," "Lovie Brown," "Bobbie White"), her age, a brief physical description, and a summary of her time "on the line" in the "sporting life." There were fifty recorded prostitutes, thirty-seven white and thirteen black, who worked in eight houses and a number of assorted cribs. A crib was simply a shed or lean-to that provided a bit of shelter and privacy. Most of the women came from Texas, a few from New Mexico, and one each from Pocatello, Idaho, Cincinnati, Ohio, and New Orleans, Louisiana.

A careful watch was kept over the district with strict enforcement of the orders that prohibited firearms and liquor. Whites were forbidden to enter the "colored" district and blacks were forbidden access to the white district. The entire district was closed each day from midnight until noon; this resulted in the maintenance of order in an area that under other circumstances would have been a center of drunkenness, disorder, and shootings. Given the nature of the trade, however, it was difficult to control the use of alcohol and drugs (usually cocaine and opium). The women found that alcohol livened up their often dreary days, and drugs made having sex with any man off the streets bearable. Despite the best efforts of the Army and the civil authorities, prostitution, alcohol, and drugs formed a triad that was for all practical purposes unbreakable.

A rise in cases of venereal disease reported in December was traced to the cabarets and the dancing girls who worked in them. The Base Commander met with the mayor, T. H. Dabney, and requested the removal of ten of the cabaret girls who were suspected of prostituting themselves after closing hours. Since they were neither registered with the Army nor residents of the prescribed prostitution districts, there was no way of controlling the contraction and spread of venereal disease. The Army's request was approved, and ten of the dancing girls were expelled from Columbus. In the following month or two the venereal sick report was down to its usual low number, and the Army felt its policy of fighting venereal disease through regulation had been vindicated: if the percent of venereal cases is less than in similar locations where no restricted district exists, then the solution has much to commend it and should be given consideration.

Since Columbus had become a Base of Communications in addition to being the Expedition's supply depot, it was necessary to create an infrastructure suitable to the many new responsibilities: visits by General Officers, Members of Congress, and representatives of various departments of the Government, all of whom wanted to inspect the Base and to visit the troops in the field. These dignitaries generally arrived with requests that made it imperative that they be entertained, fed, housed, and transported to the areas they had come to see. The Base Commander was consequently awarded a transportation allowance for these purposes, thus freeing him from the need to divert vehicles already in official use.

At least three daily bulletins were composed from telegraphs received and from the daily newspapers, which came into Columbus by rail. When assembled, the daily bulletins were telegraphed to General Pershing and all station commanders of the Expedition. Pershing, the Adjutant, and the Base Commander were designated censors, and all printed communications sent out from the Base were censored in accordance with detailed instructions developed by the Commanding Officer. Pershing was so concerned with maintaining tight security that he cautioned the Base Commander, Lt. Colonel Farnsworth, about the work of his Intelligence Officer, Captain Van Schaik. The Captain's mess hall indiscretions and his letter writing activities made Pershing question Van Schaik's judgment, and he warned Farnsworth that unless Van Schaik was curbed there would be a new Intelligence Officer in Columbus.

The newspaper correspondents were at first noticeably upset with the censorship to which they were not accustomed. When the reasons for censorship were explained to them, they accepted the restrictions with professional fortitude and demonstrated mature responsibility in putting together their stories. The enlisted correspondents with the Militia regiments were, however, something of a different sort. These men were writing for their hometown papers and at first paid no attention to the rules of censorship. They wrote and sent home any number of wild, improbable, and outrageous tales. Intent on making their bravery, sacrifice, and heroism evident to their friends and neighbors at home, many of their stories were of the "Fighting Alone against the Villista Hordes" variety. Only when their regimental commanders were called in and reminded that the rules of censorship applied to all correspondents did the situation improve. Furthermore, many of the stories, which appeared in the hometown papers and headlined "Columbus, NM" were written either in the comforts of El Paso, Texas, or on the trains that were simply passing through Columbus to a destination elsewhere.

Even today, after the passage of over ninety years, students, scholars, and historians of the Punitive Expedition receive correspondence and e-mails from people researching their family history. They are looking for information about a grandfather or great-uncle who served in their state's National

Guard regiment and fought heroically against Mexican bandits in Chihuahua, Mexico. They would like to get more information because the old newspaper article preserved in the family Bible does not give a very detailed record of their ancestor's service, only that he fought tenaciously in the hostile environment of the desert. When informed of the truth of the matter that no state Militia regiments fought against Villistas in Mexico their disappointment is palpable. Whether they accept the truth or maintain the legend is anyone's guess.

Ten

MYTH, LEGEND, AND REALITY

In ordinary use a myth is simply a fiction, a story made up to explain what is at the time unexplainable. It is a story the substance of which is imaginary and unverifiable, a popular belief or tradition associated with something or someone, which is unfounded in reality. History on the other hand lies beyond myth, on the other side of the fulcrum of legend and the prism of folklore. Legend and folklore are so close to synonymous concepts that they are often used interchangeably, and for our purposes we need not distinguish between the two. A legend stands with one foot in myth and the other foot in history. Legends involve real people, places, and events; the subjects are heroes, battles, and desperate human struggles. Legends are larger than life itself, and often serve to inspire, to arouse, and to unite a people in a common cause. History, on the other hand, is the attempt to reconstruct the past in a methodical and scholarly manner and thus to present the reader with a reliable guide to what actually happened insofar as that is humanly possible. Ideally, the sequence of intellectual progression is from myth through legend to history, but all too often history takes a backseat to legend and on occasion, unfortunately, to myth. Both myth and legend have combined to build almost insurmountable obstacles on the road to truth in regard to Francisco Villa and the Pershing Expedition.

Villa's early life witnessed the advent of the typewriter, the telephone, lino-type, the automobile, the Kodak camera, the first motion pictures, wireless telegraphy, the airplane, and the radio. Each in its way would contribute to

Villa's legend, and oddly enough it was the American press that was responsible for much if not most of the early legend; subsequently many of the myths have been given lives of their own by American writers and, alas, by some historians. In the days before his defeat at Columbus and the subsequent routing of his bands by the Punitive Expedition, Villa had a coterie of journalists wherever he traveled, and he went to great lengths to secure their comfort. In return they provided him with what today would be called "good press," and American public opinion was shaped in a generally favorable direction. Villa instinctively realized that image was everything: it was not *what you were* that mattered but rather what you *seemed to be* that really counted. A recent study of Villa casts him as a canny propagandist: a calculating and effective manipulator of the United States press. This statement stands among the more perceptive observations regarding Pancho Villa and the press.

The early tales of his banditry and cattle raiding provided stories to be told and exaggerated by the cowboys and farm laborers of Chihuahua. Anecdotes of his violent temper and terrible vindictiveness both horrified and fascinated listeners, and narratives of his sexual athleticism were told and retold with great gusto. Villa explained his doctrine of amorous indulgences quite clearly when he said that violence must never be done to women. He recommended marrying them because church marriages did not really mean anything, and the marriage ceremony meant an easy conscience for both parties. He further recommended shooting the priest if he objected. Villa did not, however, always follow his own advice regarding women.

Following his defeat at Horcasitas and the subsequent evacuation of Chihuahua City in late 1916, he captured Camargo and began to execute the captured Carrancistas. A woman approached him and on her knees pleaded for her husband's life. When she was told that her husband had already been shot, she began verbally to abuse Villa. Enraged by her harangue he shot her and then ordered the execution of the ninety Carrancista women taken prisoner. Their bodies were simply heaped in a pile, and perhaps the most lasting image of the atrocity was that of a two-year-old baby laughing and happily playing, his hands full of the blood of his dead mother, on whose body he was sitting. Following Pershing's evacuation of Chihuahua in 1917, Villa sought revenge against the members of the Namiquipa militia, but in anticipation of his arrival they had fled to the mountains. He had their wives assembled and ordered his men to rape them all. A few were spared this hideous treatment, however, as one of his officers offered his protection and ordered his men to shoot anyone who tried to harm them.

In addition to the American newspaper press, both Mexican and American photographers have contributed to Villa's role as a legendary hero. A photographic record unprecedented in the annals of bandit-heroes spread the legend, and motion pictures gave an extraordinary boost to his notoriety. It seems that everywhere Villa went his activities were recorded in both still and motion pictures, many of them as mundane as simply showing the great man sitting on the steps of a train's passenger car. Libraries and archives contain literally thousands of his photos, and today the Internet browsers provide easy access to virtually all of them. He is arguably the most widely recognized Mexican in America, and his picture is often found on the walls of Mexican-American restaurants. Motion pictures about his life and times are now available in both tape and disc formats from major Internet vendors, and it is probably not much of an exaggeration to assert the he has become Mexico's Billy the Kid.

In Mexico hundreds of ballads celebrated Villa as the hero of the common people, and of the four battle hymns of the Revolution, two, *Adelita* and *La Cucaracha*, are associated with Villa and the Division of the North. The ballads were (are) popular songs and poems. They were printed in loose-leaf song booklets or broadsides to be sold in plazas, railroad depots, and marketplaces. The poetry was unsophisticated, often vulgar, and usually popular, particularly among the common people. The melodies were well-known to the point of monotony, and the words were almost always arranged in quatrains. The mood evoked is often one of melancholy with a marked predilection for tragedy and the sad story of an oppressed people and great leaders, who have to offer up their blood in the struggle for human liberties. The events described in the songs are already familiar to the audience, and the ballads' purpose is to celebrate, to glorify, and to bring the listeners into closer touch with the events. Indeed, today the songs are regarded by folklorists as something of a popular history of the Revolution. They are folksongs in the true sense of the phrase, focus attention on a local hero, and overflow with exaggeration and vainglorious boasting. They represent one, perhaps the first, form of twentieth-century revolutionary art. In the songs, the legend grew: The hero of humble origin was raised to an apex of success and then hounded by repeated calamities—which end with that final indignity—the desecration of the hero's grave.

American newspaper press cartoonists had a field day, particularly the Republican papers, which delighted in tweaking President Wilson's pride in an election year. The Chicago *Tribune* portrayed Wilson as the "Word Wizard," hypnotizing Uncle Sam as he says, "Our Mexican policy is working out beautifully. We regard the principle of arbitration as sacred, except on Mondays, Wednesdays and Fridays, and as to our military preparations, we are adequately prepared to demand our rights as long as the ink holds out." The

Peoria *Transcript* and the Newark *Evening News* portrayed a frustrated Uncle Sam trying to swat a flea named "Villa"; in the New York *Tribune* and the New York *Evening Sun* an equally frustrated Uncle Sam unsuccessfully chased a Mexican jumping bean labeled "Villa." Editorial cartoons from around the country portrayed a frustrated and confused Army: in the Brooklyn *Eagle* a cavalryman attacked a cacti patch with his sword hoping to find a Villista; a singed Uncle Sam poured a ladle of water labeled "U.S. Army" on the raging inferno of Mexico. General Pershing was not immune: a widely circulated cartoon showed him tied to a saguaro cactus as Villa danced in front of him, his wounded leg supported by a crutch. Clearly the United States and its Army were helpless and confused when confronted by the wily Villa. For a time the European war had a competitor in the American press, and that competitor was not Carranza or the Mexican Revolution, it was Villa.

Of the many myths that have contributed to the Villa Legend, the most enduring seems to be the Myth of the Cave. In his flight from the fight at Guerrero, the wounded Villa is reported to have sought refuge in a cave (where he remained for two months) high in the Sierra Madre, while his leg healed. One day, the myth has it, he was even able to watch Pershing's troopers march by, and he could hear them as they sang "It's A Long Way to Tipperary." His bodyguards took good care of him and he was able to see Pershing's activities for miles around. Only two men stayed with Villa, according to the myth, both of them his first cousins. With great difficulty, they mounted him on a burro and proceeded to a cave known as Cuevo de Coscomate, where he holed up for two months. The entrance of the cave was concealed by branches and leaves, and his relatives regularly provided him with food and water. From there he was able to watch Pershing's columns riding by one day. No doctor treated his wounds, but Villa slowly recovered, even though (according to most reports) the only treatment he received was when Francisco Beltran, the only one of his commanders who had some knowledge of medicine, dressed his wound with a rudimentary bandage. During the approximately two months that he hid out in the cave, Villa was completely out of touch with his men, which was probably good for his morale. It would certainly not have speeded his recovery had he learned that a significant part of the small group that had remained loyal to him had been wiped out. The cave myths may have had their origin with William Randolph Hearst's newspapers. The Hearst papers told their readers that Villa from his mountain sanctuary watched the United States Army pass in review every afternoon.

From the evidence taken from Villistas who were interrogated by Pershing's intelligence officers, an almost day-by-day account of Villa's whereabouts was collected, and from the evidence produced by Pershing's spies in

Villa's entourage, we know that Villa was reluctant to commit himself to virtually any enclosure during the period of his flight from the Americans' pursuing columns. To suggest that he would remain in a cave for two months is nonsensical; to suggest that he was in a cave so close to the Americans that he could hear the words of the songs the soldiers sang is absurd. Caves most often have an entrance that is also the exit, and Villa, with his fear of capture and clever instincts for survival, would not have been foolish enough to hide in a potential trap. Furthermore, if Villa *had* hidden in a cave for two months he would have been there from shortly after the time when he was wounded (March 27–28) until near the end of May 1916, and we know that was not the case.

Two other myths in the Villa Legend have been offered to the reading public. The first is that Villa was wounded by Americans and not Carrancistas: he had not been able to stay away from the expedition, according to this myth. It had fascinated him. He kept scouting it, teasing it; and finally it had fetched him a bullet above the right knee, putting him out of action for weeks. The second is that Villa had lured the 10th Cavalry into a trap at Carrizal on June 21, 1916. Carrizal was the result of the cunning of General Villa, and his agents had deceived Pershing into believing that Villa could be taken at Carrizal. When part of the 10th Cavalry arrived there, Villa, a few miles away, was watching everything through binoculars. The available evidence supports neither myth, and it is a mystery to this writer how they got started in the first place. Villa, as we have seen, was wounded at San Ysidro by Carrancistas, or as some suggested by one of his own men. As for the Carrizal myth, by June 16 Villa and Beltran along with about thirty men had reached San Juan, six miles north of Cerro Gordo, in Durango. Villa established his headquarters in San Juan and from there attempted to contact and concentrate his scattered forces. He remained there, over 300 miles from Carrizal, until June 27 when he moved his headquarters to Hacienda de Torreon, 5 miles northeast of Canutillo.

The Cavalry Myth, or how Pancho rode into Mexican legend, began at Celaya, Guanajuato, in 1915. The cavalry of Villa swept down on a surprised Obregón and attacked the entrenched enemy in waves of valiant charges, horsemen against machineguns, until evening broke off the assaults. The following day the Villistas again rode into their own Valley of Death. After more than thirty cavalry charges, they were driven from the field. This pattern of attack, mounted cavalry gallantly charging into the deadly fire of machineguns would become Villa's stock and trade, repeated again and again. A romantic picture to be sure, but in reality simply untrue. In reality the Villistas developed their tactics under fire from modern machine guns, which made successful cavalry attacks impossible. Instead, they fought as mounted infantry. They left their horses safely behind while they advanced against the enemy, generally at night, under whatever cover they could find.[1] The Cavalry Myth began because the culture of the horse in Mexican cowboy society required it: one cannot compose and sing ballads about a "Centaur of the North" who fights on foot. The characteristics of Villista tactics were simple, and were learned empirically: avoid an open advance in the face of enemy fire, travel and attack under cover of night, use the horse for transportation and where necessary for retreat, and delegate battlefield authority to subordinates. There is no better example of these tactics than in the Villista attack at Columbus.

Another myth contributing to the Villa Legend may be called the Myth of Hostility. It is taken for granted by many (both north and south of the border) that the people of Chihuahua were united both in their support of Villa and in their hostility toward the Punitive Expedition. What is overlooked here is the success General Pershing had in securing the goodwill and cooperation of the Mexican people with whom his forces came into contact. In March the rural population of Chihuahua was hostile and uncooperative; by April attitudes had changed. In Namiquipa many farmers as well as other peasants throughout the Santa María Valley, had collaborated with the Americans, sold them supplies, and, more importantly, provided military intelligence, which aided U.S. forces. Bandit bands were dispersed, and men who had gone to Columbus were apprehended.[2] In addition to the cooperation just described, in May the Namiquipa militia was formed with 155 members. A similar peasant militia was formed in Cruces. Namiquipa's civil guard contained a significant number of the heads of prominent families, and they actively assisted American forces in arresting a number of local Villistas who had been among the raiders at Columbus. Militia were also formed in Bachineva, Guerrero, Madera, Temósachic, Santo Tomás, Matachic, San Isidro, Tosanáchic, and Bocoyna, Even after the American troops were pulled out of the Guerrero district, the militia provided Pershing with military intelligence.

By the end of the twentieth century, Villa had been characterized as a romantic hero, as a vengeful bandit, and as a social idealist. In 1993 a documentary, "The Hunt for Pancho Villa," was aired on Public Broadcasting's "The American Experience," and received reviews entitled: "The Long Hard Hunt for Pancho Villa," "U.S. Chased Villa into Mythology, Filmmaker Says," and "PBS Does Bang-up Job in Villa Documentary." The misconception of the Expedition's purpose as a mission to get Villa dead or alive is itself alive and well. His latest biographer presents Villa as a patriot who, in his attack on Columbus, attempted to sabotage an agreement he believed existed between

President Wilson and First Chief Carranza that would have made Mexico an American protectorate. There was no such agreement, but the myths, the legends, and the folklore surrounding Villa have made him a hero or a villain for all seasons, and one is free to make of him what one wants him to be. It is easy to believe that conspiracies existed to take Mexico's treasures of oil, minerals, and land. American capital had invested in oil (Vera Cruz, Tampico), minerals (Cusihuriáchic), and land (William Randolph Hearst's vast ranchlands in Chihuahua), and have we not been told by generations of economic determinists that the flag always follows capital investment? Herein resides in part the difficulty in assessing the Punitive Expedition.

Legend is the comfort food of the past. It feeds our need to have stories that speak of our strengths, not of our weaknesses. It nourishes our pride and gives sustenance to our need for dignity. It is a source of reassurance in the face of adversity. The truth is the first casualty of legend because the truth is not always what we want it to be, and the legends we embrace are always what we want them to be. If, however, we look beyond the fog of myth and the haze of legend, and beyond the folklore of ballads, we see a different story. The naked truth was that Pershing harassed Villa closely, killed his chief officers as well as most of his men, and kept him on the run. Only in legend did Pancho Villa personify the Lion of the North. By the end of May 1917 there was not one band of the original Columbus raiders that contained more than a handful of men. They were dispersed and demoralized. The Expedition had carried out its orders with great effectiveness in a period of two months. This truth, too, has become a casualty of legend.

If failure must be attached somehow to the Punitive Expedition, then let it be attached where it belongs: President Wilson's failed policy of attempting to use the Expedition as a lever with which to gain the de facto government's acceptance of his policies toward revolutionary Mexico. Until American troops were withdrawn from Mexico, First Chief Carranza's government persistently refused to discuss policies of primary concern to Wilson: securing border stability, compensation for American financial losses, and the nature and location of future commissions to discuss issues of mutual concern. Wilson's desire to gain some degree of control over the course of the Mexican Revolution had been successfully impeded by Carranza's strong message of Mexican nationalism, and his December decision to withdraw American forces from Mexico was delayed until he could find a plausible reason to offer the American people. In January 1917 Carranza's Constitutionalist forces under Generals Eugenio Martínez, Fortunato Maycotte, and Ernesto García gave Wilson his opening, the victory over Villa at Torreón. The defeat of Villa and the growing aggressiveness of the Carrancista forces against the Villistas enabled the

"Via Villa!" The Legend in Art (Palomas, Chihuahua, Mexico 2001) [Jonathan D. Hurst].

President to announce the withdrawal of the Expedition with the assurance that First Chief Carranza was now in control of the situation in northern Mexico and the border would in the future be safe from bandit depredations.

NOTES

1. Jeffrey M. Pilcher, "Pancho Villa Rides into Mexican Legend or, The Cavalry Myth and Military Tactics in the Mexican Revolution," *Military History of the West* 26(1) (Spring 1996): 3.

2. Ana Maria Alonso, "U.S. Military Intervention, Revolutionary Mobilization, and Popular Ideology in the Chihuahuan Sierra, 1916–1917," in Daniel Nugent, ed., *Rural Revolt in Mexico and U.S. Intervention* (San Diego, CA: Center For Mexican-U.S. Studies, 1988), 216.

EPILOGUE

The Punitive Expedition left a strange, perhaps singular, legacy to American history. It was not part of the earlier jingoist, Kiplingesque, "imperialist" epoch of Pacific or Caribbean expansion, which brought the Philippines and Puerto Rico under American control, although many of the men who were a part of the Expedition had been involved in those areas. It was a far cry from earlier incursions into Mexico in pursuit of hostile or rampaging Apaches, although many of the Expedition's officers and men had been key figures in the Southwest Indian Wars. It was, rather, a response to what was seen as a foreign invasion of American territory, the first such invasion since the War of 1812. The civilian and military casualties and the extensive loss of property caused by Villa's raid infuriated the American public, coming as it did at a time of national anxiety over possible involvement in a war in Europe, and prompt action was demanded.

The legacy is one of ambiguity. Newspaper headlines from coast to coast had trumpeted the "Villa Dead or Alive" theme so popular, particularly in the newspapers of William Randolph Hearst, and yet Villa was neither captured nor brought back to New Mexico for trial. The embarrassment of Parral and the fiasco at Carrizal caused a great deal of apprehension over both the Army's leadership and its competence. The Expedition's inactivity and apparent immobility during most of its time in Mexico was perceived by many as proof of its ineffectiveness and of Villa's cleverness; as time passed the enthusiasm generated by the early exploits of Colonel Dodd and the 7th Cavalry waned and the American public became disenchanted. The reasons for Pershing's in-activity were unknown to the public, as were the mind games Carranza and Wilson played with each other. Election year politics and the growing threat of involvement in Europe's war gradually diminished interest in the Expedi-tion in much of the country. When in February 1917 it finally came home and crossed the border at Columbus with neither a clear victory nor with Villa in chains, in the eyes of the nation that spelled defeat.

The legacy for Pershing's protagonists, Villa, Carranza, and Obregón was quite different. They remain classic examples of the aphorism born in the French Revolution of 1789: *Revolution eventually consumes its own.* Carranza was designated as constitutional President the month after the Expedition returned to the United States, but he was soon caught in the tide of revolu-tionary social and political change. As a gradualist Carranza had no sympathy for the demands of workers and peasants, and enthusiastic intellectuals con-sumed by visions of a New Jerusalem left him cold. With the economy in shambles, Zapata in control of Morelos, Villa alive and roaming the North, Carranza found it impossible to govern. He survived until May 1920 when under pressure from a coalition of Sonorans led by Obregón, he looted the national treasury and fled to Veracruz. He died a miserable death on the dirt floor of a hut in the secluded village of Tlaxcalantongo, murdered in a drum-fire of bullets orchestrated by a man to whom he had granted amnesty several weeks earlier.

General Obregón became president in November and faced most if not all of the old problems that constituted the revolution's inheritance: rela-tions with the United States; outside capital investments, particularly in oil; questions of damage claims from Europe and the United States; land and labor reform; the role of the Catholic Church in Mexico's social and political life; the irregular revolutionary military forces and their federal coun-terparts; and, finally, forging a stable government under the new constitu-tion. Despite his successes in bringing some stability to Mexico's revolutionary turmoil, Obregón faced rebellion late in 1923. With aid from the United States and loyal *norteño* soldiers, he crushed the revolt in less than three months. He exacted a terrible revenge upon the rebels, nothing less than a military reign of terror. Rebel generals were swiftly sent before firing squads, and a large part of the army was destroyed. In time these men were replaced by younger officers from the new national military academy, men who had been inculcated with the values of nationalism in place of the legends and lore of the revolution. This may have been Obregón's greatest legacy.

He was succeeded by fellow-Sonoran Plutarco Elías Calles in 1924 but re-mained a power in Mexican national politics until his assassination on July

17, 1928, at the hands of a young artist whose deadly intentions were cloaked beneath the pretext of making a sketch. The artist, José de León Toral, was branded a Catholic fanatic by the press, while others have hinted at a conspiracy directed by Calles himself.

In July 1920 Francisco Villa retired to the *Hacienda de Canutillo*, a large cattle ranch in Chihuahua and Durango states given to him by the government as the price of removing him and his followers from further political involvement in Mexico's affairs. His followers gave up their arms in exchange for a year's wages, and Pancho settled in as a gentleman rancher. He had, however, made too many enemies. He was regarded by men of power as a threat to the delicate status quo. Some contend that he was killed at the order of Obregón and Calles, both of whom feared a possible political resurgence. Others claim he was killed by family members of men he had executed and of women he had raped, a classic case of frontier justice and of family honor. Whichever argument is true, Villa died on July 20, 1923, in a fusillade while driving his car through Parral. The Villa Legend began almost immediately as ballad-singers, filmmakers, mythicists, and assorted scribblers transformed his memory beyond any reasonable recognition. Forty-four years later, when the myth and legend had become history, his name was entered in the Hall of Congress alongside those of Madero and Zapata as a Hero of the Revolution.

General Pershing returned from Mexico with an understanding of the new technological nature of warfare and of the need for a well-organized staff of officers to provide both advice and assistance in the formulation of tactics and strategy. The airplane had given him a picture of the future of reconnaissance. No cavalry unit could scout farther and faster than a single plane. Mechanized transport and wireless communication opened new possibilities for the imaginative commander. He realized that mechanical and technical dependability presented a new challenge, but he remained convinced that his field experience in Mexico had given him a glimpse of the new battlefield. The Expedition had acquainted him with most of the younger officers in the army, and he knew the type of man he wanted on his staff and in command in the field.

Following America's declaration of war against Germany on April 6, 1917, he was selected by President Wilson to organize and command the American Expeditionary Force to France. His choice was a relatively simple one for Wilson: in Mexico Pershing had demonstrated his ability to take orders and carry them out without hesitation and without allowing his personal views to interfere. Once committed to entering the war, Wilson wanted the United States to have a major role in both the war and the peace to follow, and he believed that Pershing's brand of leadership would be an invaluable asset. To that end,

Secretary of War Newton D. Baker gave the new commander of the American Expeditionary Force the assurance that Washington would interfere as little as possible in his, Pershing's, job.

Upon his return from Europe after the war, Pershing unsuccessfully entered the presidential election campaign in 1920 as a Republican dark horse candidate in Nebraska. In 1921 he was made Chief of Staff of the Army and retired in 1924. His health began to fail in 1941 and he entered Walter Reed Hospital where he remained until his death on July 15, 1948, at the age of eighty-eight. He was buried in Arlington Cemetery in a location now called "Pershing Hill."

Clio, the ancient Greek Muse of History, dubbed The Proclaimer, smiles. It was believed that she came to earth from Mount Parnassus on occasion, to visit men she had chosen and to arouse in them a passion for investigating old manuscripts. Under her auspices these men would then write down what they believed had happened. Clio did not tell them, however, that their writings would come into conflict with myth and legend; nor did she tell them that despite all their efforts at bringing the old manuscripts to life, myth and legend would not only survive, would not only endure, but would often win. Clio smiles, and so, too, does Francisco "Pancho" Villa.

APPENDICES

THE CONFERENCE OF THE TWENTY-SEVEN GENERALS[1]

The following are among those known to have attended the Conference:

Arroyo, Isaac
Beltran, Francisco
Beltan, Gregorio
Bracamonte, Pedro F.
Diaz, Pablo
Dominguez, Cruz
Fernandez, José Maria
Garcia, Augustin
Granados, Julian
Gutierrez, Indalecio
Jurado, José Maria
Licon, Rafael
Medinaveitia, Manuel

Ocaranza, Eduardo
Oreales, Porfirio
Orozco, Antonio
Orozco, Porfirio
Pedrosa, Juan
Prieto, José
Reina, Francisco
Reza, Natividad
Reza, Serero
Ruiz, José
Seanez, Pablo

GRAND JURY INDICTMENT OF FRANCISCO VILLA

Sixth Judicial District Court, Luna County
Deming, New Mexico

COUNTY CRIMINAL CASES
#656

STATE OF NEW MEXICO
SIXTH JUDICIAL DISTRICT
COUNTY OF LUNA

In the Sixth Judicial District Court of the State of New Mexico, for Luna County, at the April A.D. 1916 term thereof, holden at the town of Deming, in said county, district and state.

Before the Honorable Edward L. Medler, Judge of the Third Judicial District Courts of the State of New Mexico, within and for the County of Luna in the place and stead of the Honorable Colin Neblitt, Judge of the Sixth Judicial District Courts of the State of New Mexico, in the absence of the said Honorable Colin Neblitt.

The Grand Jurors of the State of New Mexico, taken from the body of the good and lawful men of the County of Luna aforesaid, duly chosen, empaneled [sic], sworn and charged at said April A.D. 1916 term, upon their oaths do present:

That Francisco Villa, late of the County of Luna, in the state of New Mexico, on the ninth day of March, in the year one thousand and sixteen, at the said County of Luna, in the State of New Mexico aforesaid, with force and arms, in deliberately, premeditatedly, of his malice aforethought, and from a deliberate and premeditated design then and there unlawfully and maliciously to effect the death of the said James T. Dean, did make an assault; and that the said Francisco Villa a certain gun, then and there loaded and charged with gunpowder and diverse leaden bullets, which gun he, the said Francisco Villa then and there in his hands had and held, to, at, against and upon the said James T. Dean, then and there unlawfully, feloniously, wilfully [sic], deliberately, premeditatedly, of his malice aforethought, and from a deliberate and premeditated design, then and there unlawfully and maliciously to effect the death of him, the said James T. Dean, did shoot and discharge, and that the said Francisco Villa, with the leaden bullets aforesaid, out of the gun aforesaid, then and there by force of the gunpowder shot and sent forth as aforesaid, him, the said James T. Dean, in and upon the body of him, the said James T. Dean, then and there unlawfully, feloniously, wilfully [sic], deliberately, premeditatedly, of his malice aforethought, and from a deliberate and premeditated design then and there unlawfully and maliciously to effect the death of him, the said James T. Dean, did strike, penetrate and wound, giving to him, the said James T. Dean, then and there, with the leaden bullets aforesaid, so as aforesaid shot, discharged and sent forth out of the gun aforesaid by the said Francisco Villa, in and upon the body of him, the said James T. Dean, one mortal wound, of which said mortal wound, he, the said James T, Dean, then and there died.

And so the Grand Jurors aforesaid, upon their oaths aforesaid, do say: That the said Francisco Villa, him, the said James T. Dean, in manner and form aforesaid, unlawfully, feloniously, wilfully [sic], deliberately, premeditatedly, of his malice aforethought, and from a deliberate and premeditated then and there unlawfully and maliciously to effect the death of said James T. Dean, did kill and murder; contrary to the form of the Statute in such case and provided and against the peace and dignity of the State of New Mexico.

SECOND COUNT

And the Grand Jurors aforesaid, taken from the body of the good and lawful men of the County of Luna aforesaid, duly chosen, impaneled, sworn and charged, as aforesaid, at the term aforesaid, to due presentment make as aforesaid, upon their oaths aforesaid, due further present:

That a person who, and whose name, are to the Grand Jurors unknown, late of the County of Luna, in the State of New Mexico, on the ninth day of March in the year One Thousand Nine Hundred and Sixteen, at the said County of Luna, in the State of New Mexico aforesaid, with force and arms in an upon one James T. Dean, then and there being unlawfully, wilfully [sic], feloniously, deliberately, premeditatedly, of his malice aforethought, and from a deliberate and premeditated design then and there unlawfully and maliciously to effect the death of said James T. Dean, did make an assault; and that the said person, who, and whose name, are, as aforesaid, to the Grand Jurors unknown a certain gun, then and there loaded and charged with gunpowder and divers leaden bullets, which gun he, the said person, who and whose name, are, as aforesaid, to the Grand Jurors unknown, then and there in his hands had and held, to, at, against and upon the said James T. Dean, did shoot and discharge, and that the said person, who, and whose name, are, as aforesaid, to the Grand Jurors unknown, with the leaden bullets aforesaid, out of the gun aforesaid, then and there by the force of the gunpowder shot and sent forth as aforesaid, him, the said James T. Dean, in and upon the body of him the said James T. Dean, then and there unlawfully, feloniously, wilfully [sic], deliberately, premeditatedly, of his malice aforethought, and from a deliberate and premeditated design then and there unlawfully and maliciously to effect the death of him, the said James T. Dean, did strike, penetrate and wound, giving to him, the said James T. Dean, then and there, with the leaden bullets aforesaid, so as aforesaid shot, discharged and sent forth our of the gun aforesaid, by the same person, who, and by whose name are, as aforesaid, to the Grand Jurors unknown, in and upon the body of him, the said James T. Dean, one mortal wound, of which said mortal wound, he, the said James T. Dean, then and there died; and that Francisco Villa, late of the County of Luna, in the State of New Mexico, then and there, unlawfully, wilfully [sic], feloniously, deliberately, premeditatedly, of his malice aforethought, and from a deliberate and premeditated design, then and there unlawfully and maliciously to effect the death of the said James T. Dean, was concerned in, and was present, aiding, helping, abetting and comforting, assisting and maintaining the said person who, and whose name, are, as aforesaid, to the Grand Jurors unknown, the felony of murder aforesaid, in manner and form aforesaid to do and commit.

And so the Grand Jurors aforesaid, upon their oaths aforesaid, do say: That the said Francisco Villa, him, the said James T. Dean, in manner and form aforesaid, unlawfully, feloniously, wilfully [sic], deliberately, premeditatedly, of his malice aforethought, and from a deliberate and premeditated design then and there unlawfully and maliciously to effect the death of the said James T. Dean, did kill and murder; contrary to the form of the Statute in such case made and provided and against the peace and dignity of the State of New Mexico.

> [Signed] *Jas. R. Waddier*
> District Attorney within and for
> Sixth Judicial District of the
> State of New Mexico in and for
> Luna County.

ORGANIZATION OF THE PUNITIVE EXPEDITION[2]

HEADQUARTERS PUNITIVE EXPEDITION, U.S. ARMY,
Columbus, NM, March 14, 1916

General Orders,
No. 1.

1. The forces of this command are organized into a provisional division to be called "Punitive Expedition, U.S. Army."
2. The following staff is announced:

Chief of Staff:	Lt.Col. DeR[DeRosy] C. Cabell, 10th Cav.
Asst. to Chief of Staff:	Captain Wilson B. Burtt, 20th Inf.
Adjutant:	Major John L. Hines, Adj. Gen. Dept.
Intelligence Officer:	Major James A. Ryan, 13th Cavalry
Inspector:	Col. Lucien G. Berry, 4th F.A.
Judge Advocate	Capt. Allen J. Greer, 16th Infantry
Quartermaster:	Major John F. Madden, Qr. Mr. Corps
Surgeon:	Major Jere B. Clayton, Medical Corps
Engineer Officer:	Major Lytle Brown, Corps. of Engrs.
Signal Officer:	Capt. Hanson B. Black, Sig. Corps
Commander of the Base:	Major William R. Sample, 20th Inf.

3. The Provisional Division will consist of:
   (a) First Provisional Cavalry Brigade, Colonel James Lockett, Commanding.
   —Troops
   11th Cavalry   13th Cavalry
   Battery C, 6th Field Artillery (attached)
   (b) Second Cavalry Brigade, Colonel George A. Dodd, Commanding
   —Troops
   7th Cavalry   10th Cavalry
   Battery C, 6th Field Artillery (attached)
   (c) First Provisional Infantry Brigade, Colonel John H. Beacom, Commanding
   —Troops
   6th Infantry   16th Infantry
   Cos. E and H 2nd Battalion of Engineers (attached)
   (d) Ambulance Company No. 7. Field Hospital No. 7.
   (e) Signal Corps Detachments, First Aero Squadron.
   Detachment Signal Corps
   (f) Wagon Companies, Number I and 2.
4. Lieut. Colonel Euclid B. Frick, Medical Corps, will report to the Commanding Officer (Major Sample) as surgeon in charge of Medical Base Group.

DISTANCES FROM COLUMBUS, NEW MEXICO, FOR KEY LOCATIONS IN CHIHUAHUA, MEXICO, REACHED BY THE EXPEDITION FORCES

Boca Chica	40 miles
Casas Grandes	120 miles
El Valle	140 miles
Las Cruces	210 miles
Namiquipa	240 miles
San Geronimo	260 miles
Lake Itascate	272 miles
San Antonio de los Arnales	304 miles
Miñaca	310 miles
Satevó	394 miles
Santa Cruz de Villegas	484 miles
Parral	516 miles

REGARDING CASUALTIES[3]

1. The mission assigned the Punitive Expedition upon taking the field in Mexico was, primarily, to punish Mexicans who under "General" Francisco Villa, participated in the attack on Columbus, New Mexico, March 9, 1916. The material (as distinguished from the political and moral) success of the expedition, therefore, must be measured to a great degree by the casualties inflicted on the Villa followers, who in any form or manner took part in the attack.

2. The difficulty of rendering an accurate statement of casualties due to recognized causes in any campaign should be fully realized; increased difficulties arise in the consideration of the number of the list of loses in this campaign because the Carranzistas, or pretended allies, have successfully concealed information necessary to making this report more thorough and accurate. The difficulties are further increased by the enrolment of a number of Carranzistas and fresh recruits with the Villistas (Columbus raiders) during the course of the operations of the Punitive Expedition and in treating of the casualties incurred it has been found impractical to eliminate them from the total losses incurred.

3. For our purpose, however, in determining the number of casualties, or more strictly speaking, the number of Columbus raiders, who by participating in that raid paid the penalty, it is immaterial whether the casualties arose as a result of encounters with the U.S. troops or Carranzistas; this estimate also includes the capture of Columbus raiders made both by U.S. troops or Carranzistas as by such capture proper punishment can be meted out to them. In the engagements in which Carranzistas or Villistas have joined the Villistas who participated in the Columbus raid against the U.S. troops, these facts have been taken into consideration and allowance in the casualties made therfor [sic].

VILLISTA DETACHMENTS; VILLA'S STAFF AND ESCORT[4]

Colonia Dublan, Mexico
June 30, 1916

Names of Villistas, by detachments, reported to have participated in the attack on Columbus, New Mexico, March 9, 1916.

AGGREGATE

Cervantes	80
[Majority from Namiquipa]	
Pedrosa	40
[Majority from Durango)]	
Lopez	100
[Majority from San Andres]	
Escolta	80
[Majority from Durango]	
Fernandez	60
[Majority from Durango]	
Beltran	125
[Entire detachment from Sonora]	

Aggregate 485

"General" Francisco Villa's Staff and Escort; estimated strength in attack on Columbus, New Mexico, March 9, 1916, eighty; majority were from Durango.

Staff

Colonel	Manuel Vaca
"	Juan Martinez
Lieut. Col.	Sixto Valenzuela
" "	Juan Alvarez
" "	Cipriano Vargas
" "	Antonio Angel
" "	Jesus Baeza
Major	Ysmael Medina
Captain	Juan Valasquez
"	Ernesto Rios
"	Feliz Alamos
Lieut.	Lucio Vaca
"	Anestacio Contreras

Escort

Colonel	Ramon Tarango
"	Mauro Dominguez
Major	Pablo Vasquez
Major	Marcano Chumones
"	Marcus Corral
Captain	Margarito Corral
"	Manuel Sanchez
"	Joquin Velasquez
Lieut.	Anacelto Brecada
"	Jesus Arambula
"	Domingo Moreno
"	Ernesto Rios
"	José Alfaro
"	Raphael Bustimante
"	José Hierro
"	Rosalio Medina
"	Celso Apodaca
"	Santos Morales
"	Jesus Baeza
"	Ysabel Chavez
"	Mariano Jimenez
"	Albarario Marquez
"	Ygnacio Corral
"	Ornesimo Espinoza
"	Jacinto Mahoma
"	José Gonzales
"	Emitario Muńoz
"	Quinino Reyes
Pvt.	Miguel Gryalva
"	Adolpho Lopez
"	_____, Carillo
"	Emiliano Rivera
"	Frederico Mendez
"	Manuel Ariola
"	Rafael Bustamente
"	Eduardo Marques

LIST OF VILLISTAS IN THE COLUMBUS RAID[5]

March 9, 1916

Name	Rank	Residence	Remarks
Abizo, Refugio	Pvt.	Namiquipa	Cervantes' detachment
Acosta, Faustino	"	"	Killed at Tomochic in a brawl with comrades about April 15, 1916
Agapita, N.	Capt.	Sonora	Beltran's detachment
Aguirre, Julian	"	Namiquipa	Killed at Columbus, March 9
Alamos, Felix	"	Iaguna	"Dorado"
Alderete, _____	Col.	Sonora	Beltran's detachment
Alfaro, José	Lieut.	Chihuahua	"Dorado"
Alvarez, Francisco	Pvt.	Durango	"Dorado" captured at El Valle. Convicted by New Mexico Court and hanged, Deming, June 10, 1916
Alvarez, Juan	Lt. Col.	Durango	"Dorado"
Alvarez, _____	"	Sonora	Beltran's detachment
Alviso, Lauro	Pvt.	Namiquipa	Cervantes' detachment
Angel, Antonio	Lt. Col.	Durango	"Dorado" wounded at Tomochic, May 8, 1916
Apodaco, Celso	Lieut.	Namiquipa	"Dorado" held by Carranzistas at Madera
Arambula, Jesus	"	Bachineva	Rios' detachment, former "Dorado"
Arame, Enrique	Pvt.	San Geronimo	Denies reaching Columbus, prisoner since June 16, 1916
Arana, _____	Major	Sonora	Beltran's detachment
Arsola, Manuel	Pvt.	Zacatecas	Killed at Columbus, March 9
Armenta, Pablo	Capt.	Sonora	Beltran's detachment
Arsola, _____	Major	Durango	Pedrosa's detachment
Baca, Dionicio	Pvt.	Cruces	Killed at Columbus, March 9
Baca, Manuel	Pvt.	Santa Clara	With Morales, May 28, 1916
Baca, Concepcion	Pvt.	"	With Morales, May 28, 1916
Baca, Manuel	General	Santo Tomas	Killed at Santo Tomas, April 22, 1916
Baeza, Jesus	Col.	Durango	Killed at Columbus, March 9
Baldaneo, Arcadeo	Capt.	Namiquipa	Wounded at Columbus, March 9
Barron, _____	Capt.	Sonora	Beltran's detachment

Beltran, Francisco	General	"	Killed by Carranzistas, July 15, 1916
Bencome, José	Lt. Col.	Cruces	Wounded at Guerrero, May 25, killed in action El Alamio near Cruces, May 27, 1916
Boncos, Siriaco	Pvt.	Namiquipa	
Bonifacio, Torres	Col.	Durango	Fernandez's detachment
Borciaga, Reyes	Pvt.	Namiquipa	Held by Carranzistas at Madera
Borciaga, Pedro	"	Namiquipa	Held by Volunteer Guard Namiquipa
Breceda, Anceleto	Lieut.	Durango	"Dorado"
Bustamente, Raphael	"	Bachineva	Rios' detachment
Bustillos, Ramon	Pvt.	Namiquipa	Volunteered, captured by Home Guard held in Namiquipa
Caballero, Juan	Lieut.	Durango	Pedrosa's detachment
Caballero, Juan	Capt.	Guadalajara	Fernandez's detachment
Camargo, Alberto	Sgt.	Hidalgo	"Dorado" killed at Guerrero March 27
Carrillo, Trinidad	Lieut.	Durango	Killed at Columbus, March 9
Carrillo, Juan	Pvt.	Durango	"Dorado" from El Valle
Castillo, Antonio	Capt.	Bustillos	"Dorado" killed at Guerrero, March 27
Castillo, José	Lieut.	Ojo Caliente	Killed at Columbus, March 9
Castillo, Juan	Pvt.	Namiquipa	Wounded at Columbus; tried in New Mexico Court, executed June 1916
Cervantes, Candelario	Lt. Col.	Namiquipa	Killed in action, May 25, 1916, at El Alamio, near Cruces
Chavez, Cruz	Lt. Col.	Cruces	Wounded at Columbus, died and buried at Ascencion

COLUMBUS RAIDERS KILLED AND WOUNDED IN ACTION[6]

Colonia Dublan, Mexico
June 30, 1916

NAME	*RANK*	*PLACE*
Acosta, Faustino	Pvt.	Tomochic, April 15, 1916.
Aguirre, Julian	Capt.	Columbus, NM, March 9, 1916.
Areola, Mauel	Pvt.	" " " "
Baca, Deonicio	"	" " " "
Baca, Manuel	Col.	Santo Tomás, April 22, 1916.
Baeza, Jesus	"	Columbus, NM, March 9, 1916.
Beltran, Francisco	Gen.	Corro Blanco, July 15, 1916.
Bencomo, José	Lt. Col.	Alamío, May 25, 1916.
Camargo, Alberto	Sergt.	Guerrero, March 27, 1916.
Crarrilo, Trinidad	Lieut.	Columbus, NM, March 9, 1916.
Castillo, Antonio	Capt.	Guerrero, March 27, 1916.
Castillo, José	Lieut.	Columbus, NM, March 9, 1916.
Cervantes, Candelario	Col.	Alamío, May 25, 1916.
Chavez, Cruz	Lt. Col.	Columbus, NM, March 9, 1916.
Chavez, Ysabel	Lieut.	" " " " "
Cordova, Eugenio	Pvt.	" " " " "
Delgado, Carmen	Capt.	Santa Clara Mountains, June 1, 1916.
Dominguez, Carmen	Col.	Guerrero, March 27, 1916.
Enriquez, _____	"	Columbus, NM, March 9, 1916.
Fierro, Jesus	Lieut.	" " " " "
Francisco, _____	"	" " " " "
Gutierrez, Isador	Pvt.	Picacho, June 2, 1916.
Hernandez, Elijio	Lt. Col.	Guerrero, March 27, 1916.
Hernandez, Francisco	Pvt.	Columbus, NM, March 9, 1916.
Lopez, Pablo	Gen.	Chihuahua City, June 5, 1916.
Marquez, Abalario	Pvt.	La Junta, May 26, 1916.
Ortiz, Carmen	Major	Columbus, NM, March 9, 1916.
Perea, Gabriel	Pvt.	" " " " "
Perez, José Antonio	Lieut.	" " " " "
Perez, Tranquililario	Pvt.	" " " " "
Pissario, Manuel	"	" " " " "
Rascon, José A.	Major	" " " " "
Sanchez, Pablo	Lieut.	" " " " "

Saurez, [Suarez?] Candelario	Capt.	Las Animas, March 19, 1916.
Turango, Ramon	Col.	Guerrero, March 27, 1916.
Vargas, Cipriano	Lt. Col.	Columbus, NM, March 9, 1916.
Vasquez, Pablo	Major	” ” ” ” ”
Angel, Antonio	Col.	Tomochic, May 8, 1916.
Baldaneo, Arcadie	Capt.	Columbus, NM, March 9, 1916.
Castillo, Juan	Pvt.	” ” ” ” ”
Equado, Pedro	”	Guerrero, March 27, 1916.
Gonzales, José	Lieut.	Columbus, NM, March 9, 1916.
Jimenez, Mariano	”	Guerrero, March 27, 1916.
Marquez, Trinidad	Pvt.	Columbus, NM, March 9, 1916.
Pedrosa, Emilio	Major	Guerrero, March 27, 1916.
Pedrosa, Juan	Gen.	” ” ” ”
Perea, Francisco Antonio	Pvt.	Columbus, NM, March 9, 1916.
Rodriguez, David	Lieut.	” ” ” ” ”
Soto, Antonio	Pvt.	” ” ” ”
Silvino	”	Guerrero, March 27, 1916.
Tena, Fortunato	”	Columbus, NM, March 9, 1916.
Villa, Francisco	Gen.	Guerrero, March 27, 1916.
Ybarra, Pedro	Pvt.	” ” ” ”

COLUMBUS RAIDERS WHO SURRENDERED TO CARRANZISTA FORCES[7]

Fourteen of the Columbus raiders can be accounted for by name who surrendered to the Mexican military authorities and were held in confinement by them. Since the entry of U.S. troops in Mexico, many other Columbus raiders have accepted amnesty from the Carranzista government and are now under its protection. No other information is available on the subject. The following is a list of names of Villistas [who] surrendered to the Carranzista authorities, at Madera, in order to escape capture by the U.S. troops.

NAME	*RESIDENCE*
Apodoca, Selco	Namiquipa
Reyes, Bociaga	"
Simon, Castillo	"
Rascon, Emeregildo	"
Quirino, Reyes	"
Treviso, Lauro	"
Navarez, Miguel	"
Felix, Pias	"
Blas, Ramire	"
Nevarez, Jesus José	"
Marcus, Gregorio	"
Marcus, Trinidad	"
Montes, Pedro	"
Santos, Moreles	"

CASUALTIES AMONG COLUMBUS RAIDERS[8]

The aggregate of known casualties among Villistas who participated in the attack on Columbus, since March 9, 1916, killed or captured by the U.S. Troops and Carranzistas, is as follows:

Columbus, New Mexico	69
Las Animas, March 19, and Namiquipa	7
Battle of Guerrero, March 27	15
Battle of Guerrero, March 29	46
Engagement at Aguas Calientes, April 1	3
Engagement at La Cienegitta, April 3	26
Skirmish in the vicinity of La Joyo, about April 10	7
The engagement at Verde River and Green Road	4
Battle of Tomochic, April 22	25
Ojos Azules	42
Los Alamios, May 25	2
Santa Clara Cañon, June 10	2
Prisoners held by Carranzistas	14
Prisoners held by the United States	19
Total	281

CASUALTIES AMONG THE LEADERS OF THE COLUMBUS RAIDERS[9]

As a matter of reference and interest a list has been compiled of the names of leaders who participated in the attack on Columbus, NM, on March 9, 1916, and those who have been reported killed or wounded at the places and on the dates indicated.

"General"	Francisco Villa	Wounded at Guerrero, March 27.
"	Juan Pedroza	" " " " "
"	Pablo Lopez	Captured near Santa Ysabel and executed at Ciudad Chihuahua.
"	Francisco Beltran	Killed at Cerro Gordo, July 16, 1916.
"Colonel"	Mauel Baca	Killed at Santo Tomás, April 22.
"	Ramon Tarango	Killed at Guerrero, March 29.
"	Candelario Cervantes	Killed at Alamio, May 25.
"	Enriquez	Killed at Columbus, March 9.
"	Mauro Dominguez	Killed at Guerrero, March 27.
"	Alberto Camargo	Killed at Guerrero, March 27.
"	Antonio Castillo	Killed at Guerrero, March 27.
"	Elisio Alvarez	Captured at Estado, April 7, reported executed by General Cavazos.
"Lt.Col."	Pablo Sanchez	Killed at Columbus, March 9.
"	Cruz Chavez	" " " " "
"	Carmen Ortiz	" " " " "
"	Elijio Hernandez	Killed at Guerrero, March 27.
"	Cipriano Vargas	Killed at Columbus, March 9.
"	José Bencome	Killed at Alamio, May 25.
"Major"	Emilio Pedrosa	Wounded at Guerrero, March 27.
"	Pablo Vasquez	Killed at Columbus, March 9.
"	Pablo Chavez	" " " " "
"	Trinidad Castillo	" " " " "
"	Jesus Baeza	" " " " "
"Captain"	Francisco	" " " " "
"	Francisco Antonio Perez	" " " " "
"	Silvino Sato	Wounded at Guerrero, March 27.
"	José Gonzales	Wounded at Columbus, March 9.
"	Arcadio Baldanio	Wounded at Columbus, March 9, 1916.
"	Julian Aguirre	Killed at Columbus, March 9.

COLUMBUS RAIDERS TAKEN PRISONER IN MEXICO[10]

The following is a list of nineteen names of prisoners held in confinement by the U.S. Troops on June 30, 1916, who admitted having participated in the attack on Columbus, New Mexico, on March 9, 1916.

NAME	*RESIDENCE*
Burciaga [sic] Borciaga, Pedro	Namiquipa
Bustillos, Ramon	"
Camarena, Tomás	Cruces
Chavez, Guadalupe	Namiquipa
Gutierrez, Lorenzo	San Andres
Herras, Francisco	Namiquipa
Jimenez, Mariano	San Luis Potosi
Lopez, Pedro	Mexico City
Marqunez [sic] Marquez, José de la Luz	Rancho Rivera
Mejia, Francisco	Jalisco
Mesa, Juan	Sonora
Monoz [sic] Muñoz, Juan	Namiquipa
Tena, Jese [sic] José	"
Rodriguez, David	"
Rodriguez, Raphael	"
Solis, Francisco	"
Torres, Juan	"
Torres, Santos	"
Vargas, Silvino	Cruces

Columbus raiders held in confinement by U.S. troops; Camp near Colonia Dublan, Mexico, June 30, 1916 [National Archives].

DISPOSITION OF THE REMAINS OF DECEASED OFFICERS, ENLISTED MEN, AND CIVILIANS[11]

The organization of the Burial Corps consisted of a chief embalmer and such laborers, or assistants, as were from time to time required. On June 4, 1916, the Burial Corp made its first trip into Mexico, and subsequent trips were made as directed by the Commanding General of the Expedition. The final trip was made on December 5, 1916, and returned to Columbus, New Mexico, on February 5, 1917.

The records indicate that the remains of thirty-one persons were recovered and transported by truck from Mexico to Columbus, where they were prepared for shipment in accordance with regulations and the instructions of the next of kin.

The remains of the following are still in Mexico, interred as follows:

NAME AND UNIT	BURIED AT
Saddler Ralph A. Ray, Troop "L" 7th Cavalry	Minaca
Private Kirby, Troop "M" 11th Cavalry	Lajoya
Private Oliver Boushe, Troop "H" 7th Cavalry	Minaca
Saddler Hudnall, Troop "B" 10th Cavalry	Musica
Private Herbert Ledford 13th Cavalry	Santa Cruz de Villagas
Civilian Scout D. H. Holly	El Rubio

EXPENDITURES FOR THE EXPEDITION, MARCH 17, 1916 TO FEBRUARY 10, 1917[12] (in dollars)

Pay of the Army, 1916	349,629.39
Pay of the Army, 1917	1,300,380.22
Army Deposit Fund	47,843.81
Quartermaster Corps, 1916	514,960.03
Quartermaster Corps, 1917	1,070,999.44
Barracks and Quarters, 1916	3,512.68
Miscellaneous	323.58
Bills due for supplies	31,537.74
	Total: 3,287,649.82

NOTES

1. RO, 5. National Archives, "Report of Operations of 'General' Francisco Villa Since November 1915, Headquarters Punitive Expedition in the Field, Mexico, July 31, 1916" (hereinafter cited as RO).

2. *ROPE*, 4–5.

3. *ROPE*, Appendix, "Statement of Casualties among Villistas Who Participated in the Attack on Columbus, New Mexico, March 9, 1916."

4. *ROPE*, Appendix, Exhibit "B."

5. *ROPE*, Exhibit "A," Colonia Dublan, Mexico, June 30, 1916.

6. *ROPE*, Appendix, Exhibit "C."

7. *ROPE,* Appendix, 5–6.

8. *ROPE,* Appendix, 7.

9. *ROPE,* Appendix L, 96.

10. *ROPE,* Appendix, 6. Following a brief trial, eighteen of these men were incarcerated in the New Mexico State Penitentiary, Santa Fe, New Mexico. Their prison photos are in the Appendixes. For more about them see James W. Hurst, "The Villista 19," *The Villista Prisoners of 1916–17* (Las Cruces, NM; Yucca Tree Press, 2000), 35–40.

11. Record Group 407, National Archives and Records Service, College Park, Maryland, Adjutant General's Office, Central Decimal Files Bulky Files 1917–1925, Mexican Expedition 370.22, Box 2020.

12. Record Group 407, National Archives and Records Service, College Park, Maryland, Adjutant General's Office, Central Decimal Files Bulky Files 1917–1925, Mexican Expedition 370.22, Box 2020.

BIBLIOGRAPHY

ARCHIVES AND MANUSCRIPT COLLECTIONS

National Archives and Records Service, Washington, DC and College Park, Maryland

Record Group No. 94, Records of the Adjutant General's Office, 1780–1917. *General Funston's Annual Report for the Southern Department, 1916.*

Record Group 120, Box 2F. World War I Organization Records: Punitive Expedition to Mexico, "Report of Colonel Slocum of Columbus Raid."

Record Group No. 165, Box 138, Records of the Adjutant General's Office, 1780–1917, Report No. 13137. *Memorandum: Office of the Chief of Staff,* "Office of the Chief of Staff Correspondence, 1907–1919."

———. *Memorandum: Intelligence Section, Headquarters, Punitive Expedition, U.S. Army, in Camp Near Colonia Dublan, Mexico, September 1, 1916.* War Department, War Plans Division, 1919.

———. Military Intelligence Division Correspondence, 1913–1941.

Record Group 395, Entry 1218, DF 144, 1–7, Base Intelligence Office Report, "Prostitutes in Columbus, New Mexico."

Record Group 407, Records of the Adjutant General's Office, Central Decimal Files, Bulky Files, 1917–1925, Mexican Expedition, 370.22, Box 2020.

    1) Final Report of the Division Surgeon, Punitive Expedition, U.S. Army, Folder I.

    2) Final Report of Major Frank C. Baker, Medical Corps, U.S. Army, Folder I.

    3) Final Report of William R. Eastman, Medical Corps, U.S. Army, Folder I.

4) Final Report of the Judge Advocate, Punitive Expedition, Palomas, Mexico, February 5, 1917.

Library of Congress

Pershing Papers, Box 372, Folder 1. Clarke, Walter L (Major). "Final Report of the Signal Corps Troops with the Punitive Expedition," Columbus, New Mexico, February 6, 1917.

Pershing Papers, Box 372, Folder 2, Part 1. "Data Relating to the Criminal Life of Francisco Villa."

Pershing Papers, Box 372, Folder 1. Kromer, Leon B. (Captain). "Report of the Quartermaster, Punitive Expedition into Mexico for the Period July 1, 1916 to February 5, 1917."

Pershing Papers, John J. Pershing "Scrapbooks," Conts. 381–384; 385–387, Mss. 19,612, Reels 1 and 2.

Pershing Papers, Box 372. "Report of Operations, Base of Communications, Mexican Punitive Expedition, June 19, 1916 to February 5, 1917," Columbus, New Mexico, February 12, 1917.

Pershing Papers, Box 372. "Report of the Quartermaster, Punitive Expedition into Mexico for the Period July 1, 1916 to February 4, 1917."

Pershing Papers, Box 372, Folder 3. "Special Application of the Plans of the Quartermaster Corps for Operations along the Border and in the Interior of Mexico," War Department, Office of the Quartermaster General of the Army, Washington, March 21, 1916.

Government Documents

Department of State. *Papers Relating to the Foreign Relations of the United States, 1915.* Washington, DC: Government Printing Office, 1924.

———. *Papers Relating to the Foreign Relations of the United States, 1916.* Washington, DC: Government Printing Office, 1925.

———. *Papers Relating to the Foreign Relations of the United States, 1917.* Washington, DC: Government Printing Office, 1926.

Library of the United State Army Sergeants Major Academy, Fort Bliss, Texas. Secret Service Report: "Memorandum for the Chief of Staff," Office of the Chief of Staff, April 21, 1916.

"Report of the Intelligence Section, Headquarters, Punitive Expedition in Camp near Colonia Dublan, September 1, 1916."

"Report of Operations of the First Aero Squadron, Signal Corps," with the Punitive Expedition, USA, March 15 to August 15, 1916.

War Diary, First Aero Squadron, Signal Corps, U.S. Army, March 12–April 23, 1916.

BOOKS

Anderson, Mark Cronlund. *Pancho Villa's Revolution by Headlines*. Norman, OK: University of Oklahoma Press, 2000.

Atkin, Ronald. *Revolution! Mexico 1910–20*. New York: The John Day Company, 1970.

Beede, Benjamin R. *Intervention and Counterinsurgency: An Annotated Bibliography of the Small Wars of the United States*. New York and London: Garland Publishing, Inc., 1985.

Birtle, Andrew J. *U.S. Army Counterinsurgency and Contingency Operations Doctrine 1860–1941*. Washington, DC: Center of Military History, U.S. Army, 1998.

Boot, Max. *The Savage Wars of Peace: Small Wars and the Rise of American Power*. New York: Basic Books, 2002.

Braady, Haldeen. *Pershing's Mission in Mexico*. El Paso, TX: Texas Western Press, 1966.

———. *The Paradox of Pancho Villa*. El Paso, TX: Texas Western Press, 1978.

Calhoun, Frederick S. *Power and Principle*. Kent, OH: Kent State University Press, 1986.

———. *Uses of Force and Wilsonian Foreign Policy*. Kent, OH: Kent State University Press, 1993.

Callahan, James M. *American Foreign Policy in Mexican Relations*. New York: Macmillan Co., 1932.

Calzadiaz Berrera, Alberto. *Contra Todo y Contra Todos: en pos de la Venganza Sobre Columbus, N.M.* Mexico, DF: Editorial Libros de Mexico, SA, 1960; 1963; 1965.

———. *Hechos Reales de la Revolucion*. Mexico: Editorial Patria, SA, 1977.

Canfield, Bruce N. *U.S. Infantry Weapons of the First World War*. Lincoln, RI: Andrew Mowbray Inc., 2000.

Carranza, Alberto S. *La Expedicion Punitiva*. Mexico, DF: Ediciones Botas, 1937.

Cervantes, Federico M. *Francisco Villa y La Revolucion*. Mexico, DF: Ediciones Alonso, 1960.

Chinn, George W. *The Machine Gun*. Washington, DC: U.S. Government Printing Office, 1951.

Clendenen, Clarence C. *Blood on the Border: The United States Army and the Mexican Irregulars*. London: Macmillan Co., 1969.

———. *The United States and Pancho Villa: A Study in Unconventional Diplomacy*. Ithaca, NY: Cornell University Press, 1961.

Coffman, Edward M. *The Regulars*. Cambridge, MA: The Belknap Press of Harvard University Press, 2004.

Cooke, James J. *Pershing and His Generals: Command and Staff in the AEF*. Westport, CT: Praeger Publishers, 1997.

Deman, Ralph H. Van. *The Final Memoranda: Major-General Ralph H. Van Deman, USA, Ret., 1865–1952, Father of U.S. Military Intelligence*. Ralph W. Weber, ed. Wilmington, DE: Scholarly Resources, 1988.

Farnsworth, Charles S. *Diary of Lt. Colonel Charles Stewart Farnsworth, March 12–June 2–16, 1916.* Santa Fe, NM, Palace of the Governors History Library.

Finnegan, John P. *Military Intelligence.* Washington, DC: Center of Military History, U.S. Army, 1998.

Fosdick, Raymond B. *Chronicle of a Generation: An Autobiography.* New York: Harper & Brothers Publishers, 1958.

Friedman, Leon. *The Law of War: A Documentary History.* New York: Random House, Inc., 1972.

Funston, Frederick. *Memories of Two Wars: Cuban and Philippine Experiences.* New York: Charles Scribner's Sons, 1911.

Gilderhus, M. T. *Diplomacy and Revolution: U.S.-Mexican Relations under Wilson and Carranza.* Tucson, AZ: University of Arizona Press, 1977.

Goldhurst, Richard. *Pipe Clay and Drill: John J. Pershing: The Classic American Soldier.* New York: Thomas Y. Crowell Company, 1977.

Gonzales, Michael. *The Mexican Revolution 1910–1940.* Albuquerque, NM: University of New Mexico Press, 2002.

Griensen, Armando Camacho. *Elisa Griensen y la nueva Expedición Punitiva en Parral.* Mexico: Chihuahua, Chihuahua, 2001.

Haley, P. Edward. *Revolution and Intervention: The Diplomacy of Taft and Wilson with Mexico, 1919–1917.* Cambridge, MA: MIT Press, 1970.

———. *Revolution on the Border.* Albuquerque, NM: University of New Mexico Press, 1988.

Harris, Charles H., and Louis R. Sadler. *The Archaeologist Was a Spy: Sylvanus G. Morley and the Office of Naval Intelligence.* Albuquerque, NM: University of New Mexico Press, 2003.

———. *The Texas Rangers and the Mexican Revolution: The Bloodiest Decade, 1910–1920.* Albuquerque, NM: University of New Mexico Press, 2004.

Harris, Larry A. *Pancho Villa and the Columbus Raid.* El Paso, TX: McMath Company, 1949.

Horne, Charles F. *Source Records of the Great War.* Indianapolis, IN: The American Legion, 1930.

Howe, Jerome W. *Campaigning in Mexico.* Tucson, AZ: Arizona Pioneers Historical Society, 1968.

Hurst, James W. *The Villista Prisoners of 1916–17.* Las Cruces, NM: Yucca Tree Press, 2000.

John J. Pershing: A Selected Bibliography of MHI Sources, United States Army Military History Institute, Reference Branch, August 1989, August 1994.

Justice, Glenn. *Revolution on the Rio Grande: Mexican Raids and Army Pursuits, 1916–19.* El Paso, TX: Texas Western Press, 1992.

Katz, Friederich. *The Life & Times of Pancho Villa.* Stanford, CA: Stanford University Press, 1998.

Knight, Alan. *The Mexican Revolution,* 2 vols. Cambridge: Cambridge University Press, 1986.

———. *U.S.-Mexican Relations, 1910–1940: An Interpretation.* Center for U.S.-Mexican Studies, San Diego, CA: University of California, San Diego, 1987.

Lansford, William D. *Pancho Villa.* Los Angeles, CA: Shelbourne Press, 1965.

Link, Arthur S. *The Higher Realism of Woodrow Wilson and Other Essays.* Nashville, TN: Vanderbilt University Press, 1971.

———. *The Papers of Woodrow Wilson.* Princeton, NJ: Princeton University Press, 1981.

———. *Wilson: Campaigns for Progressivism and Peace.* Vol. 5. Princeton, NJ: Princeton University Press, 1965.

———. *Wilson: Confusions and Crises.* Vol. 4. Princeton, NJ: Princeton University Press, 1964.

Lister, Florence C., and Robert H. *Chihuahua: Storehouse of Storms.* Albuquerque, NM: University of New Mexico Press, 1966.

Mexican Punitive Expedition, 1916–17: A Bibliography of MHI Sources, United States Military History Institute, Reference Branch, July 1989, March 1992, November 1994.

Mexican Revolution, 1911–1921: A Working Bibliography of MHI Sources, United States Army Military History Institute, Reference Branch, October 1988.

O'Conner, Richard. *Black Jack Pershing.* Garden City, NY: Doubleday, 1961.

Ogg, Frederick A. *National Progress 1907–1917.* New York and London: Harpers & Brothers, 1918.

Palmer, Frederick. *Newton D. Baker, America at War*, 2 vols. New York: Dodd, Mead & Company, 1931.

Patton, George. *Patton Papers I: 1885–1940.* Martin Blumenson, ed. Boston, MA: Houghton Mifflin Company, 1972.

Pershing, John J., Major General. *Punitive Expedition Report*, Colonia Dublan, Chihuahua, Mexico, October 10, 1916, Carlisle Barracks, PA: Army War College.

Peterson, Jessie, and Thelma Cox Knoles. *Pancho Villa: Intimate Recollections of People Who Knew Him.* New York: Hastings House, 1977.

Plana, Manuel. *Pancho Villa and the Mexican Revolution.* New York and Northampton: Interlink Books, 2002.

Rodney, George Brydges. *As A Cavalryman Remembers.* Caldwell, ID: Caxton Printers, 1944.

Sandos, James A. *Rebellion in the Borderlands and the Plan of San Diego, 1904–1923.* Norman, OK: University of Oklahoma Press, 1992.

Scott, Hugh L. *Some Memories of a Soldier.* New York: Century Publishers, 1928.

Slattery, Matthew T. *Filipe Angeles and the Mexican Revolution.* Dublin, IN: Prinit Press, n.d.

Smith, Robert Freeman. *The United States and Revolutionary Nationalism in Mexico, 1916–1932.* Chicago and London: University of Chicago Press, 1972.

Smythe, Donald. *Guerilla Warrior: The Early Life of John J. Pershing.* New York: Scribner's, 1973.

Stout, Joseph A., Jr. *Border Conflict: Villistas, Carrancistas, and the Punitive Expedition, 1915–1920.* Fort Worth: Texas Christian University Press, 1999.

Taibo II, Paco Ignatio. *Pancho Villa: Una Biografia Narrativa.* Colonia Florida, Mexico, D.F.: Editorial Planeta Mexicana, 2006.

Thomas, Robert S., and Inez V. Allen. *The Mexican Punitive Expedition under Brigadier General John J. Pershing.* Washington, DC: War Histories Division, Department of the Army, 1954.

Tomkins, Frank (Col.). *Chasing Villa: The Last Campaign of the U.S. Cavalry.* Silver City, NM: High-Lonesome Books, 1996.

Toulman, H. L., Jr. *With Pershing in Mexico.* Harrisburg, PA: Telegraph Press, 1935.

Tuck, Jim. *Pancho Villa and John Reed: Two Faces of Romantic Revolution.* Tucson, AZ: University of Arizona Press, 1985.

Wilke, James W., and Albert L. Michaels. *Revolution in Mexico: Years of Upheaval, 1910–1940.* Tucson, AZ: University of Arizona Press, 1984.

ARTICLES

Adams, Cyrus C. "Northern Mexico, the Scene of Our Army's Hunt for Villa." *Review of Reviews* 53(April 1916): 137–138.

Alonso, Ana María. "U.S. Military Intervention, Revolutionary Mobilization, and Popular Ideology in the Chihuahuan Sierra, 1916–1917." *Rural Revolt in Mexico and U.S. Intervention.* Daniel Nugent, ed. San Diego, CA: Center for U.S.-Mexican Studies, University of California, San Diego, 1988.

"Apache Scouts in the Punitive Expedition." *Huachuca Illustrated* 1(1993): 1–5.

Bidwell, Bruce W. "History of the Military Intelligence Division, Department of the Army, General Staff, 1775–1941." Contract study, Georgetown University, 1959.

Blumenson, Martin. "Patton in Mexico: The Punitive Expedition." *American History Illustrated* 12(October 1977): 34–42.

"Border Spy Network." *Huachuca Illustrated* 1(1993): 1–3.

Braady, Haldeen. "Dr. Husk on Pancho Villa." *Western Review: A Journal of the Humanities* 2(Spring 1964): 50–54.

———. "General Scott on Pancho Villa." *Password* 13(2) (Summer 1968): 3–4.

———. "Myths of Pershing's Mexican Campaign." *Southern Folklore Quarterly* 27(3) (September 1963): 181–195.

———. "Pancho Villa at Columbus: The Raid of 1916." *Southwestern Studies* 3(1) (Spring 1965): Monograph No. 9, 1–44.

———. "Pancho Villa: The Making of a Modern Legend." *The Americas* 21(1) (July 1964): 146–162.

Braady, Haldeen, and John H. McNeely. "Francisco Villa in Folk-Songs." *Arizona Quarterly* 10(1) (Spring 1954): 5–16.

"Carranza Mentions the Door." *Literary Digest* (June 10, 1916): 1689–1690.

"Carranza's Cry of 'Halt.'" *Literary Digest* (April 22, 1916): 1134–1135.

Clendenen, Clarence C. "The Punitive Expedition of 1916: A Re-Evaluation." *Arizona and the West* 3(4) (Winter 1961): 311–320.

Cramer, Stuart W. "The Punitive Expedition from Boquillas." *The Cavalry Journal* 27(112) (November 1916): 200–227.

Cumberland, Charles C. "Border Raids in the Lower Rio Grande." *Southwestern Historical Quarterly* 57(3) (January 1954): 285–311.

Dallum, Samuel F. "The Punitive Expedition of 1916." *The Cavalry Journal* 36(148) (July 1927): 382–398.

Elser, Frank B. "General Pershing's Mexican Campaign." *Century* 99(February 1920): 433–447.

———. "Pershing's Lost Cause." *The American Legion Monthly* (July 1932): 14–15, 44–47.

Evans, Ellwood W. "Cavalry Equipment in Mexico." *Cavalry Journal* 27(November 1916): 171–182.

"Field Notes from Mexico and Border." *Cavalry Journal* 27(November 1916): 171–182.

Fleming, Lawrence J. "The Automatic Pistol in the Punitive Expedition." *The Cavalry Journal* 27(114) (April 1917): 497–514.

Fuentes, Andrés Reséndez. "Battleground Women: Soldaderas and Female Soldiers in the Mexican Revolution." *The Americas* 51(4) (April 1995): 525–553.

"Funston and Pershing, the Generals in Charge of the Chase after Villa." *Current Opinion* 60(May 1916): 318–320.

Furman, Necah S. "Vida Nueva: A Reflection of Villista Diplomacy, 1914–1915." *New Mexico Historical Review* 53(2) (April 1978): 171–192.

Gerlach, Allen. "Conditions along the Border—1915: The Plan of San Diego." *New Mexican Historical Review* 43(3) (July 1968): 195–212.

Gilliam, Ronald R. "Turning Point of the Mexican Revolution." *Military History Quarterly* 15(3) (Spring 2003): 40–51.

Hager, William M. "The Plan of San Diego." *Arizona and the West* 5(4) (Winter 1963): 327–336.

Hall, Linda B., and Don M. Coerver. "Woodrow Wilson, Public Opinion, and the Punitive Expedition: A Re-Assessment." *New Mexico Historical Review* 72(2) (April 1997): 171–194.

Harper, James W. "The El Paso-Juarez Conference." *Arizona and the West* 20(2) (Autumn 1978): 231–244.

Harris, Charles H., and Louis R. Sadler. "Termination with Extreme Prejudice: The United States versus Pancho Villa." *The Border and the Revolution: Clandestine Operations of the Mexican Revolution, 1910–1920*. Silver City, NM: High Lonesome Press, 1990.

———. "The Plan of San Diego and the Mexican-United States War Crisis of 1916: A Reexamination." *Hispanic American Historical Review* 58(3) (August 1978): 381–408.

———. "The Witzke Affair: German Intrigue on the Mexican Border, 1917–18." *Military Review* 59(February 1979): 36–49.

Hollyday, Worthington. "When the Motor Transport Was Young." *Baltimore Sun Sunday Magazine*, Pershing Papers, Library of Congress, Box 372.

Hopper, James. "New Columbus and the Expedition." *Collier's* 57(August 5, 1916): 10–11, 35.

Hurst, James W. "Columbus New Mexico's Soiled Doves." *Southern New Mexico On-line* (History and Nostalgia), www.southernnewmexiconline.com.

———. "The Pershing Punitive Expedition of 1916–1917: Mission Misunderstood." *Southern New Mexico Historical Review* 11(1) (February 2004): 9–18.

"Invading Mexico to Avert Intervention." *Literary Digest* 52(13) (March 25, 1916): 801–802.

Jore, Jeff. "Pershing's Mission in Mexico: Logistics and Preparation for the War in Europe." *Military Affairs* 52(3) (July 1988): 117–121.

Katz, Friedrich. "Communications." *American Historical Review* 84(1) (February 1979): 304–307.

———. "Pancho Villa and the Attack on Columbus, New Mexico." *The American Historical Review* 83(1) (February 1978): 101–130.

———. "Pancho Villa." *Essays on the Mexican Revolution: Revisionist Views of the Leaders,* George Wolfskill and Douglas W. Richmond, eds. Austin and London: University of Texas Press, 1979.

Kirkpatrick, Charles E. "The Mexican Border Campaign." *Encyclopedia of the American Military*, vol. 2. New York: Charles Scribner's Sons, 1994.

Lininger, Clarence. "The Type of Cavalry Horse for Campaign." *Cavalry Journal* 27(April 1917): 581–586.

MacAdam, George. "The Life of General Pershing." *The World's Work* 7(June 1919):148–158.

Mahoney, Tom. "The Columbus Raid." *Southwest Review* 17(2) (January 1932): 161–171.

Martin, C. H. "Rapid Transportation of Infantry." *Infantry Journal* 13(November-December, 1916): 333–337.

Marvin, George. "Bandits and the Borderland." *World's Work* 32(6) (October 1916): 656–663.

———. "Invasion or Intervention." *World's Work* 32(1) (May 1916): 40–62.

McGaw, Bill. "Was Pancho Villa Paid $80,000 for Making a Raid on Columbus?" *Southwesterner* (May 1964): 1–5.

McMaster, Richard K. "Letters From Mexico." *Password* I(1) (February 1956): 8–14.

Melzer, Richard. "On Villa's Trail in Mexico." *Military History of the Southwest* 21(2) (Fall 1991): 173–190.

Meyer, Michael C. "The Mexican-German Conspiracy of 1915." *The Americas* 32(1) (July 1966): 76–89.

————. "Albert Bacon Fall's Mexican Papers: A Preliminary Investigation." *New Mexico Historical Review* 40(2) (April 1965): 165–174.

Millard, George. "Mexican Expedition, U.S. Army Logistics during the Punitive Expedition." *Military Review* 60(October 1980): 58–68.

Morey, Lewis S. "The Cavalry Fight at Carrizal." *Cavalry Journal* 27(January 1917): 405–408.

Munch, Francis J. "Villa's Columbus Raid: Practical Politics or German Design?" *New Mexico Historical Review* 40(3) (July 1916): 189–214.

Norell, James O.E. "The National Match '03." *American Rifleman* 151(7) (July 2003): 38–43, 65.

"Notes From Here and There in Mexico." *Infantry Journal* 13(February 1917): 457–462.

O'Malley, Ilene V. "The Public Image of Pancho Villa." *The Myth of the Revolution: Hero Cults and the Institutionalization of the Mexican State, 1920–1940.* Westport, CT: Greenwood Press, 1986.

Pickering, Abner. "The Battle of Agua Prieta." *Infantry Journal* 12(January 1916): 707–710.

Pilcher, Jeffrey M. "Pancho Villa Rides into Mexican Legend or, The Cavalry Myth and Military Tactics in the Mexican Revolution." *Military History of the West* 26(1) (Spring 1996): 1–22.

Pope, Francis H. "Motor Transport Experiences with the Mexican Punitive Expedition." Appendix C, in Frank Tompkins, *Chasing Villa: The Last Campaign of the U.S. Cavalry.* Silver City, NM: High-Lonesome Books, 1996.

Richmond, Douglas W. "*La Guerra de Texas se renova:* Mexican Insurrection and Carrancista Ambitions, 1900–1920." *Aztlán: International Journal of Chicano Studies Research.* 11(1) (Spring 1980): 1–32.

Rippy, J. Fred, "Some Precedents of the Pershing Expedition into Mexico." *Southwestern Historical Quarterly* 24(4) (April 1921), 292–316.

Sandos, James A. "German Involvement in Northern Mexico, 1915–1916: A New Look at the Columbus Raid." *Hispanic American Historical Review* 50(1) (February 1970): 70–88.

————. "Pancho Villa and American Security: Woodrow Wilson's Mexican Diplomacy." *Journal of Latin American Studies* 13(2) (November 1981): 293–311.

————. "The Plan of San Diego: War and Diplomacy on the Texas Border 1915–1916." *Arizona and the West* 14(1) (Spring 1972): 5–24.

————. "Prostitution and Drugs: The United States Army on the Mexican-American Border, 1916–1917." *Pacific Historical Review* 49(4) (November 1980): 621–645.

Scott, James B. "The American Punitive Expedition into Mexico." *American Journal of International Law* 10(2) (April 1916): 337–340.

Shaw, W. B. "Pershing on the Trail." *Review of Reviews* 53(April 1916): 419–421.

Tate, Michael L. "Pershing's Punitive Expedition: Pursuer of Bandits or Presidential Panacea." *The Americas* 32(1) (July 1975): 46–71.

"The Cavalry Fight at Columbus." *Cavalry Journal* 27(112) (November 1916), 183–185.

"The Columbus Raid." *Cavalry Journal* 37(114) (April 1917), 490–496.

"The Mexican Murders." *The Literary Digest* 52(4) (January 22, 1916): 157–159.

"The Mexican Situation Again Becomes Acute." *Current Opinion* LX(2) (February 1916): 73–75.

"The 'Necessity' of War with Mexico." *Literary Digest* 52(July 8, 1916): 51–52.

"Verdict of the Press." *Literary Digest* 52(January 29, 1916): 213.

Villa, Francisco. "Carta de Francisco Villa al Señor General Emiliano Zapata." *Ediciones de Cultura Popular,* Chihuahua, Chihuahua, n.d.

"Villa's 'American Allies.'" *Literary Digest* (April 8, 1916): 951–954.

"War with Mexico Averted." *Literary Digest* (July 15, 1916): 116–118.

"We Can Wait No Longer." *The Independent* (March 20, 1916): 404.

"What to Do with Mexico." *Literary Digest* (May 20, 1916): 1438–1439.

Williams, S. M. "The Cavalry Fight at Ojos Azules." *Cavalry Journal* 27(January 1917): 405–408.

Williams, Vernon. L. "Lieutenant George S. Patton, Jr., and the American Army on the Texas Frontier in Mexico, 1915–16." *Military History of Texas and the Southwest* 17(1882): 1–76.

Wilson, Woodrow. "The Mexican Question." *Ladies Home Journal* 33(October 1916): 9.

Wolff, Leon. "Black Jack's Mexican Goose Chase." *American Heritage* 13(4) (June 1962): 22–17, 100–106.

Yockelson, Mitchell. "The United States Armed Forces and the Mexican Punitive Expedition." *Prologue* 29(3) (Fall 1997): Part 1, 1–9.

———. "The United States Armed Forces and the Mexican Punitive Expedition." *Prologue* 29(4) (Winter 1997): Part 2, 1–12.

Young, Karl. "A Fight That Could Have Meant War." *The American West* 3(2) (Spring 1966): 16–23; 90.

UNPUBLISHED STUDIES

Dillow, Daniel John. "Mission in Mexico: Logistical Operations during the Punitive Expedition into Mexico, 1916–1917." Unpublished MA thesis, New Mexico State University, 1993.

Gilderhus, Mark T., "The United States and the Mexican Revolution, 1915–1920: A Study of Policy and Interest." Unpublished PhD dissertation, University of Nebraska, 1968.

Johnson, Robert B. "The Punitive Expedition: A Military, Diplomatic and Political History of Pershing's Chase After Pancho Villa." Unpublished PhD Dissertation, University of Southern California, 1964.

Kestenbaum, Justin L. "The Question of Intervention in Mexico, 1913–1917." Unpublished PhD dissertation, Northwestern University, 1963.

Lou, Dennis Wingson, "Fall Committee: An Investigation of Mexican Affairs." Unpublished PhD dissertation, Indiana University, 1963.

Trow, Clifford W., "Senator Albert B. Fall and Mexican Affairs." Unpublished PhD dissertation, University of Colorado, 1966.

CONTEMPORARY PERIODICALS

Current Opinion
The Independent
Literary Digest
Outlook
The World's Work

INDEX

About the Author

JAMES W. HURST is Professor Emeritus, Joliet Junior College, Illinois. He is the author of *The Villista Prisoners of 1916–17* (2000).